# ALTERNATIVE APPROACHES TO HUMAN RIGHTS

This book explores the comparative historical evolution of the European, Inter-American and African regional human rights systems. The book devotes attention to various factors that have shaped the systems: the different circumstances in which they were founded; the influence of major states and inter-state politics within their respective regions; gradual processes of institutional evolution; and the impact of human rights advocates and claimants. Throughout, the book devotes careful attention to the impact of institutional and procedural choices on the functioning of human rights systems. Overarchingly, the book explores the contextually generated differences between the three systems, suggesting that human rights practice is less unitary than it might at times appear. Prescriptively, the book proposes that, contrary to the received wisdom in some quarters, the Inter-American system's dual-track approach may provide the most promising model in regards to future human rights system design.

CHRISTOPHER ROBERTS is an assistant professor at the Chinese University of Hong Kong. He has worked with several human rights organizations and mandates, including the Cairo Institute for Human Rights Studies, the Egyptian Initiative for Personal Rights, and the United Nations Special Rapporteur on the rights to freedom of peaceful assembly and of association.

## ASCL Studies in Comparative Law

*ASCL Studies in Comparative Law* publishes monographs and collections that broaden theoretical and practical knowledge of the world's many legal systems. Published under the direction of the American Society of Comparative Law, the *ASCL Studies* examine legal problems in a comparative light to advance legal science, develop technical insights, and promote greater cooperation across jurisdictional and cultural boundaries. This book series serves legal practitioners and those seeking to improve law and justice by publishing in-depth comparative studies of specific legal problems in every area of law.

The series has two general editors. David Gerber is Distinguished Professor of Law and Co-Director of the Program in International and Comparative Law at Chicago-Kent College of Law, Illinois Institute of Technology. He is past President of the American Society of Comparative Law. Mortimer Sellers is Regents Professor of the University System of Maryland and Director of the Baltimore Center for International and Comparative Law. He is past President of the Internationale Vereinigung für Rechts-und Sozialphilosophie.

# ALTERNATIVE APPROACHES TO HUMAN RIGHTS

## The Disparate Historical Paths of the European, Inter-American and African Regional Human Rights Systems

CHRISTOPHER ROBERTS
*Chinese University of Hong Kong*

CAMBRIDGE
UNIVERSITY PRESS

**CAMBRIDGE**
**UNIVERSITY PRESS**

University Printing House, Cambridge CB2 8BS, United Kingdom

One Liberty Plaza, 20th Floor, New York, NY 10006, USA

477 Williamstown Road, Port Melbourne, VIC 3207, Australia

314–321, 3rd Floor, Plot 3, Splendor Forum, Jasola District Centre, New Delhi – 110025, India

103 Penang Road, #05–06/07, Visioncrest Commercial, Singapore 238467

Cambridge University Press is part of the University of Cambridge.

It furthers the University's mission by disseminating knowledge in the pursuit of education, learning, and research at the highest international levels of excellence.

www.cambridge.org
Information on this title: www.cambridge.org/9781316512753
DOI: 10.1017/9781009071154



First published 2023

*A catalogue record for this publication is available from the British Library.*

*Library of Congress Cataloging-in-Publication Data is available*

ISBN 978-1-316-51275-3 Hardback

# CONTENTS

# ACKNOWLEDGMENTS

Thanks are due to all the friends and intellectual interlocutors who provided suggestions and provocations along the way, conversations with whom helped to determine both the substance and the limits of this work. More substantively still, gratitude is owed to numerous participants in the regional rights systems, including former and current judges, commissioners, members of secretariats and registries, litigants, advocates, academics, and others, who shared their time and thoughts. Thanks are particularly due to Grainne de Burca, Nehal Bhuta, and above all Philip Alston, who provided invaluable insights and encouragement across the innumerable iterations of this work. Any insights are due to the wisdom these different parties imparted; any limitations or oversights, the author's alone. The most extensive debt of gratitude goes to my parents, Michael and Linda Roberts, and to my wife, Aneesa Walji, for their support throughout the process and beyond.

# TABLE OF CASES

## European Court of Human Rights

## Inter-American Court of Human Rights

Atala Riffo and Daughters v. Chile, App. No. 12.502, Int.-Am. Ct. H.R., Merits, Reparations, and Costs (February 24, 2012) 138

Barreto Leiva v. Venezuela, App. No. 11.663, Int.-Am. Ct. H.R., Merits, Reparations, and Costs (November 17, 2009) 137

Barrios Altos v. Peru, App. No. 11.528, Int.-Am. Ct. H.R., Merits (March 14, 2001) 133, 178

Blake v. Guatemala, App No. 11.219, Int.-Am. Ct. H.R., Preliminary Objections (July 2, 1996) 130, 177

Blanco-Romero et al. v. Venezuela, App. Nos. 12.256, 12.258, & 12.307, Int.-Am. Ct. H.R., Merits, Reparations, and Costs (November 28, 2005) 136

Cabrera García and Montiel Flores v. Mexico, App. No. 12.449, Int.-Am. Ct. H.R., Preliminary Objections, Merits, Reparations, and Costs (November 26, 2010) 138

Caracazo v. Venezuela, Int.-Am. Ct. H.R., Reparations and Costs (August 29, 2002) 136

Case of Gonzalez et al. ("Cotton Field") v. Mexico, App. Nos. 12,496, 12,497, & 12,498, Int.-Am. Ct. H.R., Preliminary Objections, Merits, Reparations, and Costs (November 16, 2009) 143

Certain Attributes of the Inter-American Commission on Human Rights, Int.-Am. Ct. H.R., Advisory Opinion No. OC-13/93 (July 16, 1993) 148

Chocrón Chocrón v. Venezuela, App. No. 12.556, Int.-Am. Ct. H.R., Preliminary Objections, Merits, Reparations, and Costs (July 1, 2011) 137

Claude-Reyes v. Chile, App. No. 12.108, Int.-Am. Ct. H.R., Merits, Reparations, and Costs (September 19, 2006) 137

Compulsory Membership in an Association Prescribed by Law for the Practice of Journalism (Arts 13 and 29), Int.-Am. Ct. H.R., Advisory Opinion OC-5/85 (November 13, 1985) 127

Contreras and others v. El Salvador, App. Nos. 12,494, 12,517, & 12,518, Int.-Am. Ct. H.R., para. 122 (August 31, 2011) 205

Cuscul Pivaral and Others v. Guatemala, App. No. 12.484, Int.-Am. Ct. H.R., Preliminary Objections, Merits, Reparations, and Costs (August 23, 2018) 222

Dismissed Congressional Employees v. Peru, App. Nos. 11.830 & 12.038, Int.-Am. Ct. H.R., Preliminary Objections, Merits, Reparations, and Costs (November 24, 2006) 138

El Amparo v. Venezuela, App. No. 10.602, Int.-Am. Ct. H.R., Reparations (September 14, 1996) 131, 177

El Amparo v. Venezuela, App. No. 10.602, Int.-Am. Ct. H.R., Interpretation of Reparations (April 16, 1997) 131

Environment and Human Rights, Int.-Am. Ct. H.R., Advisory Opinion No. OC-23/17 (November 15, 2013) 222

Fernandez Ortega et al. v. Mexico, App. No. 12.580, Int.-Am. Ct. H.R., Preliminary Objections, Merits, Reparations, and Costs (August 30, 2010) 144, 182

Fontevecchia and D'Amico v. Argentina, App. No. 12.524, Int.-Am. Ct. H.R., Merits, Reparations, and Costs (November 29, 2011) 151

## Inter-American Commission on Human Rights

## African Court of Human and Peoples' Rights

## African Commission on Human and Peoples' Rights

## International Court of Justice



## Human Rights Committee



## Court of Justice of the European Union



## African Committee of Experts on the Rights and Welfare of the Child



## Economic Community of West African States Court of Justice

## East African Court of Justice



## Southern African Development Community Tribunal

# 1

## Introduction

This study explores the comparative historical evolution of the world's three most institutionally developed regional human rights systems: the European, the Inter-American, and the African. The history of the systems is important for several reasons. Between them, the three regional systems have been responsible for a great deal of the human rights work that has been conducted on the supranational level in the post–World War II period. Thanks both to the fact that they are closer to the ground, as it were, than the global human rights mechanisms, and thanks also to the fact that they are more "bottom-up" – with a major part of their work dedicated to responding to communications and complaints from individuals or groups – the regional human rights systems have been dynamic institutions, involved in extensive ongoing interactions with rights advocates and organizations.

The history of the regional human rights systems is also important because they have been less studied than the global-level rights system.[1] To be sure, there is a dedicated body of work focused on each of the three regional systems. This work is often closely focused on one component of caselaw or institutional development or another, however, and rarely examines the systems from a broader perspective. Against this backdrop, examining the development of the European, Inter-American, and African systems collectively and comparatively is helpful both in that it allows each system to be understood in novel ways, and insofar as it helps to clarify the significance of the collective work of those systems relative to the post–World War II development of the field of international human rights considered on the whole.

[1] As another pair of authors who have considered the history of the regional human rights systems have observed, "the broader debate on the history of human rights" that took off in the 2010s "paid surprisingly little attention to regional human rights systems, thereby missing some of the most salient strands of the larger history." Alexandra Huneeus and Mikael Madsen, "Between Universalism and Regional Law and Politics: A Comparative History of the American, European and African Human Rights Systems," 16 *International Journal of Constitutional Law* (2018), 136.

Bringing greater attention to the work of the regional human rights systems is valuable for another reason as well. Many of the explorations of human rights to date, whether considering post–World War II developments or broader histories of "the idea" of human rights, tend to focus on particular component parts of the broader field of rights: exploring the influence of important thinkers, the drafting of international conventions, the development of particular human rights organizations and/or of the broader "human rights movement," or the like. Less explored and emphasized are the forms that different human rights institutions have taken, the manner in which they have approached their work, and the impacts such institutions have had on the human rights field, and on understandings of the meaning of rights, over time. In squarely focusing on the development of some of the most complex and dynamic human rights institutions, this work aims to address that deficit.

In addition, a great deal of the work on international human rights to date has tended to imagine human rights as a western concept, rooted in the European experience. On one level, the ability of various parties to form such an impression is rooted in and closely connected to the history of European imperialism. On another, it has been facilitated by the fact that the European human rights system has produced the greatest volume of caselaw, has the largest body of literature devoted to it, and has often been unreflectively lauded and held up as a model to follow. A focus on the work of the Inter-American and African systems is particularly helpful in this context, in that it helps to expand and complicate that picture, complimenting work that has been done in other contexts, focused for instance on the use made of rights in decolonization struggles,[2] or on the more radical approaches to rights work that have developed in various national contexts.[3]

To observe that the regional systems have been comparatively understudied does not mean, of course, that scholarship is lacking; rather, a rich and informative body of work has addressed each system, from a number

[2] A model text here is Ibhawoh's *Imperialism and Human Rights*, which highlights both the manner in which invocations of rights were used to attempt to resist repressive components of British rule, as well as the manner in which rights language was used by the British in order to attempt to justify their rule, capturing the polyvalent potential inherent in rights discourse. Bonny Ibhawoh, *Imperialism and Human Rights: Colonial Discourses of Rights and Liberties in African History* (State University of New York Press, 2007). See also Bonny Ibhawoh, *Human Rights in Africa* (Cambridge University Press, 2017).

[3] See, e.g., Daniel Bonilla Maldonado ed., *Constitutionalism of the Global South: The Activist Tribunals of India, South Africa, and Colombia* (Cambridge University Press, 2013).

of different angles. In the European context, the most comprehensive historical overview is Ed Bates' *The Evolution of the European Convention on Human Rights*,[4] which provides a progressivist narrative of the first several decades of the system's development, together with an account of the challenges faced by the system since the turn of the millennium. Extensive detail concerning the system's founding is provided both by Brian Simpson's lengthy *Human Rights and the End of Empire*[5] as well as by Marco Duranti's *The Conservative Human Rights Revolution*,[6] both of which adopt critical lenses relative to the circumstances in which the European human rights system was formed. Important information concerning specific periods and components of the system's evolution can be found in a number of other more tightly focused works.[7]

To date, the Inter-American system lacks comparably comprehensive historical chronicling. Cecilia Medina Quiroga's *The Battle of Human Rights*[8] provides a general overview of the system's formation up to the late 1980s, highlighting the significance of the system's struggle with "gross, systematic violations" to the formation of its approach to rights work.

[4] Ed Bates, *The Evolution of the European Convention on Human Rights: From Its Inception to the Creation of a Permanent Court of Human Rights* (Oxford University Press, 2010).

[5] Brian Simpson, *Human Rights and the End of Empire: Britain and the Genesis of the European Convention* (Oxford University Press, 2004).

[6] Marco Duranti, *The Conservative Human Rights Revolution: European Identity, Transnational Politics, and the Origins of the European Convention* (Oxford University Press, 2017).

[7] See, e.g., Franz Matscher and Herbert Petzold eds., *Protecting Human Rights: The European Dimension: Studies in Honour of Gérard J Wiarda* (Carl Heymanns Verlag KG, 1988); Rick Lawson and Matthijs de Blois eds., *The Dynamics of the Protection of Human Rights in Europe: Essays in Honour of Henry G Schermers* (Springer, 1994); Andrew Drzemczewski, "A Major Overhaul of the ECHR Control Mechanism: Protocol No 11," in *Collected Courses of the Academy of European Law Volume VI Book 2* (Kluwer, 1995), 162–75; Denis Huber, *A Decade Which Made History: The Council of Europe 1989–1999* (Council of Europe, 1999); Paul Mahoney, Franz Matscher, Herbert Petzold, and Luzius Wildhaber, eds., *Protecting Human Rights: The European Perspective: Studies in memory of Rolv Ryssdal* (Carl Heymanns, 2000); Philip Leach, Helen Hardman, Svetlana Stephenson, and Brad K. Blitz, *Responding to Systemic Human Rights Violations: An Analysis of "Pilot Judgments" of the European Court of Human Rights and their Impact at National Level* (Intersentia, 2010); Steven Greer, *The European Convention on Human Rights: Achievements, Problems and Prospects* (Cambridge University Press, 2006); Stephan Breitenmoser, Bernhard Ehrenzeller, Marco Sassoli, Walter Stoffel, and Beatrice Wagner Pfeifer, eds., *Human Rights, Democracy and the Rule of Law: Liber Amicorum Luzius Wildhaber* (Nomos, 2007); Rudiger Wolfrum and Ulrike Deutsch eds., *The European Court of Human Rights Overwhelmed by Applications: Problems and Possible Solutions* (Springer, 2009).

[8] Cecilia Medina Quiroga, *The Battle of Human Rights: Gross, Systematic Violations and the Inter-American System* (Brill, 1988).

Tom Farer's article-length piece extends this history by another decade or so, considering the system's growing strength over the 1990s in particular.[9] Robert Goldman's "History and Action" provides a brief but compelling exploration of the system's history up to the end of the first decade of the twenty-first century,[10] while Victor Abramovich explores the manner in which the system moved from a focus on gross and systematic violations, as highlighted by Quiroga, to an emphasis on entrenched, structural patterns of violation, over the course of the 2000s.[11] Other authors have explored other aspects of the system. Klaas Dykmann's work examines the relationship between the regional human rights endeavor and the Organization of American States as a whole.[12] Pioneering work on the role of civil society in developing human rights in the region was done by Kathryn Sikkink, while more recent important studies along similar lines have been conducted by authors such as Vania Markarian and Patrick William Kelly.[13] Thomas Antkowiak and Jo Pasqualucci have highlighted the importance of the system's jurisprudence on indigenous peoples,[14] in

9 Tom Farer, "The Rise of the Inter-American Human Rights Regime: No Longer a Unicorn, Not Yet an Ox," 19 *Human Rights Quarterly* (1997), 510–46.

10 Robert Goldman, "History and Action: The Inter-American Human Rights System and the Role of the Inter-American Commission on Human Rights," 31 *Human Rights Quarterly* (2009), 856–87.

11 See Victor Abramovich, "From Massive Violations to Structural Patterns: New Approaches and Classic Tensions in the Inter-American Human Rights System," 6 *Sur International Journal of Human Rights* (2009), 7–37.

12 See Klaas Dykmann, *Philanthropic Endeavors or the Exploitation of an Ideal? The Human Rights Policy of the Organization of American States in Latin America, 1970–1991* (Iberoamericana Vervuert, 2004).

13 See Kathryn Sikkink, "The Emergence, Evolution, and Effectiveness of the Latin American Human Rights Network," in Elizabeth Jelin and Eric Hershberg eds., *Constructing Democracy: Human Rights, Citizenship and Society in Latin America* (Westview Press, 1996), 59–84; Margaret Keck and Kathryn Sikkink, *Activists Beyond Borders: Advocacy Networks in International Politics* (Cornell University Press, 1998); Vania Markarian, *Left in Transformation: Uruguayan Exiles and the Latin American Human Rights Networks, 1967–1984* (Routledge, 2005); Patrick William Kelly, *Sovereign Emergencies: Latin America and the Making of Global Human Rights Politics* (Cambridge University Press, 2018).

14 See Jo Pasqualucci, "The Evolution of International Indigenous Rights in the Inter-American Human Rights System," 6 *Human Rights Law Review* (2006), 281–322; Thomas Antkowiak, "Rights, Resources, and Rhetoric: Indigenous Peoples and the Inter-American Court," 35 *University of Pennsylvania Journal of International Law* (2013), 113–87; Thomas Antkowiak, "A Dark Side of Virtue: The Inter-American Court and Reparations for Indigenous Peoples," 25 *Duke Journal of Comparative and International Law* (2014), 1–80.

addition to which Thomas Antkowiak has chronicled the development of the system's expansive approach to remedies.[15] James Cavallaro has provided the most comprehensive accounts exploring the practical efficacy of some of the more unique components of the Inter-American system's approach.[16] Other works have highlighted various other important aspects of the system's work and evolution.[17]

Compelling histories of the African system have been provided by Evelyn Ankumah[18] and Kofi Kufuor.[19] Rachel Murray has recounted the relationship between Africa's human rights systems and Africa's regional political bodies, the Organization of African Unity and the African Union.[20] Frans Viljoen has provided an authoritative study on the drafting of the Charter, among other important works.[21] Chidi Odinkalu has

15 See Thomas Antkowiak, "Remedial Approaches to Human Rights Violations: The Inter-American Court of Human Rights and Beyond," 46 *Columbia Journal of Transnational Law* (2008), 351–419.

16 See James Cavallaro and Emily Schaffer, "Less as More: Rethinking Supranational Litigation of Economic and Social Rights in the Americas," 56 *Hastings Law Journal* (2004), 217–82; James Cavallaro and Stephanie Brewer, "The Virtue of Following: The Role of Inter-American Litigation in Campaigns for Social Justice," 8 *SUR International Journal of Human Rights* (2008), 85–97; James Cavallaro and Stephanie Brewer, "Reevaluating Regional Human Rights Litigation in the Twenty-First Century: The Case of the Inter-American Court," 102 *American Journal of International Law* (2008), 768–827.

17 See, e.g., Jose Cabranes, "The Protection of Human Rights by the Organization of American States," 62 *American Journal of International Law* (1968), 889–908; Thomas Buergenthal, "The Inter-American Court of Human Rights," 76 *American Journal of International Law* (1982), 231–45; S. James Anaya and Claudio Grossman, "The Case of Awas Tingni v. Nicaragua: A New Step in the International Law of Indigenous Peoples," 19 *Arizona Journal of International and Comparative Law* (2012), 1–15; Daniel Toda Castan, *The Transformation of the Inter-American System for the Protection of Human Rights: The Structural Impact of the Inter-American Court's Case Law on Amnesties* (EUIC Global Campus Europe, 2013); DPLF: Magazine of the Due Process of Law Foundation, Issue on The Reform of the Inter-American Commission on Human Rights (2014); Ariel Dulitzky, "An Inter-American Constitutional Court? The Invention of the Conventionality Control by the Inter-American Court of Human Rights," 50 *Texas International Law Journal* (2015), 45–93; DPLF: Magazine of the Due Process of Law Foundation, The Inter-American Human Rights System: Changing Times, Ongoing Challenges (2016).

18 Evelyn Ankumah, *The African Commission on Human and Peoples Rights* (Brill, 1996).

19 Kofi Oteng Kufuor, *The African Human Rights System – Origin and Evolution* (Palgrave, 2010).

20 See Rachel Murray, *Human Rights in Africa: From the OAU to the African Union* (Cambridge University Press, 2004).

21 See Frans Viljoen, "The African Charter on Human and Peoples' Rights/the Travaux Préparatoires in the Light of Subsequent Practice," 25 *Human Rights Law Journal* (2004), 313–26.

chronicled the system's procedural evolution.[22] Other works have highlighted various other key components of the system's evolution.[23]

The history of the regional human rights systems cannot be understood without at least some understanding of other developments in the history of human rights, including developments on the international level. The creation of the United Nations human rights system was particularly important, of course, and has been explored extensively; key works in that context include Johannes Morsink's *The Universal Declaration of Human Rights,* Mary Ann Glendon's *A World Made New,* Elizabeth Borgwardt's *A New Deal for the World,* and Christopher N. J. Roberts' *The Contentious History of the International Bill of Human Rights.*[24] Other scholars have turned their attention to the preparation of the international covenants and the International Convention on the Elimination of All Forms of Racial Discrimination,[25] and the development and impact

[22] See Chidi Odinkalu, "The Individual Complaints Procedures of the African Commission on Human and Peoples' Rights: A Preliminary Assessment," 8 *Journal of Transnational Law and Contemporary Problems* (1998), 359–402; Chidi Odinkalu and Camilla Christensen, "The African Commission on Human and Peoples' Rights: The Development of Its Non-State Communication Procedures," 20 *Human Rights Quarterly* (1998), 235–80; Chidi Odinkalu, "The Role of Case and Complaints Procedures in the Reform of the African Regional Human Rights System," 1 *African Human Rights Law Journal* (2001), 225–46.

[23] See, e.g., Emmanuel Bello, "The African Charter on Human and Peoples' Rights: A Legal Analysis," in *Collected Courses of the Hague Academy of International Law, Volume 194* (Brill, 1985); Makua Mutua, "The African Human Rights Court: A Two-Legged Stool?," 21 *Human Rights Quarterly* (1999), 342–63; Nsongurua Udombana, "Towards the African Court on Human and Peoples' Rights: Better Late Than Never," 3 *Yale Human Rights and Development Law Journal* (2000), 45–111; Frans Viljoen, "A Human Rights Court for Africa, and Africans," 30 *Brooklyn Journal of International Law* (2005), 1–66; Malcolm Evans and Rachel Murray eds., *The African Charter on Human and Peoples' Rights* (2nd edn Cambridge University Press, 2008).

[24] Johannes Morsink, *The Universal Declaration of Human Rights: Origins, Drafting and Intent* (University of Pennsylvania Press, 1999); Mary Ann Glendon, *A World Made New: Eleanor Roosevelt and the Universal Declaration of Human Rights* (Random House, 2001); Elizabeth Borgwardt, *A New Deal for the World: America's Vision for Human Rights* (Harvard University Press, 2007); Christopher N. J. Roberts, *The Contentious History of the International Bill of Human Rights* (Cambridge University Press, 2015).

[25] For key scholarship on the drafting of those conventions, see Daniel J. Whelan and Jack Donnelly, "The West, Economic and Social Rights, and the Global Human Rights Regime: Setting the Record Straight," 29 *Human Rights Quarterly* (2007), 908–49; Roland Burke, "Putting the Stamps Back On: Apartheid, Anticolonialism, and the Accidental Birth of a Universal Right to Petition," in *Decolonization and the Evolution of International Human Rights* (University of Pennsylvania Press, 2010), 59–91; Roland Burke, "Some Rights Are More Equal than Others: The Third World and the Transformation of Economic and Social Rights," 3 *Humanity: International Journal of Human Rights, Humanitarianism and*

of the international movement against apartheid.[26] A number of more recent works have highlighted the importance of the 1970s to the history of human rights, including Samuel Moyn's *The Last Utopia*, Jan Eckel and Samuel Moyn's co-edited volume *The Breakthrough* and Barbara Keys' *Reclaiming American Virtue*.[27] Other authors have focused on the evolution of particular institutions, such as Human Rights Watch,[28] Amnesty International[29] and the International Commission of Jurists.[30]

*Development* 3 (2012), 427–48; Steven Jensen, *The Making of International Human Rights: The 1960s, Decolonization, and the Reconstruction of Global Values* (Cambridge University Press, 2016).

26 See Hakan Thorn, *Anti-Apartheid and the Emergence of a Global Civil Society* (Palgrave, 2006); David Hostetter, *Movement Matters: American Apartheid Activism and the Rise of Multicultural Politics* (Routledge, 2006); Carol Anderson, "International Conscience, the Cold War, and Apartheid: The NAACP's Alliance with the Reverend Michael Scott for South West Africa's Liberation," 19 *World History Journal* (2008), 297–325; Hakan Thorn, "The Meaning(s) of Solidarity: Narratives of Anti-Apartheid Activism," 35 *Journal of South African Studies* (2009), 417–36; Ryan Irwin, *Gordian Knot: Apartheid and the Unmaking of the Liberal World Order* (Oxford University Press, 2012); all the papers in the special 2014 edition of *Radical History Review* on "The Global Anti-Apartheid Movement"; and Robert Skinner, "The Dynamics of Anti-Apartheid: International Solidarity, Human Rights and Decolonization," in Andrew W.M. Smith and Chris Jeppesen eds., *Britain, France and the Decolonization of Africa: Future Imperfect?* (UCL Press, 2017), 111–30.

27 Samuel Moyn, *The Last Utopia: Human Rights in History* (Harvard University Press, 2010); Jan Eckel and Samuel Moyn eds., *The Breakthrough: Human Rights in the 1970s* (University of Pennsylvania Press, 2013); Barbara Keys, *Reclaiming American Virtue: The Human Rights Revolution of the 1970s* (Harvard University Press, 2014). See also Jan Eckel, "'Under a Magnifying Glass': The International Human Rights Campaign Against Chile in the Seventies," in Stefan-Ludwig Hoffmann ed., *Human Rights in the Twentieth Century* (Cambridge University Press, 2011), 321–42; Barbara Keys, "Anti-Torture Politics: Amnesty International, the Greek Junta, and the Origin of the Human Rights 'Boom' in the United States," in Akira Iriye, Petra Goedde and William I. Hitchcock eds., *The Human Rights Revolution: An International History* (Oxford University Press, 2012), 201–21; Jan Eckel, "The International League for the Rights of Man, Amnesty International, and the Changing Fate of Human Rights Activism from the 1940s through the 1970s," 4 *Humanity: International Journal of Human Rights, Humanitarianism and Development* (2013), 183–214.

28 See Peter Slezkine, "From Helsinki to Human Rights Watch: How an American Cold War Monitoring Group Became an International Human Rights Institution," 5 *Humanity: International Journal of Human Rights, Humanitarianism and Development* (2014), 345–70.

29 See Jonathan Powers, *Against Oblivion: Amnesty International's Fight for Human Rights* (Fontana, 1981); Jonathan Powers, *Like Water on Stone: The Story of Amnesty International* (Northeastern University Press, 2001); Tom Buchanan, "'The Truth Will Set You Free': The Making of Amnesty International," 37 *Journal of Contemporary History* (2002), 575–97; Stephen Hopgood, *Keepers of the Flame: Understanding Amnesty International* (Cornell University Press, 2006).

30 See Howard Tolley, *The International Commission of Jurists: Global Advocates for Human Rights* (University of Pennsylvania Press, 1994).

Above and beyond this literature on the history of the regional systems and international human rights more broadly, several important pieces, largely penned over the course of the new millennium, have considered how the regional human rights systems might best reorient their efforts in the face of contemporary challenges. This literature contains some of the sharpest analysis of the various systems, due both to its attention to and grounding in the manner in which the systems in question actually function, and to its willingness to squarely examine the challenges the systems face. In the European context, compelling work calling for a rethinking of the system's approach has been produced by Steven Greer and Luzius Wildhaber, a former president of the Court.[31] In a 2012 piece, Greer and Wildhaber observed the co-existence of several different visions of the European human rights system's work: an "individual justice" perspective, a "constitutional justice" perspective, and the perspective of "pluralism." The "individual justice" perspective, on their account, "maintain[ed] that the Court exists primarily to redress Convention violations for the benefit of the particular individual making the complaint."[32] Greer and Wildhaber argued this was a largely untenable position, given the Court's limited resources. The "constitutional justice" perspective, in contrast, involved cases being

> selected and adjudicated by the [European Court of Human Rights] in a manner which contributes most effectively to the identification, condemnation, and resolution of violations, particularly those which are serious for the applicant, for the respondent state (because, for example, they are built into the structure or *modus operandi* of its public institutions), or for Europe as a whole (because, for example, they may be prevalent in more than one state).[33]

The "pluralist" perspective, finally, was one in which "the Court has many functions and not the binary alternatives suggested by the models of individual and constitutional justice," which are all "part of an interlocking plurality of legal systems in both contemporary Europe and beyond."[34]

[31] Steven Greer and Luzius Wildhaber, "Revisiting the Debate about 'constitutionalising' the European Court of Human Rights," 12 *Human Rights Law Review* (2012), 655–87. See also Luzius Wildhaber, "A Constitutional Future for the European Court of Human Rights?," 23 *Human Rights Law Journal* (2002), 161–5; Steven Greer, "What's Wrong with the European Convention on Human Rights?," 30 *Human Rights Quarterly* (2008), 680–702.

[32] Greer and Wildhaber, "Revisiting the Debate," 663.

[33] Ibid., 671.

[34] Ibid., 677.

Practically, Greer and Wildhaber argued the system should adopt a "constitutional pluralis[t]" approach, in which the Court would take a more active role in shaping its docket in order to attempt to achieve the maximum possible efficacy, and to be able to respond to the most severe rights violations.[35] Regardless of one's take on this recommendation or the potential for it to be fulfilled in practice, Greer and Wildhaber's piece provides a valuable analytical service, by helping to clarify the coexistence, and frequent tension, between different visions of what human rights work may entail.

In the Inter-American system, one key subject of attention has been whether or not to import the European system's margin of appreciation approach. One early contemplator of the issue was Pablo Contreras, who highlighted the manner in which "the European Court has been a pioneer in the creation of deferential standards," while the Inter-American Court "ha[d] not yet developed a theory of deference to domestic authorities."[36] While Contreras presented arguments both for and against the adoption of such an approach,[37] other scholars have since weighed in more forcefully on one side or the other. A subsequent piece by Jorge Contesse, for instance, more directly made the case for the importation of a more deferential approach. Like others, Contesse observed that the Inter-American Court had "embrace[d] a maximalist model of adjudication – one that [left] very little, if any, room for states to reach their own decisions."[38] This made sense, Contesse suggested, in the Court's early years, when it regularly had to confront serious and widespread violations. More recently, however, in Contesse's view, the type of cases brought before the court had changed; in light of that changing context, Contesse contended the Inter-American Court should "embrac[e] normative subsidiarity" in order to "foster, as a less aggressive and interventionist approach, a more collaborationist model for the enforcement of international human rights law,"

[35] Greer and Wildhaber were pessimistic as to reform efforts at the time, however, which they saw as bogged down "by a mixture of confusion about, and hostility and indifference towards, constitutionalisation." Ibid., 659.

[36] Pablo Contreras, "National Discretion and International Deference in the Restriction of Human Rights: A Comparison between the Jurisprudence of the European and the Inter-American Court of Human Rights," 11 *Northwestern Journal of International Human Rights* (2012), 28, 30. Contreras made clear that while the Inter-American system had occasionally referenced the idea of a margin of appreciation, it had not deployed it in a consistent manner.

[37] See ibid., 61–7.

[38] Jorge Contesse, "Contestation and Deference in the Inter-American Human Rights System," 79 *Law and Contemporary Problems* (2016), 123–45, 124.

and to thereby avoid the blowback that would likely arise should member states repeatedly run up against an overly confrontational system.[39] A similar position was adopted by Andreas Follesdal, who argued that "a margin of appreciation doctrine, duly developed and specified, [could] contribute to alleviating the tension between human rights protection and due deference to sovereignty in a defensible way."[40] As with Greer and Wildhaber's observations in the European context, whatever one's position on these debates, they are broadly instructive insofar as they help to highlight central tensions underlying human rights practice in general, and the difference between the European system's more cautious, "margin of appreciation"-inflected approach and the more directly confrontational posture adopted by the Inter-American system in particular.

In the African context, insightful work probing institutional possibilities has been done by Chidi Odinkalu, a prominent litigator before both the African Commission and Court. In a piece from 2003, Odinkalu observed that "the quite complex problems of human and group survival in Africa do not easily lend themselves to diagnosis or solutions within the human rights frame of analysis."[41] The heart of the problem, Odinkalu suggested, was the fact that "[t]he African State – in its colonial and post-colonial formations – has been disabled by a combination of historical and contemporary factors from being able to play its role as a guarantor of rights, rendering it instead, for the most part, a force for their violation."[42] As Odinkalu further observed, traditional approaches to human rights work assumed "violations of human rights [were] the exception rather than the rule."[43] In Africa, in contrast, such violations were the norm, and therefore it was necessary to adopt a different approach to rights work.[44] Odinkalu's

39 Ibid., 144.

40 Andreas Follesdal, "Exporting the Margin of Appreciation: Lessons for the Inter-American Court of Human Rights?," 15 *International Journal of Constitutional Law* (2017), 362.

41 Chidi Odinkalu, "Back to the Future: The Imperative of Prioritizing for the Protection of Human Rights in Africa," 47 *Journal of African Law* (2003), 1.

42 Ibid., 2.

43 Ibid., 4.

44 In particular, it was necessary to attempt to "address the vectors and causes that predispose the peoples of the continent to violations instead of concentrating on the symptoms," including through focusing on "state building and the construction of civic citizenship," as only by establishing "institutions credible enough to prevent [serious] violations or to effectively address them when they occur" would rights fulfillment be enabled. Ibid., citing Abdullahi An Na'im, "The Legal Protection of Human Rights in Africa: How to Do More with Less," in Austin Sarat and Thomas Kearns eds., *Human Rights: Concepts, Contests, Contingencies* (University of Michigan Press, 2001), 105.

work is essential not only in the African context but also more broadly, due to the manner in which it upends traditional human rights assumptions, including both the assumption that violations are the exception, rather than the norm, and the assumption that rights work is concerned with limiting state power, rather than expanding it.

Such works help draw attention to internal diversity in the functioning of human rights systems and visions, including the contrast between more individualized and more constitutionalized perspectives, the tension between more conciliatory and more confrontational approaches, and the different positions rights systems and advocates may adopt relative to the significance of, and the appropriate attitude toward, state power. Other essential work, relative to understanding the regional human rights systems more broadly, has investigated the forces that have driven the systems' development. Mikael Rask Madsen, drawing on Bourdieu and with attention primarily to the European system, has argued that the growing strength of the transnational judiciary has been due in significant part to the power and self-interest of members of the legal profession.[45] Madsen has also explored the impact of political factors on the development of the European regional human rights system, including the significance of the European system's foundation in the Cold War context, and the manner in which the system's supporters have had to pay careful attention to political factors in order to protect and advance the system's legitimacy.[46] Along such lines, Madsen has suggested that key players within the European system relied upon a careful "legal diplomacy" in the system's early decades, enabling the system to move from a cautious initial position to a more entrenched and powerful one.[47] In addition, drawing

[45] See Mikael Rask Madsen, "Reflexivity and the Construction of the International Object: The Case of Human Rights," 5 *International Political Sociology* (2011), 259–75; Yves Dezalay and Mikael Rask Madsen, "The Force of Law and Lawyers: Pierre Bourdieu and the Reflexive Sociology of Law," 8 *Annual Review of Law and Social Science* (2012), 433–52.

[46] See, e.g., Mikael Rask Madsen, "From Cold War Instrument to Supreme European Court: The European Court of Human Rights at the Crossroads of International and National Law and Politics," 32 *Law and Social Inquiry* (2007), 137–59; Mikael Rask Madsen, "Legal Diplomacy: Law, Politics, and the Genesis of Postwar European Human Rights," in Hoffmann ed., *Human Rights in the Twentieth Century*, 62–81.

[47] See Mikael Rask Madsen, "The Protracted Institutionalization of the Strasbourg Court: From the Diplomacy of Law to Integrationist Jurisprudence," in Jonas Christoffersen and Mikael Madsen eds., *The European Court of Human Rights between Law and Politics* (Oxford University Press, 2011), 43–60; Mikael Rask Madsen, "The Challenging Authority of the European Court of Human Rights: From Cold War Legal Diplomacy to the Brighton Declaration and Backlash," 79 *Law and Contemporary Problems* (2016), 141–78.

upon evolutionary theory, Madsen has argued that the development of international courts should be understood as taking place through a process involving "punctuated equilibria" – in other words, the development of such bodies has been characterized by long periods in which little changes, interrupted by brief periods in which new systems are formed or dramatic reforms are made to existing systems.[48]

Alexandra Huneeus has engaged in similarly analytical work, focused most centrally on the Inter-American system. Huneeus has explored the various manners in which judicial actors on different levels have interacted with one another,[49] highlighting the extent to which the strength of the Inter-American Court's authority in different national contexts has been determined by the nature of domestic legal communities.[50] Huneeus has also investigated the European and Inter-American systems' attempts to develop a more structural approach to their work, and the obstacles those supporting such an approach have faced.[51]

Huneeus and Madsen produced an article-length overview of the history of all three regional human rights systems, constituting, as the authors put it, "a first systematic attempt to compare the institutional histories of the regional human rights systems in Europe, the Americas, and Africa."[52] Huneeus and Madsen emphasized two factors as important to the development of the regional systems. First, as Madsen had done previously, they emphasized "legal diplomacy," which they argued prevailed in the European Court's early work "as a means to play the double game of, on the one hand, affirming the Court's position as having the final say on the interpretation of the rules while, on the other, finding solutions

[48] See Mikael Rask Madsen, "Explaining the Power of International Courts in Their Contexts: From Legitimacy to Legitimization," in Adriana De Klor, Miguel Maduro and Antoine Vauchez eds., *Courts, Social Change and Judicial Independence* (European University Institute, 2012), 23. The reference is to Steven J. Gould, "Episodic Change Versus Gradualist Dogma," 2 *Science and Nature* (1978), 5–12.

[49] See Alexandra Huneeus, "Rejecting the Inter-American Court: Judicialization, National Courts, and Regional Human Rights," in Rachel Sieder, Alexandra Huneeus and Javier Andres Couso eds., *Cultures of Legality: Judicialization and Political Activism in Latin America* (Cambridge University Press, 2010), 112–38; Alexandra Huneeus, "Courts Resisting Courts: Lessons from the Inter-American Court's Struggle to Enforce Human Rights," 44 *Cornell International Law Journal* (2011), 493–534.

[50] Alexandra Huneeus, "Constitutional Lawyers and the Inter-American Court's Varied Authority," 79 *Law and Contemporary Problems* (2016), 179–207.

[51] See Alexandra Huneeus, "Reforming the State from Afar: Structural Reform Litigation at the Human Rights Courts," 40 *Yale Journal of International Law* (2015), 1–40.

[52] Huneeus and Madsen, "Between Universalism and Regional Law and Politics," 136.

that did not alienate the existing or prospective member states."[53] Second, Huneeus and Madsen emphasized the importance of political factors, including the Cold War in particular, to the regional systems' evolutions.

Huneeus and Madsen's piece ended with two major conclusions. First, they emphasized how all three regional systems:

> followed common institutional and legal models and ideas that emerged at the level of world society, and were in place as the first regional institutions were debated and imagined. Thus, while it is the case that the European human rights system became influential in its region earlier, all three systems were heir to models imagined during the inter-Cold War period. Further, their emergence cannot be explained as the product of strategic action or functional imperative alone: despite great differences in their contexts, the states of each region drew on shared ideas that have come to be widely accepted but articulated slightly differently due to regional contextual constraints.[54]

Here it is necessary to differ. There is no doubt that on a general level all three regional systems have drawn from a shared global emphasis on the importance of supranational rights oversight. At the same time, Huneeus and Madsen's account suggests a greater degree of uniformity than existed when the regional systems were formed, or than has existed since. In contrast to Huneeus and Madsen's account, this study suggests that different ideas of rights were involved in the foundational moments of each of the three regional systems, that those ideas evolved over the course of subsequent debates within each system, and that they have continued to evolve since, leading to far more diversity and contestation within and between those visions than Huneeus and Madsen suggest.

Second, Huneeus and Madsen suggest that their approach:

> throws into relief factors that helped shape the variation that nonetheless exists among the three systems. In particular, each system's distinct position within global politics and particularly the geopolitics before, during, and after the Cold War shaped the evolution of its institutions. Notably, the close of the Cold War led to an initial convergence between the European and Inter-American systems, both of which became more judicialized and gained influence in national law.[55]

[53] Ibid., 147. While Huneeus and Madsen primarily argue legal diplomacy was important to the early development of the European system, they also observe that later, post-Brighton Declaration developments suggest "that the rights-oriented jurisprudence that the Court carefully distilled beginning in the late 1970s is being attenuated by new forms of strategic judging reminiscent of the legal diplomacy of the early ECtHR." Ibid., 156.

[54] Ibid., 159–60.

[55] Ibid., 160.

Huneeus and Madsen's suggestion that the end of the Cold War has seen a convergence between the systems contains some truth; certainly, it gave all three systems increased political space, and led to a relatively receptive period for international human rights work, as well as for international judicialization. At the same time, and contrary to Huneeus and Madsen's suggestion, while the European and Inter-American systems may have converged in some ways following the end of the Cold War, this convergence was both partial and accompanied by new forms of differentiation, such that once again the actual picture is one of greater differentiation, and less convergence, than Huneeus and Madsen suggest.

Huneeus and Madsen's work is path-breaking, helping to clarify many of the dynamics involved in the evolution of the regional human rights systems. This is especially the case relative to the dynamics they identified as having shaped the systems' evolutions, including, for example, the importance of political factors, reliance on "judicial diplomacy," and the force and power of juridification. At the same time, Huneeus and Madsen's work leaves many questions unexplored. First, while they explore political factors and moments of major system evolution, Huneeus and Madsen devote less attention to ongoing, everyday processes of system evolution, and to the ways in which encounters with different forms of rights violations have shaped the systems in different ways. Second, Huneeus and Madsen, in common with the majority of the scholarship focused on the regional human rights systems, have tended to devote far more attention to the work of the regional courts, and far less to other components of regional rights work, including the work of multifunction commissions in particular.

Most overarchingly, Huneeus and Madsen's work focuses on similarities in the forces that have driven the evolution of each of the systems. In this, it is not dissimilar from much of the work of rights historians, which tends to suggest and to rely upon a unitary vision of human rights, referring to concepts and categories such as "the idea of human rights" or "the human rights movement." Such scholarship fails to recognize or fully draw out the extent to which human rights work encompasses, and has always encompassed, a variety of different visions and approaches. The comparative historical evolution of the European, Inter-American and African regional human rights systems is particularly fertile terrain in such regards, insofar as the three systems have each produced different visions of and approaches to human rights, constituted and shaped by their different foundational moments, the diverging struggles for rights that have taken place in each, and the varying institutional design features and procedural approaches that have developed in response to such concrete histories and struggles over time. This study, in contrast, devotes more focused attention to the alternative approaches to human rights that have evolved in each system. The result of such an investigation is to produce an alternative, more diverse and more internally contested understanding of the history of human rights.

Exploring the history of human rights through the history of human rights institutions poses a challenge not faced by many historians of the field, including those who focus on the preparation of major documents or on the contributions of particular prominent individuals, or who rely on the conceit that "human rights" as such constitutes a readily identifiable, unified object of study. This is because it is not immediately apparent in what particular actions or component features the character of international institutions consists. The approach of this study to this challenge is straightforward: in order to understand the character, significance and impact of any particular international human rights institution, it is not sufficient to focus solely on its provenance, the rights struggles with which it has contended, or its internal institutional design alone. Rather, all three must be considered. These three different aspects must be considered not merely through a synchronic snapshot view of the systems' present forms, moreover, but rather through an assessment of the manner in which such details have changed and evolved over time.

The following study does not merely examine the historical evolution of one regional human rights institution, of course, but rather three. Exploring those histories side-by-side allows for a recognition of both similarities and differences, not only in a formal sense, such as for instance relative to the rights guaranteed by the foundational documents of each, but also relative to the factors that have driven the evolution of each system over time. The similarities between the systems are interesting, encompassing for instance the structural constraints rights institutions are inevitably under, as well as the dynamics that characterize the manner in which dispute resolution bodies evolve over time. It is the differences that will be given pride of place here, however. To the extent diversity in human rights visions has been explored to date, the emphasis has typically been on substantive differences – on the purported difference between civil and political and social and economic rights, for instance. While there are certainly substantive differences between the rights protected by the systems, in many ways the primary difference, foregrounded by the account that follows, pertains not to the substantive rights each guarantees, but rather to the manner in which each goes about advancing its mandate. In short, in other words, the difference between the systems primarily concerns their different modes of approaching human rights work.

The first manner in which the differences between the three systems are explored in this study is through reference to their different foundational moments, a subject explored in the second chapter. This emphasis on foundational moments, naturally, covers the periods in which each system was initially formed. None of the systems is the product of a solitary foundational moment alone, however – rather, the contemporary form of each is due to numerous such "moments," including not only that in which the system was initially forged, but also subsequent moments in which each system was recomposed, in light of the particular challenges, opportunities and understandings of the day. The text explores the nature of these processes within each system. While there are parallels, the foundational processes within each have also been distinct, with differences pertaining *inter alia* to the circumstances in which the different systems were formed, the background contexts that led to and shaped their initial developments, the nature of key players involved, and how rapidly or slowly the relevant developments took place.

There is no doubting that foundational moments have been important to the shape each regional human rights system has taken. At the same time, it is also possible to give founding moments too much attention. Much of the existing literature on the history of human rights has, in fact, conformed to such a pattern, presenting one or another period or context as "the origin" of human rights.[56] Human rights is anything but a static field, however, and while such moments form an important part of the broader story, that story is incomplete without exploration of the ongoing tensions and processes that have followed such founding moments, and of the manner in which rights visions have constantly been shaped and reshaped by the emergence of new political formations and the rise to prominence of new struggles.

While foundational moments form one key site for investigation, therefore, the systems cannot be understood through reference to foundational moments alone. The third chapter focuses on a particularly important element, often – paradoxically and perversely – sidelined within human rights histories. Too often, the evolution of human rights ideas

[56] Similarly recognizing the tendency of human rights histories to take the form of origin stories, see Dan Edelstein, "Is There a 'Modern' Natural Law Theory? Notes on the History of Human Rights," 7 *Humanity: International Journal of Human Rights, Humanitarianism and Development* (2016), 345–64.

is presented and understood as if rights ideas evolved in a vacuum, disconnected from background circumstances and social contestations. In reality, much of the gradual evolution of the regional human rights institutions has been driven not by abstract rights theories, but rather by and through the efforts and struggles of rights advocates, working to address one concrete situation of violation or another.[57] Chapter 3 focuses on this component of system evolution – the different rights struggles that have caught the regional systems' attentions at different times, and the manner in which such struggles have contributed to the systems' broader modes of understanding and responding to rights violations.

On first reflection, it might seem that the struggles that appear before a particular regional system are simply a reflection of the nature of the rights challenges faced in that region, and indeed, background regional context is the most significant factor in terms of shaping the cases with which each system has contended. The matter is not quite so simple, however – rather, various factors determine when, whether, how and to what extent particular struggles can be advanced as rights struggles in the first place.[58] Among other factors, the procedural rules and institutional forms a particular rights system adopts do a great deal to determine what sorts of issues can and cannot be brought to a system's attention, and in what manner. The fourth chapter explores this question of comparative institutional design. Institutional design is not static, of course. Rather, each system has, to a certain degree, been responsive to its background context, with institutional and procedural design evolving over time in response to the demands made. In short, the institutional form of the various regional rights systems should be understood as both constituting and constituted by the rights struggles that have come before them. They have been

57 Not all of the literature has ignored such actors; for similar emphasis on the need to understand human rights and international law and institutions as constructed "from below," out of concrete political struggles and thanks to the efforts of social movements, see, e.g., Neil Stammers, "Social Movements and the Social Construction of Human Rights," 21 *Human Rights Quarterly* (1999), 980–1008; Balakrishnan Rajagopal, "From Resistance to Renewal: The Third World, Social Movements, and the Expansion of International Institutions," 41 *Harvard International Law Journal* (2000), 529–78; Balakrishnan Rajagopal, *International Law from Below: Development, Social Movements and Third World Resistance* (Cambridge University Press, 2003); and Neil Stammers, Robert Jupe and Jane Andrew, *Human Rights and Social Movements* (Pluto, 2009); Ibhawoh, *Human Rights in Africa*, 24–8.

58 For the classic, general account concerning such issues, see William Felstiner, Richard Abel and Austin Sarat, "The Emergence and Transformation of Disputes: Naming, Blaming, Claiming …," 15 *Law and Society Review* (1980), 631–54.

constituted by those struggles insofar as each struggle has left its mark, defining the manners in which the systems have developed over time and the ways they have come to think about their functions as well as about the meaning and purpose of human rights work writ large. At the same time, they have constituted those struggles, by imposing frames that have limited and shaped the manner in which such struggles may be presented and advanced.

As the above lays out, this work breaks from standard practice in multiple ways, including by centering an investigation of "human rights" on the development of human rights institutions, and by considering the development of those institutions from a more polyvalent perspective than that from which they are typically approached. The result is an account of "human rights" as more internally diverse and contested than it is typically presented, and of that diversity itself as more closely linked to institutional and procedural choices than a historian of ideas alone might immediately recognize. Recognition of that diversity should give pause both to advocates and critics of an overly simplified vision of rights, highlighting the alternative possibilities already existing or which have been explored in the past, and foregrounding the extent to which alternative visions may continue to evolve – or may be rediscovered – in the future.

# 2

# Foundational Moments

## I Introduction

One of the places to which scholars have most frequently turned in order to better understand the nature of human rights systems, and indeed, various components of international legal order in general, are the moments in which the relevant systems were initially formed. Among other things, such moments have been of particular interest, and are particularly fertile in terms of the insights they can help bring to the surface, because they offer a site in which the interactions between state parties possessed of major political interests, advocacy campaigns run by civil society organizations and rights advocates, background structural and circumstantial factors, and major global historical events come together, creating, at particular moments and in particular times and places, the conditions of possibility for negotiation, agreement, and the development of international and supranational systems. The interaction between these factors in the context of a system's foundational moment or moments, moreover, is at least in substantial part responsible for the vision and approach to human rights that becomes normalized within and enabled by that system going forward.

It is important in this context not to imagine that a system may only have one foundation. Initial moments exist, of course – in the context of the regional human rights systems, they took place in the late 1940s and early 1950s in Europe and the Americas and the late 1970s and early 1980s in Africa. Complex international systems often have more than one "foundational" moment, however. This is clearly apparent in the context of the Inter-American and African systems, both of which were constructed gradually over time, with the initial system augmented in the Americas for instance by agreement on the Inter-American Convention in the 1960s, and in Africa by the incorporation of a court into the system in the 1990s and 2000s. Even in the European system, which emerged from its initial moments most fully formed, later moments had a major impact on the system's shape as well, including most prominently the system's transition to more fully judicialized form in the 1990s. Recognizing the periodic nature of such moments is also important in and of itself, recalling Madsen's notion of evolution by punctuated equilibria,[1] as well as Ackerman's emphasis on the need to consider multiple constitutional moments in the context of a particular constitutional order.[2] In order to understand the "foundation" of each of the systems, therefore – itself merely one of several key facets that must be understood in order to grasp the broader nature of any particular supranational human rights system, as the following chapters will argue – it is necessary to examine each system's multiple births and rebirths. This chapter will examine the key foundational moments of the European, Inter-American, and African systems in turn.

## II Europe

### *II.1 The European Convention for the Protection of Human Rights and Fundamental Freedoms*

The modern international human rights regime was born in the wake of World War II.[3] Emphasis on the importance of rights gathered steam during the war. Roosevelt's 1941 "Four Freedoms" address constituted one important wartime precedent, US and British agreement on the Atlantic

[1] Madsen, "Explaining the Power of International Courts".

[2] See Bruce Ackerman, *We the People, Vol. 1: Foundations* (Harvard University Press, 1991); Bruce Ackerman, *We the People, Vol. 2: Transformations* (Harvard University Press, 1998); Bruce Ackerman, *We the People, Vol. 3: The Civil Rights Revolution* (Harvard University Press, 2014).

[3] On that birth, see, from a voluminous literature, Morsink, *The Universal Declaration*; Glendon, *A World Made New*; Mark Mazower, "The Strange Triumph of Human Rights, 1933–1950," 47 *The Historical Journal* (2004), 379–98; Borgwardt, *A New Deal for the World*; Roger Normand and Sarah Zaidi, *Human Rights at the UN: The Political History of Universal Justice* (Indiana University Press, 2008); Roberts, *The Contentious History*. Rights as such, of course, can be connected to a much longer history, as can the idea that the international community and international law should recognize such rights. Among the many forerunners of later developments, for example, one might point to Russian international lawyer Fedor Fedorovich Martens' emphasis on the existence of rights which "découlent de la nature et des conditions de l'humanité," including the rights to "respect de sa personne, à l'inviolabilité de sa famille et de sa propriété" in the late nineteenth century. Fedor Fedorovich Martens, *Traité de Droit International*, Volume 1 (Librairie Marescq Aine, 1883), 14. One could also point to the insistence of Elihu Root, the American Secretary of State, that states are obliged to conform to "an established standard of civilization" in their treatment of foreigners, followed shortly thereafter by Edwin Borchard, an American international

Charter, later that year, another. Wartime enthusiasm for human rights was expressed by a number of organizations that prepared draft bills of rights and otherwise worked to promote the "human rights" cause. On the American side of the Atlantic these included organs of the US government, such as the State Department and the National Resources Planning Board, inter-governmental bodies, such as the Inter-American Juridical Committee and the International Labour Organization (ILO) (core staff from which had relocated to Canada during the war), and a number of civil society groups, including Christian and Jewish groups, the World Citizens' Association, the International League for Human Rights, the Commission to Study the Organization of Peace, the American Law Institute,[4] and the Committee on Human Rights of the Universities' Committee on Post-War International Problems.[5] On the European side

lawyer, who emphasized this meant that states must ensure foreigners "a certain minimum of rights necessary to the enjoyment of life, liberty and property." See Elihu Root, "The Basis of Protection to Citizens Residing Abroad," 4 *American Journal of International Law* (1910), 521; Edwin M. Borchard, *The Diplomatic Protection of Nationals Abroad; or, The Law of International Claims* (Banks Law Publishing, 1915), 39. Similarly, in an address to the American Society of International Law in 1912, Pasquale Fiore emphasized that individuals have "certain rights, which are independent of the state and sometimes in opposition to the rights of the sovereign power" – emphasizing the prohibition of slavery, and the rights to property, freedom of conscience, and freedom of movement. See Pasquale Fiore, "Some Considerations on the Past, Present and Future of International Law," 6 *American Society of International Law Proceedings* (1912), 15–36. For more, see Stephen C. Neff, *Justice Among Nations: A History of International Law* (Harvard University Press, 2014), 273–4. Even more directly, in 1929 the International Law Institute adopted the "Declaration of the International Rights of Man," which emphasized the rights to life, liberty, property, nondiscrimination, religious freedom, language, and nationality. The new Declaration was endorsed by the International Federation of Leagues for the Defense of the Rights of Man and Citizens in 1931, and formed an important precedent for several of the bills of rights drafted during the war.

4 The American Law Institute's draft was notable for its recognition and inclusion of a number of socioeconomic rights, including the rights to social security, employment, decent working conditions, food, and shelter.

5 The American Law Institute was founded in 1923, with the aim of promoting the clarification and simplification of American common law. The World Citizens Association was founded in 1939, intended as an American branch of the World Foundation, founded by Spanish author and diplomat Salvador de Madariaga in 1936. The Commission to Study the Organization of Peace was also founded in 1939, by history professor James Shotwell, international relations professor Quincy Wright, and peace activist Clark Eichelberger. The International League was founded in 1941, largely by French exiles from the Fédération Internationale des Droits de l'Homme (itself founded in 1898, in response to the Dreyfus affair). For more, see Jan Herman Burgers, "The Road to San Francisco: The Revival of the

of things, Hersh Lauterpacht's 1945 *An International Bill of the Rights of Man* was particularly significant.[6] In addition to formulating his own bill of rights and advancing the cause of rights in general, Lauterpacht's work was perhaps most notable for its forceful emphasis on the importance of ensuring that any international rights document be overseen by effective institutional mechanisms.

Such efforts were motivated in part by the horrors and injustices of the war itself, which provided a powerful background context in relation to which the new rights project could be promoted. As the war came to an end, many of those who came to power in Europe knew those horrors only too well, having spent time in the resistance, in prison, or both during the war, where they suffered not only from the policies of the Axis powers, but also from repressive policies adopted by allied local authorities.

In the wake of the war, attention turned to the international level. While rights were referenced in the Charter of the United Nations, those references were not as strong as rights advocates would have wished. Primary responsibility for rights issues was bestowed upon the Economic and Social Council, which promptly delegated such responsibility to a newly created subsidiary body, the Human Rights Commission. While creation of the Commission prompted the immediate submission of a number of rights-based communications from around the world, the Commission quickly determined that it would be inappropriate to respond to such communications.[7]

Human Rights Idea in the Twentieth Century," 14 *Human Rights Quarterly* (1992), 468; William Irvine, *Between Justice and Politics: The Ligue des Droits de l'Homme, 1898–1945* (Stanford University Press, 2007); Glenn Tatsuya Mitoma, "Civil Society and International Human Rights: The Commission to Study the Organization of Peace and the Origins of the UN Human Rights Regime," 30 *Human Rights Quarterly* (2008), 607–30; Hanne Hagtvedt Vik, "Taming the States: The American Law Institute and the 'Statement of Essential Human Rights,'" 7 *Journal of Global History* (2012), 481; Eckel, "The International League for the Rights of Man."

[6] See Hersch Lauterpacht, *An International Bill of the Rights of Man* (Oxford University Press, 1945/2013). Among the notable features of Lauterpacht's work is that while he advocated the inclusion of socioeconomic rights among those rights that were guaranteed internationally, he considered them nonjusticiable.

[7] While delegates of the Philippines, Lebanon, and India supported the consideration of the complaints, and Lauterpacht argued that the United Nations was legally bound to receive them, such positions lost out. For more, see Ton Zuijdwijk, *Petitioning the United Nations: A Study in Human Rights* (Palgrave, 1982); Hersch Lauterpacht, "The International Protection of Human Rights," 70 *Hague Recueil* (1947), 1–108; International Law Association, *Report of the Forty-Third Conference Held at Brussels University 29 August–4 September 1948* (ILA, 1950); Hersch Lauterpacht, *International Law: Being the Collected Papers of Hersch*

Instead, the Commission busied itself with the task of preparing a list of the rights that were to be recognized by the international community. Initially, it was unclear whether this would involve drafting a declaration or a convention, and in either case what kind of mechanisms would be developed to oversee rights protection. Some voices echoed Lauterpacht's views on the need for strong mechanisms. Toward the conclusion of the Human Rights Commission's mid-1948 meetings, Cassin proposed the creation of a commission of eleven members to examine compliance with rights obligations, which might receive petitions and propose draft rights resolutions.[8] For key state parties, however, not only was the idea of creating oversight institutions seen as a step too far, but even the idea of producing a binding rights guarantee proved too much, with consensus solidifying instead around the idea of a declaration. The Universal Declaration of Human Rights was accordingly drawn up by the Commission and passed on to the General Assembly, which adopted it at end of 1948. While conversations on a follow-up convention commenced immediately thereafter, they quickly became bogged down.

The outcome of discussions concerning the possibility of ensuring strong human rights protections on the international level was thus to prove a disappointment for many of human rights strongest advocates – as, rather than a hard law convention that would be overseen by a court with the power to issue binding judgments, only the aspirational "Universal Declaration" was produced. Many in Europe, therefore, turned their attention to the regional level. In doing so, they were able to link up their campaign for greater rights protections with the increasingly popular campaign for greater regional unity. Early momentum in such a direction had come from many quarters. In Britain, for instance, the Federal Union, a

*Lauterpacht* (Cambridge University Press, 1976); Simpson, *Human Rights and the End of Empire*, 352–63; Burke, *Decolonization*, Chapter 3.

8 See Simpson, *Human Rights and the End of Empire*, 442–3. Earlier proposals for the consideration of petitions by working groups of the Human Rights Commission, as well as for an international human rights court, were made in a working group established to consider implementation, but were met with hostility from the great powers. See ibid., 480–6. The French government initially allowed Cassin to argue in favor of petition, although they were opposed to it, because they were confident that other countries would oppose it, and indeed in short order both Britain and France expressed firm opposition, both because of their belief that the petition would harm them politically more than it would harm their Cold War opponents – they imagined, rightly, that no complaints would be allowed by the authoritarian governments of the Eastern block – and because of their fear that anticolonial forces would be able to advance complaints against them through such a system. See ibid., 514–7, 522–5.

member-based organization, had called during the war for a post-bellum federation of democratic states under a constitution including a bill of rights. Similar ideas had been floated within the British government, with the idea of a European rights convention debated in the House of Lords in 1944, though it was opposed by the government at the time.

In continental Europe as well the desire for greater unity had been around since the war. Within occupied France both the Conseil National de la Resistance and Le Mouvement de Libération Nationale emphasized the importance of post-war European federation and with it a program in support of human rights. The same idea was given more formal voice and support by a conference held in Geneva in 1944, attended by representatives of Denmark, France, Italy, Holland, Poland, Czechoslovakia, Yugoslavia, and Germany. Following the war, groups such as the European Parliamentary Union, the European League for Economic Cooperation, the French Council for a United Europe, the Nouvelles Équipes Internationales, and the Socialist Movement for the United States of Europe all took up the call for greater unity. The Union of European Federalists and the United Europe Movement, later known as the European Movement, were formed thereafter as umbrella organizations, including these and other groups.[9] This new federalist movement held a major conference in The Hague in May 1948. The conference resulted in agreement to work toward two ends – the establishment of a "European Parliamentary Assembly," and the production of a "European Charter of Human Rights." In accordance with the wishes of rights advocates, the latter was to be overseen by a court, to which individuals might apply. France, Italy, Belgium, and the Netherlands were all supportive, as, from afar, was the United States. The British remained wary at best.

[9] For more, see European Movement, *The European Movement and the Council of Europe* (1949); Arnold Zurcher, *The Struggle to Unite Europe 1940–58* (Greenwood, 1958); Henri Brugmans, *L'Idée Européenne 1920–1970* (De Temple, 1970); Frank Willis ed., *European Integration* (New Viewpoints, 1975); Richard Vaughan, *Post War Integration in Europe* (Palgrave, 1976); James Wilkinson, *The Intellectual Resistance in Europe* (Harvard University Press, 1981); Walter Lipgens, *A History of European Integration: 1945–1947* (Clarendon, 1982); Walter Lipgens, *Documents on the History of European Integration* (de Gruyter, 1985); Derek Heater, *The Idea of European Unity* (Palgrave, 1992). As Kaiser, Moyn, and Duranti have shown, more conservative forces, including in particular Christian religious groups, played a key role in promoting both the European and the global human rights projects in this period. See Wolfram Kaiser, *Christian Democracy and the Origins of the European Union* (Cambridge University Press, 2007); Samuel Moyn, *Christian Human Rights* (University of Pennsylvania Press, 2014); Duranti, *The Conservative Human Rights Revolution*.

While the federalist project had been born out of the immense violence of World War II, it would soon derive even greater momentum from the gathering tensions of the Cold War.[10] The period following the May 1948 Hague Conference saw communists take power in Czechoslovakia, civil war break out in Greece, and the imposition of the "Berlin Blockade" in Germany. Against such a backdrop, regional unity came to appeal not so much on the basis of the high ideals the idea potentially embodied, as due to widespread belief in the need to confederate in order to more forcefully resist the Soviet Union. At the same time, security concerns began to take precedence, with the Treaty of Brussels agreed in March 1948, and NATO established in April 1949.

From late 1948 to early 1949 the inter-governmental "Committee for the Study of European Unity" met to consider the idea of a European parliamentary assembly. Progress was difficult, however, in large part thanks to British resistance. The compromise ultimately agreed upon was to create a "Council of Europe," which would consist of both a "Consultative Assembly," which would give voice to the people, and a "Committee of Ministers," to ensure a role for governments. Naturally, the assembled state representatives thought it appropriate that the "Committee of Ministers" should be the more powerful body, and accordingly gave it the power to control the agenda, while further stipulating that no progress might be made on any key issue without unanimous consent of the assembled ministers. With these parameters agreed, the Council of Europe was created in May 1949, bringing together the United Kingdom, France, Italy, Belgium, the Netherlands, Luxembourg, Norway, Sweden, Denmark, and Ireland in a novel regionalist endeavor.

While security concerns were now firmly on top of the agenda, the human rights project was not forgotten. Rather, in fact, it came to take on a new appeal for the states of Western Europe, as emphasizing human rights was seen as a useful strategy through which Western European states could publicize their high ideals and respectful treatment of their citizens, while denouncing the rights abuses of the Soviet Union. From early 1949 on, various subgroups formed by the European Movement began to contemplate in more detail the shape Europe's human rights system might take. Early proposals imagined the creation of a commission, to which individuals might bring their claims, as well as of a court,

[10] As M. Spaak once reportedly put it, "the man who did most to bring about the union of Western Europe was Joseph Stalin." See Arthur Robertson, *Human Rights in Europe* 4–5 (1st edn., Manchester University Press, 1963).

to which the commission might advance claims as and when it deemed appropriate.

While the institutional imagination at this stage was moderately ambitious, other components of the initial draft text were more conservative. The list of rights that was drawn up carefully excluded social and economic rights. In addition, states were only to be required to protect the rights in question "to the extent that [they] were secured by the constitution, laws and administrative practice existing in each country at the date of the signing of the Convention"[11] – limiting the Convention's scope, in other words, to the prevention of backsliding, and foreclosing the possibility of interpreting the text in a progressive, evolutive manner.[12]

On the formal level, as of early 1949 the Consultative Assembly seemed content to leave the question of rights as a pending issue for the future. The following months saw a series of maneuvers through which the Consultative Assembly forced the Committee of Ministers to move rights into a more prominent place on its agenda, however. Ultimately, this pressure led to the convening of a special commission, tasked with preparing a draft convention, with the European Movement's draft to be taken as a starting point. While a minority within the special commission argued that the Council of Europe should confine itself to protecting democracy, the majority rejected this view, in favor of a fuller set of rights protections. The commission took the further crucial step of removing the clause that had limited the previous draft to the prevention of backsliding. The draft then passed into the hands of the Consultative Assembly, where a debate broke out over the potential inclusion of social and economic rights. Under the influence of Britain's Labour government, the right to property was dropped, in favor of the right to form trade unions freely.

[11] European Movement, European Convention of Human Rights, INF/5/E/R (1949).

[12] The draft convention also included a clause stipulating that states must "Faithfully … respect the fundamental principles of democracy … hold at reasonable intervals free elections by universal suffrage and secret ballot … [and] take no action which will interfere with the right of political criticism and the right to organize a political opposition." This clause was ultimately removed from the convention, however, to be replaced in the Convention's first protocol by a more limited provision calling only for the "hold[ing of] free elections at reasonable intervals by secret ballot, under conditions which will ensure the free expression of the people," without making any reference to political criticism and/or the political opposition. The impacts of this decision could be seen, among other places, in the Commission's early refusal to accept an application from the German Communist party following its dissolution by Germany in 1956, on the basis that the party's commitment to a proletarian revolution constituted a contradiction with democratic ideals. See German Communist Party v. Germany, App. No. 250/57, Eur. Comm. H.R. (July 20, 1957).

The decision not to exclude social and economic rights more broadly from the draft convention was affirmed, however.

The draft produced by the Consultative Assembly was referred to the Committee of Ministers in November 1949. From this stage on the British would play a key limiting role. While the British government had previously supported calls for some form of international rights convention in Western Europe, in significant part due to its belief that agreement on such a convention might provide a useful tool of foreign policy, as that convention increasingly took shape, the government became more and more concerned with the domestic implications of supranational human rights oversight. British resistance took several forms. In the first place, the British often contended that external rights protection was simply unnecessary, as no external institution could offer better protection than that which Britain's common law rights heritage offered. Linked to this, the British also suggested the proposed new European rights convention lacked substance, consisting rather of rhetorical declarations which would have little meaning or effect in practice.[13] In addition, and somewhat at odds with their other contentions, the British expressed concern with the idea that a European body might be able to force changes to the law of England. Finally, most seriously, the British government was aware that its empire was anything but a model of rights enjoyment, and that the imperial project would be seriously challenged should it be subjected to rights-based review.[14]

British concerns grew into several forms of opposition to the proposed text: the British demanded that the text be more specific; they called for a strengthened role for the Committee of Ministers; they resisted the idea that the Convention might apply to colonial territories; they opposed the idea of strong domestic legal applicability; and they resisted the ability of individuals to bring petitions, and the existence of a court with mandatory oversight. This resistance was successful on all fronts. In terms of the text, British appeals were broadly supported, as a new draft convention, heavily

[13] This critique drew upon a long tradition in Britain of dismissing rights guarantees in such terms; see, e.g., Jeremy Bentham, *Anarchical Fallacies* (William Tait, 1843); Jeremy Waldron, *"Nonsense Upon Stilts": Bentham, Burke and Marx on the Rights of Man* (Routledge, 1987).

[14] Adding insult to injury, the British delegate at the time presented this argument under the hypocritical guise that "constitutional reasons prevented the United Kingdom government from accepting international obligations on behalf of colonial governments without prior consultation and agreement." Bates, *Evolution of the European Convention*, 94. For more on British objections in general, see Simpson, *Human Rights and the End of Empire*, 655–93.

influenced by ongoing discussions on the International Covenant on Civil and Political Rights, was agreed upon. The Committee of Ministers was strengthened by being given the power to decide, by two-thirds majority, whether or not to convert a Commission decision into a binding judgment, and whether Commission reports might become public, as well as being entrusted with oversight of the implementation of decisions and judgments. A stipulation that the provisions of the Convention should be given full effect in domestic law was removed and replaced by the weaker suggestion that state parties must guarantee everyone within their jurisdiction the rights and freedoms defined therein, while a further article (Article 50) limited the remedial powers of the Court to declaratory statements. British concern that their colonial governance might be subjected to oversight – a concern shared by the Belgians and the French[15] – were addressed through the inclusion of a provision preventing the Convention from applying to colonial territories unless a separate declaration was made. Finally, and most significantly of all, the ability of individuals to bring forward complaints to the system, as well as acceptance of the court's oversight, were made optional, opt-in features. As if that were not enough, a derogations clause was also added, as was a clause stipulating that friendly settlements were to be encouraged.

The European "Convention for the Protection of Human Rights and Fundamental Freedoms," that was ultimately signed on November 4, 1950, was hence marked by an extensive set of limitations: failure to include social and economic rights; a weak vision of its own powers; a dominant role for state parties through the Committee of Ministers; lack of direct applicability to the colonial context; a strong derogation clause; and, most centrally of all, the optional nature of two key mechanisms, the right of individual petition and the possibility of court oversight. Above and beyond all these more concrete limitations, the Convention was also perhaps constrained by something more intangible, adhering in and flowing from the conditions in which it was formed. Unlike the work that was done on the international level, the European Convention was not imagined as a document for all humanity. Rather, its framing was more exclusionary, aimed at demonstrating Western Europe's exceptionality and underscoring the distinction between Western Europe as a space of rights-protection and the lack of rights protection elsewhere. Hamstrung by the

[15] See *Collected Edition of the "Travaux Préparatoires" of the ECHR* (Council of Europe, 1975–85); Duranti, *The Conservative Human Rights Revolution*, 203.

context in which it was born and the emphasis on excluding the rights of the colonized in particular,[16] the European Convention was hence marked by a worrying tendency to couple its extension of strong rights protections to some with an equally strong tendency to draw a line between those to whom such protections might apply, and those to whom they would not.[17]

16 Leopold Senghor, future president of Senegal and a member of the Parliamentary Assembly of the Council of Europe at the time the draft European Convention was debated, spoke scathingly of the decision to insert a clause making colonial applicability optional:

> Article 63 runs counter to the general principles of the Declaration of Human Rights and particularly to Article 14 which condemns all discrimination, as also to Article 1, which states that "the High Contracting Parties shall secure to each person within their jurisdiction the rights and freedoms defined in Section 1 of this Convention."
>
> In effect, Article 63 appears to be a rather clumsy way of excluding overseas territories from the Convention. It therefore appears to me to be an echo of the Colonial Pact …
>
> In adopting Article 63 the Assembly would transform the European Declaration of Human Rights into a Declaration of European Human Rights. This would be to deny the same rights to other men. This would mean betraying the spirit of European Civilisation which – as Valéry has written – made man "the measure of all things" …
>
> I can hear the experts, speaking in the name of realism, prophesying all sorts of catastrophes if we delete this Article 63. A century and a half ago, in 1789, there were also experts in France. They prophesied that to extend Human Rights to slaves would mean giving the Colonies the signal for revolt. They, the realists of those times, were mistaken, and it was their dictator – Napoleon – who caused France to lose Haiti, the finest of its colonies, in trying to re-establish slavery.

European Consultative Assembly, Second Session of the Consultative Assembly (August 7–28, 1950), reprinted in *Collected Edition of the "Travaux Préparatoires" of the ECHR*. For more on the colonial clause and its afterlife, see Barbara Miltner, "Revisiting Extraterritoriality After Al-Skeini: The ECHR and Its Lessons," 33 *Michigan Journal of International Law* (2012), 693–747.

17 As Duranti has put it,

> Whereas the historical logic of citizenship rights was one of a diffusion of rights outward to an expanding circle of once marginalized groups, the historical logic of European human rights protections was one of a movement from the outside inward.
>
> The European human rights system was directed at safeguarding those freedoms that the European unity movements described as derived from Western Europe's premodern Christian and humanist heritage within the confines of what Churchill termed "democratic European civilization." By this, he meant a bounded cultural space restricted to those nations who embraced a common set of ethical values derived from the shared history of their peoples. The Universal Declaration, by contrast, explicitly grounded its human rights principles in metaphysical assumptions regarding inherent human attributes – dignity, reason, and conscience – abstracted from any particular sociopolitical context. European human rights were, in this sense, not universal human rights.

Duranti, *The Conservative Human Rights Revolution*, 210.

While the Convention's exclusionary framing received criticism from some at the time, it was seen by many more as a positive feature of the system. The optional nature of individual petition and court jurisdiction, on the other hand, were seen as major grounds for concern. Thanks to the system's lack of an oversight infrastructure, and thanks as well to European federalists' decreasing attention to rights as the momentum of integration shifted to the economic terrain,[18] as of the end of 1950 it was unclear whether the European Council and the European Convention on Human Rights had much of a future. Perhaps, having made a symbolic statement with the Convention, states would consider they had done enough, and grand dreams of a more meaningful European human rights system would gradually fade away.

Early fears would prove excessive, however. An early sign the regime would not become moribund came through the drafting of the first optional protocol, proposing the addition of the rights to education, property, and free elections. The protocol was agreed in 1952, and by 1954 had already acquired the ten ratifications needed to enter into force. Convention ratifications also came fairly quickly. The United Kingdom took the lead, aware that it would risk serious damage to its reputation if it failed to do so, given how stubbornly it had worked to water-down the system. By 1953 ten ratifications had been received and the Convention came into force, with the first eleven-member Commission composed the following year. Even more surprisingly for those left pessimistic by the drafting process, by mid-1955 six states had signed up to allow petitions, thereby allowing the submission of individual communications to commence.[19] By the end of 1958 eight states had accepted the Court's jurisdiction,[20] paving the way for the composition of the first Court in 1959.[21]

[18] While human rights remained prominent in the negotiations on the formation of a more closely integrated European economic community in the early 1950s, by later in the decade they had largely faded from view. See Gráinne de Burca, "The Road Not Taken: The EU as a Global Human Rights Actor," 105 *American Journal of International Law* (2011), 649–93.

[19] Ireland and Denmark were leaders, followed by Belgium, Iceland, West Germany, and Sweden; Norway signed up later in 1955. Britain would only accept in 1966, after its colonial empire had all but vanished. Italy, Switzerland, and France were all late adherents, Italy signing up in 1973, Switzerland in 1974, and France in 1981.

[20] Once again Ireland and Denmark were the first states to sign up, followed by the Netherlands in 1954, West Germany and Belgium in 1955, and Austria, Luxembourg, and Iceland in 1958.

[21] The text of the Convention did not contain any precise provisions as to bureaucratic support for a future court, stipulating only that the Council of Europe would provide for the Court's expenses. The question was put to the Directorate of Human Rights, an office

While this rapid rate of acceptance of the Convention's optional features was a hopeful sign, it was tempered somewhat by the fact that states in general only ever accepted the right of individual petition or the court's oversight for a few years at a time, thereby maintaining strong pressure on both the Commission and the Court not to take up their mandates with too much enthusiasm.

### *II.2 The Colonial Question*

Understanding the conditions in which the European human rights system was initially composed helps cast light on several fundamental aspects of the system, and the enduring relevance of several aspects of the system's formation may be seen in its contemporary successes and challenges. In addition to the initial moments of the system's formation, it is worth pausing a moment to consider a major case that arose in the system's early years, concerning British colonial governance in Cyprus. While the Cyprus case might from some perspectives appear a relatively marginal affair, it is suggested here that it was particularly significant in terms of the practical precedents it set, relative to the possibilities and modes of human rights work the European system would, and would not, take up in future.

Despite what one might have expected, given their vigorous resistance to the idea the European Convention be applied in the colonial context and their insistence on the insertion of a clause stipulating that the Convention might only apply in the colonial context on a discretionary basis, the British were quick to declare that they would in fact allow the Convention to so apply. At the time this seemed a relatively safe move, since Britain had not signed up to the possibility of individual petitions or to the jurisdiction of the Court. By submitting such a declaration, therefore, the authorities likely imagined they could burnish their image at little practical cost.

If such was the thinking of the British authorities who made the decision to accept the Convention's applicability to colonial holdings, their confidence that their actions in the empire would remain unchallenged was

reporting to the Secretary General of the Council of Europe, which argued that the matter should be put in the Court's hands. The initial arrangement saw the Court's staff seconded from the Directorate of Human Rights; the Court was careful to emphasize that this was merely a practical arrangement, however, and that it had full control of the matter in accordance with the principle of judicial independence. For more, see Paul Mahoney, "The Statute of the Registry of the European Court of Human Rights: Past, Present and Future," in Mahoney et al. eds., *Protecting Human Rights* (Heyman, 2000), 849.

misplaced. The first case declared admissible by the European system, in June 1956, was an inter-state communication, brought by Greece against the United Kingdom, in relationship to British authorities' declaration of a state of emergency in Cyprus on November 26, 1955, and the aggressive measures of suppression they implemented in the period that followed.[22]

The Greek communication was expansive in tone and wide-ranging in the areas it addressed, challenging numerous policies deployed pursuant to the British emergency regime in Cyprus. The strength of the Greek case was bolstered by their appointment of Henri Rolin, a distinguished professor of international law (and later a judge in the European Court), to represent their case before the Commission. Receipt of the communication presented a novel challenge to the British foreign office, which had never before had to confront any such challenge. The substance of the case was a matter of serious concern for British colonial administrators well beyond the immediate context, as declarations of emergency rule and the implementation of repressive measures under emergency mandates were standard practice across the empire, particularly in its dying days.[23] In short, foreign office staff took the submission extremely seriously.[24] While the British government mulled the possibility of adopting an obstructivist approach, ultimately they decided to take the opposite tack, attempting to curry favor by facilitating the Commission's work, including supporting a Commission mission to Cyprus, where they hoped to demonstrate the inherent reasonableness of the measures they were taking, by carefully shepherding the delegation away from any inconvenient facts where necessary.

It is not clear to what extent the British were able to convince the Commission of the reasonableness of the measures they had adopted. What is clear, however, is that the Commission was aware that adopting

[22] The second case declared admissible by the European system, in October 1957, was also a communication from Greece concerning British actions in Cyprus, in particular forty-nine documented instances of the torture of Greek Cypriots. That case was resolved on the political level, however, as, following the establishment of an independent government in Cyprus, Greece agreed to drop the case.

[23] For earlier forms of such practice in the British Empire, see Christopher Roberts, "From the State of Emergency to the Rule of Law: The Evolution of Repressive Legality in the Nineteenth Century British Empire," 20 *Chicago Journal of International Law* (2019), 1–60; Christopher Roberts, "The Age of Emergency," 20 *Washington University Global Studies Law Review* (2021), 99.

[24] As Simpson puts it, the British were aware that if there was a negative judgment, "there would have to be a complete reappraisal of the mechanisms of repression which had been developing over the years, and which had never previously had to be justified in international proceedings." Simpson, *Human Rights and the End of Empire*, 959.

an aggressive position in its first holding, in a matter of high importance to one of Europe's most powerful states, could lead to forceful political blowback. The seriousness with which the Commission took such concerns was testified to by the fact that its finding was anything but bold and assertive. The Commission considered a range of interrelated British emergency law measures: the imposition of a curfew; prolonged detentions without warrant or trial; deportations; the entry and search of premises without warrant; new rules establishing tight control over burials; new forms of censorship and other limitations on speech and assembly; school closures; the occupation and destruction of property; the imposition of collective punishment; the authorization of corporal punishment; and the implementation of rules limiting the accountability of public officials and security forces. On all questions, the Commission did not find any violations, with the Greek commissioner often the sole voice of dissent.

In order to reach this outcome, the Commission relied on a range of avoidance strategies. Thus, for instance, the Commission found that it had no need to pass judgment on the question of collective and corporal punishment, as, subsequent to the initial communication, Britain had revoked the ordinances enabling those measures.[25] Another of the Commission's avoidances was of even greater import. As well as challenging various specific measures adopted by the British, Greece had also challenged their ability to declare a state of emergency in the first place, arguing that the situation in Cyprus had not warranted it. In response, the Commission utilized a novel formula through which to justify its failure to find a violation, observing that every government "retains, within certain limits, its discretion in appreciating the threat to the life of the nation. In the present case the [British] Government of Cyprus has not gone beyond these limits of appreciation."[26]

[25] Four members of the Commission vigorously dissented on this issue. See Greece v. United Kingdom, Eur Comm. H.R., 2 European Yearbook of Human Rights 182 (1958–1959), para. 230. The Commission itself, moreover, at least gently indicated that, had it issued a holding on corporal punishment, it would have found the United Kingdom in violation of the Convention, observing that "the trend of opinion today amongst the peoples of the Council of Europe is not sympathetic to corporal punishment as a penal sanction for young persons" – thereby also taking a first step toward the development of the system's "European consensus" approach to jurisprudence.

[26] Ibid., para. 130. The Commission did however assert that it had authority to review the question, resisting the British position that such review was inappropriate. Interestingly, as Simpson notes, behind the scenes opinion in the British Colonial Office largely overlapped with the Greek position, with many convinced Governor Armitage's declaration of a state of emergency and subsequent actions had gone too far. See Simpson, *Human Rights and the End of Empire*, 1002–5.

Thus it was that the "margin of appreciation," which has become one of the cornerstones of the European approach to human rights, was born.

Of similar importance, though less recognized, was the manner in which the Commission addressed the question of admissibility. Britain argued that the case should be found inadmissible, due to the petitioners' failure to make the case that domestic remedies had been exhausted. In reply, Greece argued that an exception to the rule of exhaustion ought to apply, since, in its view, the state of emergency in Cyprus had removed the possibility of effective remedy. In response, the Commission split the difference, accepting the British argument as to the individual claims of violation Greece had submitted, relative to which the Commission held the exhaustion rule was applicable, while accepting the Greek argument relative to those claims concerning "legislative measures and administrative practices," relative to which the Commission found the exhaustion rule inapplicable.

An important implication of this decision – and one that is easier to see in light of comparative human rights experience – was to set the European system's jurisprudence along two distinct paths. On one side, big-picture law and policy cases and cases addressed to systemic situations of violation; on the other, cases concerning more carefully individuated instances of violation. The first path was linked to inter-state communications, the second to "individual" communications. Through this decision, the Commission helped to develop, in advance of its ever having received an "individual" communication, an understanding that it would be inappropriate for too wide a lens toward human rights violations to be adopted via the individual communication procedure.[27]

The years that followed the Commission's disappointing but politically sagacious holding in the Cyprus case saw decolonization gather steam, limiting the number of further opportunities the developing European human rights system would have to confront colonial rights violations

[27] The emphasis on more carefully delimited cases in the European context can be traced to other factors as well. Given the intense contestation around individual petitions during the Convention's drafting, it was already unlikely that the Commission would allow individuals to bring broad, *actio popularis*-style complaints. More tangibly, the difference may be traced to the different language pertaining to individual and state complaints in the Convention, which observed that individuals might claim to be victims, while states might allege more general claims of violation on the part of other states. The fact that two different tracks would develop was not inevitable, however: as the experience of the other systems has shown, it is perfectly possible for a Commission to consider widespread, systematic and structural violations through an "individual complaints" procedure.

directly. Several cases in the years that followed offered the Commission the chance to address colonial-style laws and policies, if not their implementation in the colonial context. The next two major cases considered by the Commission gave it a chance to establish a more forceful rights-based position on states of emergency. The Commission's second inter-state case arose from a communication submitted by Norway, Sweden, Denmark, and the Netherlands concerning the situation in Greece after the military coup of 1967.[28] Following a lengthy investigation the Commission issued a holding accepting the applicants' allegations, rejecting the military government's claims that it had a right to overthrow the previous government, and finding that the Greek government had not had sound grounds for declaring a state of emergency. Faced with the threat of expulsion from the Council of Europe, the Greek government chose instead to leave of its own volition.

The Commission's third major inter-state case was initiated by a communication from Ireland concerning the emergency policies deployed by the United Kingdom in Northern Ireland. While in its 1976 report the Commission failed to hold that the majority of the emergency policies deployed by the United Kingdom had violated rights guarantees, it did find that the combined practices of forcing detainees to stand against walls, hooding them, subjecting them to loud and disruptive sounds, and depriving them of sleep, food, and water amounted to torture. Following this finding, the Commission referred the case to the Court, at which stage the holding became public. The Court was not willing to go quite as far as the Commission, finding only that the use of the methods in question amounted to inhuman and degrading treatment.[29]

The system had another early chance to address a different aspect of the colonial legacy through a case submitted by the "individual" application route. In the mid-1960s hundreds of thousands of British citizens of South

[28] Denmark, Norway, Sweden, & the Netherlands v. Greece, App. Nos. 3321–2/67 & 3344/67, Eur. Comm. H.R. (November 5, 1969).

[29] Ireland v. United Kingdom, App. No. 5310/71, Eur. Comm. H.R. (January 18, 1978). Between the late 1970s and early 1980s the Commission went on to issue holdings in relation to several cases submitted by Cyrus concerning Turkey. In all three, the Commission found that Turkey had committed widespread and serious violations. See Cyprus v. Turkey, App. No. 6780/74, Eur. Comm. H.R. (July 10, 1976); Cyprus v. Turkey, App. No. 6950/75, Eur. Comm. H.R. (July 10, 1976); Cyprus v. Turkey, App. No. 8007/77, Eur. Comm. H.R. (October 4, 1983). Since Turkey had not signed up to the jurisdiction of the Court, the cases were referred to the Committee of Ministers, which refused to take any serious action to follow-up on the findings. While the Committee eventually allowed publication of the reports, it refused to vote on whether or not to affirm the Commission's decisions, despite the fact that according to its own rules of procedure such a vote was obligatory.

Asian origin attempted to immigrate to the United Kingdom, primarily from East Africa. In response, the British government passed a law aimed at preventing their entry. The Commission tried for several years to promote a friendly settlement; failing that, it ultimately produced a report finding that the United Kingdom's immigration laws violated the Convention.[30] Despite the fact the United Kingdom had accepted the jurisdiction of the Court, however, the Commission did not refer the case, doubtless out of fear of the political blowback that would follow.[31] Instead the report went to the Committee of Ministers, where the British government was able to block the two-thirds majority necessary in order to take further action, or even to make the decision public, leading to the Committee's closure of the case in 1977.[32]

While such cases saw the European system moving in a more assertive direction in comparison to the weak position adopted in the *First Cyprus Case*, their outcomes remained timid. The decisions also came too late to establish European responsibility for widespread and systematic violations in the context of Empire. That failing produced several troubling legacies. In the first place, the European human rights system's failure to directly confront colonial rights violations helped to conceal the violence and inequalities of colonialism and the extent of European culpability that flowed therefrom. In addition, the system's failure to recognize the rights violations on which colonial law and policy was based – in short, the absolute incompatibility of human rights obligations and the techniques of colonial governance – helped to allow many of those same colonial governance practices to survive the process of decolonization and to persist within the legal and institutional structures of postcolonial states. Moreover, by failing to address colonial rights violations, the European system entrenched limitations on the scope of the European vision of

[30] See East African Asians v. United Kingdom, App. No. 4403/70, Eur. Comm. H.R. (December 14, 1973).

[31] The Commission's wariness was well-founded. In 1972 the United Kingdom's Home Secretary circulated an internal memo commenting on the troublesome nature of the Strasbourg system, and concluding with the observation that "it is a calculation whether we shall be exposed to greater political harm by continuing to subscribe to these articles or by withdrawing from them." For more, see Bates, *Evolution of the European Convention*, 286–9.

[32] Anthony Lester, who was a lawyer for the applicants, has argued that the pressure around the case helped to produce at least some positive changes in British law at the time, however. See Anthony Lester, "East African Asians Versus the United Kingdom: The Inside Story," Lecture (October 23, 2003).

rights, helping to inaugurate a vision of rights protection that has struggled to come to grips with transborder harms, as well as with the historical legacies of colonial violence and exploitation.

### *II.3 Judicialization*

As the previous sections have shown, many key aspects of the European system were determined in the system's early years. The contemporary system owes much of its shape and nature not only to those early moments, however, but also to another period, in which several key aspects of the system were fundamentally rewritten – the years of immense optimism among many of the system's supporters, and of political opportunity, that followed the end of the Cold War.

As we have seen, when the European system was formed, both individual petition and the Court's jurisdiction were optional features. As popular support for human rights rose in the 1970s, the Court became more confident. While the Court adopted an increasingly assertive role, its institutional position was still weak in several ways, both because of the temporary nature of states' recognitions of its jurisdiction, and thanks to the still prominent role of the Committee of Ministers.

As the 1970s transitioned into the 1980s, various actors began to consider ways to firm up and expand the position and role of the Court.[33] According to the system originally established, the Committee of Ministers had responsibility to take action on Commission holdings not referred to the Court. Individuals had no status before the Committee of Ministers, however, and were rarely informed in any detail concerning proceedings there; state parties, on the other hand, were not only privy to the proceedings, but were also able to vote on how to proceed, even when the Commission found they had violated the Convention. The potential for abuse was borne out in practice, as on multiple occasions the Committee refused to recognize the Commission's findings.

As time went on, the Committee of Ministers' overtly political interference in the European human rights system was increasingly criticized.[34]

[33] Earlier steps to expand the independence of the system's institutions included changes to the rules of procedure of first the Court and then the Commission, allowing both to assert a greater degree of control over their registry staff, following disputes with the Secretary General of the Council of Europe in 1969. See Mahoney, "The Statute of the Registry," 851.

[34] See Bates, *Evolution of the European Convention*, 413, citing David Harris, Michael O'Boyle, and Colin Warbrick, *Law of the European Convention on Human Rights* (1st edn., Oxford University Press, 1995); Ronny Abraham, "La Réforme du Mécanisme de Contrôle de la

During the course of the 1980s, this criticism became more effective, leading the Committee of Ministers to exercise its political discretion less and less, such that by the late 1980s it was rare for the Committee to dispute the Commission's holdings.[35] In the late 1980s the informal pressure the Committee had been under led to a more concrete change in the form of procedural reforms. In 1987 the Committee's rules of procedure were amended to make publication of the Commission's reports the default outcome, to make it harder for Committee processes to end up without a decision, and to regularize, at least to a degree, the Committee's role relative to the enforcement of judgments.[36]

Concurrently, pressure was building toward more fundamental reforms of the system. The most important factor driving recognition of the need for reform was the system's constantly increasing caseload. The caseload of the system was already dramatically higher in the 1970s than it had been in the 1960s; by the 1980s, it was moving in the direction of being unmanageable, without an increase in resources. Whereas in 1976 2,041 provisional files were opened, 427 applications registered, 11 cases were declared admissible and 5 judgments were delivered, in 1989 4,900 provisional files were opened, 1,445 applications were registered, 95 cases were declared admissible, and 24 judgments were delivered. Increased caseload reflected increased awareness of the Convention and its oversight system; this increased awareness not only led to a greater volume of cases, but also to a greater volume of high-quality cases. This development was thanks both to the growing number of lawyers familiar with the system and to the growing extensiveness and sophistication of the system's jurisprudence, as well as of human rights jurisprudence in general, providing lawyers with a much more extensive textual basis on which to ground their submissions. As a result, over and above the number of cases being submitted, new cases were often harder to summarily dismiss, and required a

Convention Européenne des Droits de l'Homme: Le Protocole no 11 à la Convention," 40 *Annuaire Français de Droit International* (1994), 619–32.

[35] An exception occurred in *Warwick v. United Kingdom* (App. No. 9471/81, Eur. Comm. H.R. [July 18, 1986]), a case concerning the corporal punishment of schoolchildren.

[36] Where the Committee did refuse to uphold the Commission's findings, the result might be the self-defeating one of drawing extra public attention to the matter, placing additional pressure on the state in question to reform the relevant practice. While the Committee was not as given to directly disputing Commission holdings as it once had been, much of the Committee's oversight work was undertaken by the Directorate of Human Rights, which continued to favor a gentler, behind the scenes approach to enforcement.

greater devotion of time and effort on the part of the Commission, the Court, and their respective staffs.

While this caseload pressure affected the Court, its main pressure was on the Commission, given the Commission's role as the system's frontline institution.[37] While several reforms were introduced into caseload processing to improve efficiency, such improvements could not keep up with the demands imposed by the increasing rate of submissions. Protocol 8, opened for signature and signed by the majority of state parties at a conference in Vienna in 1985, aimed to improve the efficiency of the Commission by allowing it to establish chambers and meet in committees of three to review admissibility.[38] Even as Protocol 8 was being drafted, however, it was apparent that such steps alone would not be sufficient to address the growing caseload challenge.

The 1980s thus saw two pressures coincide: normative pressure toward the increasing formality and independence of the system, on the one hand, and pressure toward efficiency-based reforms, to address the rising caseload challenge, on the other. Under the weight of these dual pressures, momentum for a more radical reconstruction of the system as a whole gradually built. The idea of major reforms was floated at the eighth meeting of the "Committee of Experts for the Improvement of the Procedure under the European Convention on Human Rights," held in July 1982.[39] The reform project began to gather political support at a conference held in Vienna three years later, where the Swiss and Austrian delegations led the way in pushing for recognition of the right of individuals to bring their cases to the Court, minimization of the role of the Committee of Ministers, and, if possible, the merger of the Commission and Court into a single judicial body.[40] Discussions on the possibility of

[37] By the late 1980s the Commission was increasingly playing a role similar to that of a court of first instance, dealing with repetitive cases and cases raising no novel legal issues, while sending cases requiring the formation of novel jurisprudence to the Court.

[38] See Arthur Robertson and John Merrills, *Human Rights in Europe: A Study of the European Convention on Human Rights* (3rd edn., Manchester University Press, 1993), 19–20. Protocol 8 also took a step toward greater judicialization of the Commission, by requiring that commissioners be persons qualified to hold high legal office.

[39] The meeting saw two commissioners, Frowein and Trechsel, suggest the merger of the Commission and the Court into a single body. The Commission as a whole, moreover, came out in support of the same idea in 1983. See Drzemczewski, "A Major Overhaul," 144.

[40] For more, see Helmut Turk, "The European Ministerial Conference on Human Rights," in Matscher and Petzold eds., *Protecting Human Rights*, 647–55.

reform continued in subsequent years.[41] Several states were not on board, however, with the British once again acting as spoilers, motivated in substantial part by reluctance to give up the measure of state control maintained through the Committee of Ministers. Despite the discussions, therefore, the political will necessary for major reform remained elusive throughout the 1980s.[42]

[41] Later in 1985, for instance, a group of deputies of the Committee of Ministers asked the Steering Committee for Human Rights to consider how the system might be improved, an issue the Committee of Experts for the Improvement of the Procedure under the European Convention took up at its seventeenth meeting at the end of the year, where the idea of a single, unified court continued to be placed front and center. The matter was discussed further at colloquies in Seville in November 1985 and in Neuchâtel, Switzerland in March 1986, where the idea of a unified Court received strong support from both system members and political representatives. See Herbert Petzold and Jonathan Sharpe, "Profile of the Future European Court of Human Rights," in Matscher and Petzold eds., *Protecting Human Rights*, 471–2. As Harmsen observes, Francies Jacobs concluded the conference by noting that "only the 'somewhat intriguing combination' of the Court Registrar and the UK government representative appeared to dissent from the prevailing consensus." Robert Harmsen, "The Reform of the Convention System: Institutional Restructuring and the (Geo-)Politics of Human Rights," in Christoffersen and Madsen eds., *The European Court*, 122, citing General Report, 8 *Human Rights Law Journal* (1987), 195–6. See also Bates, *Evolution of the European Convention*, 425. Discussions within the Committee of Experts did not lead to a decisive conclusion, however, with the Committee of Experts reporting to the Steering Committee for Human Rights at the end of 1987 that "no single and decisive argument for or against a merger had been found"; in the Committee for Human Rights as well "no consensus could be reached." Drzemczewski, "A Major Overhaul," 143. Momentum continued via the Parliamentary Assembly, however. In 1986, following the Neuchâtel colloquy, members of the Assembly presented a motion to make a recommendation on the merger of the Court and Commission. The proposal was considered by the Assembly's legal affairs committee, who prepared a text that was adopted by the Assembly in October 1988. That text, Recommendation 1087, called on the Committee of Ministers to give serious consideration to the single court idea.

[42] The United Kingdom was not the only state reluctant for things to progress rapidly. Several states were slow to ratify the modest Protocol 8, with France, Germany, Greece, and Turkey all resistant, ratifying only in 1989. As Bates observes, France and Germany also reduced their periods of acceptance of the optional clauses from five to three years in the period, while a serious debate occurred in the United Kingdom as to whether to renew at all. At the same time, states' ability to withdraw from the system was constrained; while there were frequent debates concerning renewal, as one judge put it at the time, "it would now be politically impossible for most countries to withdraw from the Convention, as it has captured the minds of the public to a great extent." See Bates, *Evolution of the European Convention*, 427–39, citing Brian Walsh, "The European Court of Human Rights," 2 *Connecticut Journal of International Law* (1987), 274. Harris, O'Boyle, and Warbrick similarly observed that any state's withdrawal from the convention system would provoke sharp criticism. See Harris, O'Boyle and Warbrick, *Law of the European Convention*.

With the collapse of the Soviet bloc beginning in 1989 everything started to change.[43] The Council of Europe reacted proactively, setting up programs to support democracy and the rule of law, and generally increasing its public presence and footprint. In 1990 the Council "not only confirmed its status as a privileged structure for dialogue with the countries of central and Eastern Europe, but turned itself into a structure for receiving them."[44] While many expressed reservations relative to both the wisdom of rapid enlargement in general and to the inclusion of new member states with less-developed national rights standards in particular, such voices were in the minority. Between 1990 and 1996 eighteen new states accepted the Convention, bringing the total number of members of the Council of Europe up to forty.[45] Meanwhile the Parliamentary Assembly, together with the European Commission for Democracy through Law, also known as the Venice Commission, worked hard to provide a diverse array of different forms of rights-based support to the countries of Eastern Europe, building upon the standards developed by the Commission and Court.[46]

[43] The idea of expanding the Council of Europe eastward had already started to gather momentum in the late 1980s. The Colombo Commission Report of 1986, Assembly Recommendation 1103 of March 15, 1989 and the Committee of Ministers Resolution of May 5, 1989 all advanced a vision of the Council as oriented to the promotion of democracy and rights in Eastern European countries. It was only with the collapse of the iron curtain and the end of the Cold War, however, that it became possible to implement this vision. See Huber, *A Decade Which Made History*, 8–16.

[44] Ibid., 26.

[45] The new states that joined the Council of Europe between 1990 and 1996 were Finland (1990), Hungary (1990), Poland (1991), Bulgaria (1992) Estonia (1993), Lithuania (1993), Slovenia (1992), the Czech Republic (1993), Slovakia (1993), Romania (1993), Andorra (1994), Latvia (1995), Albania (1995), Moldova (1995), Ukraine (1995), The former Yugoslav Republic of Macedonia (1995), Croatia (1996) and Russia (1996). German reunification of course meant that the former East Germany became part of the system as well. As Huber has noted, one telling incidental effect of this expansion was that it

> provide[d] a major headache for Sir Richard Rogers, the British architect whose design for a building to house the projected new-style machinery for supervision of the European Convention on Human Rights had just been approved after years of delay. The assumption in summer 1991 had been that the Council might expand, in the medium term, to comprise some thirty states. That estimate [would, by the next year, have to be] dramatically up-graded.

Huber, *A Decade Which Made History*, 59. Turkey, meanwhile, became a full member of the system only shortly before the expansion into Eastern Europe, accepting the right of individuals to make applications in 1987 and the jurisdiction of the court in 1990.

[46] See Andrew Drzemczewski, "The Council of Europe's Cooperation and Assistance Programmes with Central and Eastern Europe in the Human Rights Field: 1990 to

While it would be a few years before cases started to pour in from the new member states, awareness that they would soon come, together with the still growing volume of submissions from long-term member states, made reform all the more necessary. At the same time, the end of the Cold War and the rapid transitions toward more democratic governance that took place in Eastern Europe created a political atmosphere particularly conducive to the European human rights project. The new climate could be felt at a meeting in Vienna in October 1993, the first major meeting of all the state parties since the signing of the original convention.[47] The Vienna Conference highlighted the intent of the Council of Europe's long-term members to use the European human rights system as a means of supporting democratic transitions in Eastern European states. New member states were encouraged not only to sign up to the treaty, but also to immediately accept both individual petition and the jurisdiction of the Court, recommendations they proved willing to accept.

The new climate of enthusiasm for human rights[48] also provided an opportunity to advance the systemic reforms mooted in the 1980s. In 1992, the Parliamentary Assembly called by unanimous vote for the creation of a single court system,[49] and assembly members stepped up their pressure on

September 1993," 14 *Human Rights Law Journal* (1993), 335–44; Jeffrey Jowell, "The Venice Commission: Disseminating Democracy through Law," 24 *Public Law* (2001), 675–83.

47 The meeting followed closely on the heels of the 1993 World Conference on Human Rights, held in Vienna over the summer.

48 The strength of the Convention was bolstered by the increasing emphasis the European Court of Justice put on Convention rights over the course of the 1990s as well; for more, see Sionaidh Douglas-Scott, "A Tale of Two Courts: Luxembourg, Strasbourg and the Growing European Human Rights Acquis," 43 *Common Market Law Review* (2006), 629–65.

49 See Res. 1194 (1992) (October 6, 1992). The Parliamentary Assembly's vote was preceded by several other steps supportive of systemic reform. In late 1990 the Dutch and Swedish governments each separately put forward proposals for reform. In contrast to earlier calls for a single system, these new proposals suggested a two-tier system. Political impetus was provided to the process by the Committee of Ministers at its meeting in November 1991. With prompting from the Parliamentary Assembly, the Dutch/Swedish idea was considered by both the Committee of Experts of the European Council as well as both the Commission and the Court in 1992; at that time, a majority were in favor of the two-tier proposal. The idea of a single system ultimately taken up by the Assembly had not died, however, and found strong support both among states and a number of judges and members of the Court's registry as well. Despite the differences of opinion concerning the shape the new system should take, all were generally agreed that "the system of protection should be judicial, individuals should have direct access to a court (irrespective of which proposal was adopted) and that the Committee of Ministers should lose its competence to rule on the merits of cases." Drzemczewski, "A Major Overhaul," 156. See also Karel de Vey Mestdagh, "Reform of the European Convention on Human Rights in a

their respective governments to support such a reform.[50] On May 28, 1993, the Committee of Ministers finally joined them in supporting the creation of a judicial body. But while the idea of abolishing the Commission and creating a new, more powerful court was promptly accepted, the right of individual petition remained contentious. The British launched a determined rearguard action on the issue, aimed at maintaining the optional nature of individuals' ability to bring complaints to the new court.[51] The vast majority of states strongly opposed the British proposal, however, and shortly thereafter – due, it seems, to the British Foreign Office having managed to wrest the upper hand from the Home Office – the British softened their approach, and accepted the inclusion of a mandatory right of petition.

Changing Europe," in Lawson and de Blois eds., *The Dynamics of the Protection of Human Rights*, 346–9; Rudolf Bernhardt, "Reform of the Control Machinery Under the European Convention on Human Rights: Protocol No 11," 89 *American Journal of International Law* (1995), 149–50; Explanatory Report to Protocol 11, para. 1.

50 As one member of the Parliamentary Assembly recalled, "In winding up the discussions of 6 October 1992 I stated, among other things, that 'If we leave everything in the hands of the members of the Steering Committee … we will be exposing ourselves to major difficulties. We must ensure that a decision is taken at a political level'." Friedrich Vogel, "The Role of the Parliamentary Assembly of the Council of Europe in Bringing Protocol No. 11 into Being," in Mahoney et al. eds., *Protecting Human Rights*, 23.

51 The British intervention came during a meeting of the Steering Committee in March 1994. As Drzemczewski has put it, "This meeting was full of high drama, in that political considerations now evidently came into the forefront of discussions, which up to that time had been relatively well camouflaged by discussions of a technical nature." The official declaration read out by the British delegate stated

> … I therefore speak now with the full authority of the British Government. We feel that it is wrong to change the existing system, for a number of compelling reasons.
>
> The first and most important is the balance between the authority of the Court, and that of the elected governments of member States. Our governments are accountable to our parliaments and people for the powers they exercise. By contrast, the Court here at Strasbourg is accountable to no-one … My Government feels very strongly that the opportunity to review the Court's performance periodically, and make a conscious decision to renew the right of individual petition, is right and proper as a democratic safeguard …
>
> The second reason is that the new Court we are creating will be very different from the old system … The new Court is untried. My Government therefore feels that this is exactly the wrong time to take the further radical step of making the right of individual petition mandatory …
>
> The proposed change has actually nothing to do with the reform on which we have worked so hard.

Drzemczewski, "A Major Overhaul," 162–75.

Protocol 11, the document laying out the new system, was finalized and opened for signature in 1994.[52] The new protocol, and with it the new system, came into force four and a half years later, at the end of 1998. Combined with the momentum toward entrenchment of rights in national legal orders in the period, including the 1998 adoption of the Human Rights Act in the United Kingdom,[53] the coming into force of Protocol 11 was perceived as a high point for European rights advocates. In securing the Protocol, they had finally managed to fulfill the frustrated dreams of the system's founders by establishing both the right of petition and the oversight of the Court as nonnegotiable features of the European rights system. In doing so, they helped give the European system as a whole a new, more fully judicialized shape. Both the successes and challenges of the new system – explored further later – must be considered not only in the light of the system's initial moments, but also its reconstitution in the 1990s.

## III The Americas

### *III.1 The American Declaration of the Rights and Duties of Man*

In 1826, Simon Bolivar called upon those assembled at the Congress of Panama – including representatives of Gran Colombia (encompassing modern day Colombia, Ecuador, Panama and Venezuela, and parts of Peru and Brazil), Peru, the United Provinces of Central America, and Mexico – to create a confederation of Latin American states.[54] The

[52] While Protocol 11 created a single court and made individual petition mandatory, the idea of phasing out the role of the Committee of Ministers remained a step too far, with responsibility for the oversight of the new Court's judgments left in the Committee's hands. The more progressive Parliamentary Assembly did, however, start to act as an extra check on the Committee's work, by beginning to consider the extent to which state parties were implementing the Court's judgments. See Greer, *The European Convention on Human Rights*, 161–2.

[53] For more on the extension of the system's standards into national legal orders, see Anne-Marie Slaughter, Alex Stone Sweet, and Joseph Weiler eds., *The European Court and the National Courts: Legal Change in its Social, Political, and Economic Context* (Hart, 1998); Alec Stone Sweet and Helen Keller eds., *A Europe of Rights: The Impact of the ECHR on National Legal Systems* (Oxford University Press, 2008).

[54] For more on the Congress, and subsequent regional conferences, see Germán A. de la Reza, *El Congreso de Panamá de 1826 y otros ensayos de integración en el siglo XIX. Estudio y fuentes documentales anotadas* (Ediciones Eón, 2006). While some in the United States hoped to attend the conference, slave-holding Southern states were resistant, wary of involvement with Gran Colombia and other Latin American states that had outlawed slavery.

Congress resulted in the production of the ambitious "Treaty of Union, League, and Perpetual Confederation." Only Gran Colombia signed the treaty, however; shortly afterwards it descended into civil war, and thus Bolivar's dream came to a premature end.

While Bolivar's dream was never achieved, the states of the Americas continued to meet from 1826 on. Toward the end of the century, an organization that recalled the confederation of which Bolivar had dreamed, the "International Union of American Republics," was established at the first "International Conference of American States," held in Washington, DC, between 1889 and 1890. The echo of Bolivar's plan was only a faint one, however, as the Union was a loose confederation, encompassing members with significantly differing objectives. For the United States, the purpose of the new organization was to facilitate commercial exchange and peaceful relations, and to enhance their power within the Americas. From the point of view of Latin American states, on the other hand, the hope was the opposite, that the existence of a more formalized regional system would increase their ability to resist unwanted American influence.

In the decades that followed the question of rights became increasingly prominent, albeit in a very particular form. European states and jurists in the late nineteenth century placed great importance on the protection of the property of foreigners, viewed as a key component of international law, and sought to exclude those states deemed unable to protect such rights (or otherwise to protect the rights of European citizens) from full recognition as states.[55] If states failed to respect the property rights of Europeans, the aggrieved powers would often resort to force.[56] Over time,

Ultimately, this resistance was such that the United States was only able to send two delegates, Richard Clough Anderson Jr., who died on route to Panama, and John Sergeant, who arrived too late. The result was that Great Britain was the only major foreign power present, a fact that redounded to Britain's advantage, allowing the British to secure several favorable trade deals.

55 Among other modalities, European jurists and diplomats justified this treatment by arguing that various non-European states were "uncivilized." One example of such a classification was the International Law Institute's 1875 study on "Oriental" states, discussed in Martti Koskenniemi, *The Gentle Civilizer of Nations* (Cambridge University Press, 2001), 132–4. More generally, see Gerrit W. Gong, *The Standard of "Civilization" in International Society* (Clarendon, 1984), who also observes the centrality Europeans placed on "the freedoms of trade, travel, and proselytizing" (ibid., 36); and Anthony Anghie, *Imperialism, Sovereignty, and the Making of International Law* (Cambridge University Press, 2005), 251–3.

56 Thus for instance in 1838 the French blockaded Mexican ports and occupied Veracruz, after a French pastry chef allegedly had his store looted, while in 1850 Britain blockaded Greek ports, following the alleged theft from a British subject of some goods (despite the

Latin American states and others pushed back against European states' interference in their domestic affairs and against foreign military intervention in particular. In order to push back, however, Latin American states were essentially coerced into playing by the rules of the game, by demonstrating their ability to ensure the protection of foreigners' property. In doing so, though, they also attempted to alter the standard applied, arguing against the application of a more stringent universal standard of protection, in favor of a standard by which foreign citizens would be granted equal treatment to nationals.[57]

The first major contemplations of "rights" at the international level in the Americas, therefore, came in response to assertions of the rights of foreigners. In response, Latin American states argued that a standard of equal treatment be applied, an argument that served to convert the emphasis on foreigners' rights into a broader emphasis on the rights of all. In the context in which it was applied, significantly, such an argument served not as a source of limitation on sovereignty, but rather as a means through which to assert sovereignty by pushing back against the potential for foreign intervention.[58] On the regional level, the 1902 Convention Relative to the Rights of Aliens was perhaps the foremost vehicle for such

meager nature of the reported loss, testified to by the fact that the arbitration ultimately agreed upon resulted in an award of only £150). In 1902 Britain, Germany, and Italy blockaded Venezuela, in order to attempt to recover the money Venezuela owed them in state debt. For more, see Miriam Hood, *Gunboat Diplomacy: Great Power Pressure in Venezuela, 1895–1905* (Unwin Hyman, 1983).

57 The equal treatment standard was known as the "Calvo Doctrine," after the Argentinian jurist who advanced the idea. See Carlos Calvo, *Le droit international théorique et pratique* Volume 2 (3rd edn., Nabu, 1880/2012), 225–6; Donald Shea, *The Calvo Clause: A Problem of Inter-American and International Law and Diplomacy* (University of Minnesota Press, 1955). Over time, the views of United States came to align with those of Latin American states, due to the volume of claims the United States was facing from Europeans. See Elihu Root, "The Basis of Protection to Citizens Residing Abroad," *Proceedings of the American Society of International Law* (1910), 4. For further consideration of such issues, see Neff, *Justice Among Nations*, 276–7, 336–8; Benjamin Coates, *Legalist Empire: International Law and American Foreign Relations in the Early Twentieth Century* (Oxford University Press, 2016); Duranti, *The Conservative Human Rights Revolution*, 68–70.

58 As one commentator has put it,

> The persistent intervention of the United States into the domestic affairs of its Latin American neighbors in the early part of the twentieth century stimulated Latin American efforts to establish a regional public order system based on the principles of non-intervention and the sovereign equality of states. Early efforts in support of human rights were directed primarily toward this goal.

Goldman, "History and Action," 857.

a project, emphasizing as it did that "States do not owe to … foreigners, any obligations or responsibilities other than those established by their Constitutions and laws in favor of their citizens."[59]

Regional unity continued to grow in the following years. In 1907, Guatemala, El Salvador, Honduras, Costa Rica, and Nicaragua completed a Treaty of Peace and Amity, including an "Additional Convention" which committed state parties to refusing to recognize any government coming into power in any of the other states "as a consequence of a *coup d'état*, or of a revolution against the recognized Government."[60] In 1908 the Central American Court of Justice was created, with jurisdiction over the same five states. The Court was headquartered in Cartago, Costa Rica, and was the world's first standing international tribunal,[61] as

[59] Convention Relative to the Rights of Aliens (1902), Article 2. In 1906, the Pan-American Conference approved the "Convention Establishing the Status of Naturalized Citizens who Again Take up their Residence in the Country of their Origin" as well, which similarly aimed to limit the extent and force of emigrants' claims to property rights. Other efforts to push back against foreign intervention were also underway. Following the blockade of Venezuela in 1902, Luis María Drago, the Foreign Minister of Argentina, proposed the "Drago Doctrine," as a sort of supplement to the Calvo Doctrine. The Drago Doctrine stipulated that coercive measures were not appropriate in attempts to recover debts. See Luis María Drago, "State Loans in Their Relation to International Policy," 1 *American Journal of International Law* (1907), 692–726; Amos S. Hershey, "The Calvo and Drago Doctrines," 1 *American Journal of International Law* (1907), 26–45. The United States did not accept the convention, however. See Cabranes, "The Protection of Human Rights," 891 n. 9. While the Porter Convention adopted at the 1907 Hague Peace Conference prohibited the use of armed force to collect debts, that prohibition was voided if the debtor state refused to submit to international arbitration or comply with an arbitral ruling. See Edwin Borchard, "International Contractual Claims and Their Settlement," Judicial Settlement of International Disputes, No. 13, *American Society for Judicial Settlement of International Disputes* (1913); Shea, *The Calvo Clause*, 15. On the United States' use of force in the preceding decades, which was motivated or spurred by clashes pertaining to the protection of American nationals and property abroad, see Milton Offutt, *The Protection of Citizens Abroad by the Armed Forces of the United States* (John Hopkins University Press, 1928); Charles Lipson, *Standing Guard: Protecting Foreign Capital in the Nineteenth and Twentieth Centuries* (University of California Press, 1985); Ellen C. Collier, *Instances of Use of United States Forces Abroad, 1798–1993* (Congressional Research Service, 1993); Brian McBeth, *Gunboats, Corruption, and Claims* (Praeger, 2001); Cyrus Veeser, *A World Safe for Capitalism: Dollar Diplomacy and America's Rise to Global Power* (Columbia University Press, 2007); Noel Maurer, *The Empire Trap: The Rise and Fall of U.S. Intervention to Protect American Property Overseas, 1893–2013* (Princeton University Press, 2013).

[60] *See* General Treaty of Peace and Amity, 206 CTS 63 (December 20, 1907), Additional Convention, Art. 1.

[61] For more on the Court and its context, see William Spence Robertson, *Hispanic-American Relations with the United States* (Wentworth, 1923); Nicolas Politis, *La justice internationale* (Pantheon Assas, 1924/2017), 139–55; Victor Rescia and Marc Seitles, "The Development of

well as the first international tribunal to which individuals could bring claims.[62]

In 1910 the International Union of American Republics was renamed the Pan-American Union. Despite this rebranding, efforts for greater unity soon ran into difficulties. The Central American Court of Justice was forced to cease operating after a decade, after it issued a ruling challenging the construction of a US naval base in Nicaragua. Renewed momentum had to wait until US President Roosevelt's declaration of a new "Good Neighbor" policy in 1933, signaling the United States' intent to be less interventionist in Latin America.[63] The "Good Neighbor" policy was reaffirmed by the US Secretary of State at the Seventh International Conference of American States in Montevideo in December of the same year, at which the Convention on Rights and Duties of States was agreed.[64] While the convention is well known by international law scholars and practitioners as a fundamental reference point relative to the question of state recognition, it incorporated other broader matters of concern to Latin American states as well, including emphasizing the juridical equality of states and the principle of nonintervention. Other resolutions of the Montevideo Conference dealt with rights-related concerns, with Resolution LXXIV emphasizing "the civil equality of the foreigner with the national as the maximum limit of protection to which the former might aspire" and Resolution XCIII "the protection of the native races and the civilization of the tribes."

the Inter-American Human Rights System: A Historical Perspective and a Modern-Day Critique," 16 *New York Law School Journal of Human Rights* (2000), 596; Coates, *Legalist Empire*, 118–19. The new building built to house the Central American Court of Justice was one of three "temples of peace" financed by Andrew Carnegie, the other two being the Peace Palace in the Hague, and the Pan-American Building in Washington, DC.

62 For some related contemplations, see Edwin Borchard, "The Access of Individuals to International Courts," 24 *American Journal of International Law* (1930), 359–65.

63 The policy was complemented by the creation of the "Office of the Coordinator of Inter-American Affairs" in 1940, and accompanied by a broader public-image campaign aimed at changing the perception of the United States in Latin America as well as the perception of Latin American in the United States. For more, see Earl Beck, "The Good Neighbor Policy, 1933–1938," 1 *The Historian* (1939), 110–31; Bryce Wood, *The Making of the Good Neighbor Policy* (Columbia University Press, 1961); Brian O'Neil, "Carmen Miranda: The High Price of Fame and Bananas," in Vicki L. Ruiz and Virginia Sánchez Korrol eds., *Latina Legacies: Identities, Biography, and Community* (Oxford University Press, 2005), 193–208; Fredrick B. Pike, *FDR's Good Neighbor Policy: Sixty Years of Generally Gentle Chaos* (University of Texas Press, 2010); Mary E. Stuckey, *The Good Neighbor: Franklin D. Roosevelt and the Rhetoric of American Power* (Michigan State University Press, 2013).

64 Convention on Rights and Duties of States, 165 LNTS 19 (December 26, 1933).

By 1936 the potential for another global conflict was becoming increasingly clear. In response American states took a series of measures, including the creation of a new system of consultation, which would be used many times over the war years, and adoption of the "Declaration of Principles of Inter-American Solidarity and Cooperation."[65] Two years later, at the Eighth International Conference of American States in Lima, the assembled states decided to emphasize human rights, in part in order to indicate their opposition to the fascist current on the rise in Europe at the time. Thus the preamble to the declaration issued at the conference called for adherence to "individual liberty without religious or racial prejudices"; Resolution XI stressed the "preferential right" of the indigenous population to protection as "reparation for the lack of understanding with which they were treated in earlier periods"; and other resolutions called for the "Defense of Human Rights" as well as for "Freedom of Association and Freedom of Expression for Workers."[66]

As highlighted in the previous section, World War II provoked extensive discussion of human rights. Most significant, with regard to the American regional system that was to follow, was the formation in 1942 of an "Inter-American Juridical Committee," consisting of jurists from nine different states, which was tasked with preparing a report on the factors that had contributed to the breakdown of global order in 1939. Among other factors, the Committee's report emphasized the suppression of freedom of expression and access to information by fascist governments, observing that "thus the very wells of thought were poisoned, and political leaders who were promoting false theories of nationalism were able to strengthen their hold upon the loyalty of the people."[67] In its conclusion, the Committee endorsed the adoption of an international bill of rights, a call that was strongly supported by the government of Mexico in particular.

From that moment, things moved quickly. The Inter-American Juridical Committee was tasked with preparing a draft declaration, which it submitted to the Pan-American Union in 1945. Thus, when American states met in Mexico City later that year, with the aim of achieving greater

65 Approved December 21, 1936. An Inter-American Conference for the Maintenance of Peace was also held in 1936, at which, among other outcomes, the assembled states approved a resolution on the duties and rights of women with respect to peace.

66 For more, see Charles Fenwick, "Pan-American Action for Protection of Human Rights," 243 *Annals of the American Academy of Political and Social Science* (1946), 139.

67 Inter-American Juridical Committee, Preliminary Recommendation on Post-War Problems (September 5, 1942).

regional unity,[68] the idea that rights might form part of the regionalist project was already on the table. To the Juridical Committee's draft were added others, submitted by Cuba, Brazil, Uruguay, and Mexico. Different drafts contained different ideas: that of Cuba made reference to the 14th Amendment to the United States Constitution; those of Brazil and Uruguay emphasized the importance of social security; and that of Mexico underscored the need for a supervisory organ, as well as emphasizing the importance of "material well-being," which it observed could be guaranteed only by the recognition of socioeconomic rights, and through the means of a democratic structure of governance. These forceful opinions were reflected in the declaration produced by the conference, which stressed the importance of the rights to education, material well-being and equal opportunity to enjoy spiritual and material goods, while other resolutions emphasized the importance of the rights to health, the right of access to information, the right to freedom from racial discrimination, and women's rights. Resolution XL of the conference meanwhile emphasized that:

> International protection of the essential rights of man would eliminate the misuse of diplomatic protection of citizens abroad, the exercise of which has more than once led to the violation of the principles of non-intervention and of equality between nationals and aliens, with respect to the essential rights of man.[69]

The wording of Resolution XL highlighted the extent to which offering rights protections still seemed, to the states of the Americas, more a means of ensuring sovereignty than a limitation upon it.[70] Perhaps most significantly, the conference saw Mexico call on the Inter-American Juridical Committee to prepare a more formal draft rights declaration.

The foundational moment of the Inter-American human rights system came three years later, at the Ninth International Conference of American

[68] As one commentator put it, there was a general understanding that more formal regional organization was necessary in order to address the "uncertainty, confusion, duplication [and] inefficiency" of recent years. Josef Kunz, "The Bogota Charter of the Organization of American States," 42 *American Journal of International Law* (1948), 569.

[69] Pan American Union, Final Act of the Inter-American Conference on Problems of War and Peace, Mexico City, February–March, 1945.

[70] The strong support of Latin American states for human rights at the time could also be seen in their support for the incorporation of strong rights language within the United Nations Charter. See James Green, *The United Nations and Human Rights* (Brookings Institute, 1956), 16; Sandifer, *Human Rights in the Inter-American System*, Pan American Union, 1965), 510–11; Simpson, *Human Rights and the End of Empire*, 250–1.

States in Bogota, where the Organization of American States (OAS) was established. Human rights were included as one of the fundamental principles of the OAS. The conference also led to the production of the American Declaration of the Rights and Duties of Man. Support for a strong rights outcome was primarily spearheaded by Uruguay, which favored the incorporation of human rights into the Charter of the OAS directly, and the creation of a supranational judicial mechanism to oversee rights guarantees. Opposition to a strong rights outcome was led by Mexico, in a reversal of its earlier rights-supportive position. This reversal was indicative, among other things, of a shift in the perception of human rights among many of the states of the region, which were gradually coming to see a strong regional rights system not so much as an effective way to push back against the United States, but rather as a limitation on their sovereignty. This new attitude was reflected in the arguments Mexico presented against the creation of a supranational court: that it would increase the power of individuals relative to states; that complaints would multiply over time; that such a court would be insensitive to national needs; and that ultimately the existence of such a court would require states to bring their laws and constitutions into conformity with universal standards. The majority of Latin American states supported the Mexican position, as did the United States, motivated by the fear that a strong regional rights system might call into question its domestic system of racial discrimination.[71]

[71] For more on the manner in which systematic racial discrimination in the United States impacted on human (and "civil") rights debates in that country, see Mary Dudziak, *Cold War Civil Rights: Race and the Image of American Democracy* (Princeton University Press, 2000); Azza Salama Layton, *International Politics and Civil Rights Policies in the United States, 1941–1960* (Cambridge University Press, 2000); Carol Anderson, *Eyes Off the Prize: The United Nations and the African American Struggle for Human Rights, 1944–1955* (Cambridge University Press, 2003); Carol Anderson, "A 'Hollow Mockery': African Americans, White Supremacy, and the Development of Human Rights in the United States," Hope Lewis, "'New' Human Rights: U.S. Ambivalence Toward the International Economic and Social Rights Framework," and Dorothy Q. Thomas, "Against American Supremacy: Rebuilding Human Rights Culture in the United States," all in Cynthia Soohoo, Catherine Albisa, and Martha F. Davis, eds., *Bringing Human Rights Home: A History of Human Rights in the United States* (University of Pennsylvania Press, 2008), Vol. 1, 72–102; 103–44; and Vol. 2, 1–16 respectively; Risa Goluboff, *The Lost Promise of Civil Rights* (Harvard University Press, 2010); Christopher N.J. Roberts, "William H. Fitzpatrick's Editorials on Human Rights (1949)," *Quellen zur Geschichte der Menschenrechte* (2017), www.geschichte-menschenrechte.de/schluesseltexte/william-h-fitzpatricks-editorials-on-human-rights-1949; Gene Zubovich, "For Human Rights Abroad, against Jim Crow at Home: The Political Mobilization of American Ecumenical Protestants in the World War II Era," 105 *Journal of American History* (2018), 267–90. As one article notes, "W. E. B. Du

In the end, the assembled states narrowly voted against the creation of a court, and against the immediate preparation of a binding convention.[72]

While such results were disappointing, the assembled states agreed to produce a nonbinding document, the American Declaration of the Rights and Duties of Man. The American Declaration constituted a landmark text, preceding the Universal Declaration of Human Rights by eight months.[73] While the Declaration was nonbinding,[74] its text was wide-ranging, to such an extent in fact that it still forms one of the most progressive documents within the regional human rights corpus. The American Declaration covers many of most commonly agreed upon rights, including the rights to life, liberty, and security; to equality before law; to a fair trial; to protection from arbitrary arrest; to due process of law; to religious freedom; to freedom of opinion and expression; to freedom of assembly

Bois articulated an international human rights objection to domestic racial segregation as early as 1923," although the rights-based strategy was rejected at the time. Carol Bettinger-Lopez, Davida Finger, Meetali Jain, JoNel Newman, and Sarah Paoletti, "Redefining Human Rights Lawyering Through the Lens of Critical Theory: Lessons for Pedagogy and Practice," 18 *Georgetown Journal on Poverty Law and Policy* (2011), 343.

72 Eight of the twenty-one states assembled – Bolivia, Colombia, Cuba, El Salvador, Guatemala, Haiti, Honduras, and Uruguay – supported a stronger regional system of human rights incorporating both such features. Thirteen – Argentina, Brazil, Chile, Costa Rica, the Dominican Republic, Ecuador, Mexico, Nicaragua, Panama, Paraguay, Peru, the United States, and Venezuela – voted against the creation of such a system, however. The idea of creating a human rights agency within the OAS was also rejected, thanks primarily to US opposition. For more on the drafting of the Declaration, see Durward Sandifer, *Human Rights in the Inter-American System*; Lawrence LeBlanc, *The OAS and the Promotion and Protection of Human Rights* (Springer, 1977); Quiroga, *Battle of Human Rights*; David Forsythe, "Human Rights, The United States and the Organization of American States," 13 *Human Rights Quarterly* (1991), 66–98; J. Scott Davidson, *The Inter-American Human Rights System* (Darmouth Publishing, 1996).

73 Latin American states, moreover, were strong supporters of human rights at the United Nations. For more, see Morsink, *The Universal Declaration*, 157–238; Susan Waltz, "The Role of Small States in the Construction of the Universal Declaration of Human Rights," 23 *Human Rights Quarterly* (2001), 44–72; Susan Waltz, "Reclaiming and Rebuilding the History of the Universal Declaration of Human Rights," 23 *Third World Quarterly* (2002), 444; Mary Ann Glendon, "The Forgotten Crucible: The Latin American Influence on the Universal Human Rights Idea," 16 *Harvard Human Rights Journal* (2003), 27–39.

74 Had the Declaration formed part of the Charter, an argument for its binding nature could have been advanced, given the binding nature of the Charter itself. Recognizing this, states were careful to ensure that the Declaration was adopted by a resolution, and emphasized that the Declaration must not be understood as incorporated in the Charter. This position was underscored by the Inter-American Juridical Council the following year. See Inter-American Juridical Committee, *Report of the Inter-American Council of Jurists Concerning Resolution XXXI of the Bogota Conference* (1949).

and association; to voting and participation in government; to private and family life; and to property. In addition, the Declaration also recognizes an extensive array of socioeconomic rights, including the rights to special protection and care for mothers and children; to health, including through good sanitation, food, clothing, housing, and medical care; to "an education that will prepare [each individual] to attain a decent life" in accordance with the principle of "equality of opportunity in every case"; to cultural life; to work and a suitable standard of living; to leisure time; and to social security.[75] In further contrast to the European Convention, with its emphasis on states' treatment of their own citizens, and its colonialism-inspired antipathy to extraterritorial jurisdiction, the American Declaration enunciated a more universal vision of rights, even if by means of rhetorical posture as much as by substantial commitment. This was demonstrated both by the declaration's title, invoking the legacy of the French Revolution, and by the text of its introduction, which emphasized "that the essential rights of man are not derived from the fact that he is a national of a certain state, but are based upon attributes of his human personality."[76]

All things considered, the Bogota conference presented a mixed legacy. On the one hand, the more optimistic dreams of rights advocates were disappointed, as the final document produced was not binding, nor was any sort of oversight mechanism created – even one with optional oversight, as would later be created within the European system. At the same time, however, the document's nonbinding nature could be considered a

[75] While the inclusion of social rights in the document was initially considered controversial, ultimately no states opposed their inclusion. The 1917 Constitution of Mexico was an important precedent in terms of the recognition of socioeconomic rights in the American Declaration, as it was the first constitutional document to give them wide protection by recognizing the rights to organize unions, to work, to a minimum wage, to equal pay for men and women, and to welfare, education, and health care. In the following decades, countries across Latin America amended their constitutions to incorporate the same rights provisions. See Greg Grandin, "The Liberal Tradition in the Americas: Rights, Sovereignty, and the Origins of Liberal Multilateralism," 117 *American Historical Review* (2012), 68–91.

[76] The progressive character of the Declaration could also be seen in its insistence that rights should be interpreted in an evolving manner, with the text stressing that "the international protection of the rights of man should be the principle guide of an evolving American law," and its further observation that, while the rights it enumerated were to be considered "suited to the present social and juridical conditions," states "should increasingly strengthen [the] system [of rights protection] in the international field as conditions become more favorable." Women's civil and political rights were also emphasized at the Ninth International Conference of American States, via a separate resolution.

blessing in disguise, because it allowed for the adoption of a more progressive text than might otherwise have been possible, had states considered that the rights guarantees contained therein would have binding force. In addition, while states were unwilling to support the immediate adoption of a binding document or the creation of a court, neither did they foreclose such possibilities altogether – quite the opposite, in fact, as they adopted a resolution calling upon the Inter-American Juridical Committee to prepare a draft statute of a supranational human rights court, to be presented at some unspecified future time.[77]

### *III.2 The Inter-American Commission*

The initial moment in the American regional rights system's formation was hence simultaneously more attenuated and cautious than that of the European system, in terms of hard guarantees backed up by oversight mechanisms, and more expansive, in terms of the scope and breadth of rights deemed worthy of acknowledgment. Clearly, however, further steps would be necessary before the American human rights system took on a greater life of its own. Such steps would not come immediately: as the postwar era gave way to the Cold War, the development of a regional rights system in the Americas stalled. While the Inter-American Juridical Committee had been mandated to prepare a statute for a court, it declared that it was unable to do so for two reasons. First, it could not see a way to determine a formula that "would reconcile national claims to judicial autonomy with the paramount jurisdiction of an international tribunal." Second, it observed that, since the Declaration created non-binding obligations, there was no body of positive law upon which such a court could rule.

Over and above such formalistic objections, there were political challenges. The US government moved away from multilateral diplomacy in the Eisenhower years, in the face of strong threats by Congressional representatives to amend the US constitution to limit executive treaty-making power.[78] As one commentator has put it,

[77] See Resolution XXXI, Ninth International Conference of American States, Bogota, Colombia (1948).

[78] "Brickerism," as the movement was known, was a prominent progenitor of the antitreaty position that has persisted in the United States congress to the present day. See Vernon Van Dyke, *Human Rights, the United States, and World Community* (Oxford University Press, 1970); Natalie Hevener Kaufman and David Whiteman, "Opposition to Human Rights Treaties in the United States Senate: The Legacy of the Bricker Amendment," 10 *Human*

> With the advent of the Cold War, US Latin American policy underwent significant transformation. The Roosevelt administration's Good Neighbor Policy was replaced in the 1950s by a policy that sought to contain the spread of communism in the hemisphere. Accordingly, the United States began providing a variety of support to numerous authoritarian regimes with questionable human rights practices on the ground that they were bulwarks against communist expansion. Thus, despite its formal espousal of non-intervention and support for human rights, the United States began to intervene, militarily and otherwise, in the domestic affairs of those Latin American states it deemed sympathetic to communist ideologies.[79]

The United States brought its new power and single-minded Cold War purpose to bear on the OAS as well, doing everything it could to shape it into a tool to support its foreign policy objectives, in which efforts it was largely successful.[80]

*Rights Quarterly* (1988), 309–37; Duane Tananbaum, *The Bricker Amendment Controversy: A Test of Eisenhower's Political Leadership* (NCROL, 1988); David Forsythe, "Human Rights and U.S. Foreign Policy: Retrospect and Prospect," 105 *Political Science Quarterly* (1990), 435–54; David Forsythe, "The United States, the United Nations, and Human Rights," in Margaret Karns and Karen Mingst eds., *The United States and Multilateral Institutions: Patterns of Changing Instrumentality and Influence* (Routledge, 1990), 261–88; Forsythe, "Human Rights, The United States," 78; Richard Davies, *Defender of the Old Guard: John Bricker and American Politics* (Ohio State University Press, 1993). On the broader pushback against the left within the United States in the period, as evidenced by McCarthyism and other groups, see Mary Sperling McAuliffe, *Crisis on the Left: Cold War Politics and American Liberals, 1947–54* (University of Massachusetts Press, 1978); David Caute, *The Great Fear: The Anti-Communist Purge under Truman and Eisenhower* (Touchstone, 1978); David Kepley, *The Collapse of the Middle Way: Senate Republicans and the Bipartisan Foreign Policy, 1948–1952* (Praeger, 1988); Ellen Schrecker, *Many are the Crimes: McCarthyism in America* (Little, Brown and Company, 1998); Richard Lingeman, "Domestic Containment: The Downfall of Postwar Idealism and Left Dissent, 1945–1950," in Mark Carnes ed., *The Columbia History of Post-World War II America* (Columbia University Press, 2007), 201–25.

79 Goldman, "History and Action," 869.

80 As one scholar later put it, the OAS in the period "primarily presented an Inter-American instrument for the U.S. to react to expanding Socialism and through which the influence of the USSR in developing Latin American countries could be contained." Dykmann, *Philanthropic Endeavors or the Exploitation of an Ideal?*, 14. Dykmann cites similar sentiments from several other scholars, noting that "Farer portrayed the OAS as a 'gentlemen's anti-Communist club' … Booth called it a 'vehicle for containing communism' … [and] Drekonja-Kornat considered the creation of the OAS as the inclusion of Latin America as a subsystem into the imperial order of the United States." Ibid., citing Tom Farer, *The Grand Strategy of the United States in Latin America* (Transaction, 1988); John Booth, "US Influence in Central America," in Robert Biles ed., *Inter-American Relations: The Latin American Perspective* (Lynne Rienner, 1988), 28; Gerhard Drekonja-Kornat, *Grundmuster Lateinamerikanischer Außenpolitik* (Braumüller, 1986), 9. Along similar lines, Fidel Castro

The Inter-American Juridical Committee's emphasis on formal obstacles hence provided a rhetorical veneer masking deeper, political challenges. The Juridical Committee sustained themselves through a belief that progress would come with time, however; as one member of the committee put it at the time, demonstrating both a faith in gradualist progress as well as a skepticism of the value of easy but potentially empty rhetoric,

> Here, as in other slow marches towards perfection in society, impatient mankind may be tempted to relinquish existing, tangible, proven gains for uncertain, impracticable solutions which appear to promise more ... there has been far too glib and vocal acceptance of the general credo of human rights without adequate attention to practical realities. Some of the very countries that have been in the forefront of this movement will likely prove to be the last to accept a specific obligation impinging upon their national sovereignty ... Unless the nations of this planet seek to subscribe to empty phrases which must go unrealized, the progress must be made slowly, painfully, but determinedly.[81]

In line with such sentiments, the Council of Jurists continued to press for progress behind the scenes, though it met with little success. In 1954, for instance, the Council of Jurists asked the OAS whether it should place the issue of a court statute on the agenda of its tenth conference. The OAS suggested the time was not yet ripe, however, due to the ongoing lack of political support for such a step.[82]

later characterized the OAS as the "colonial office" of the United States. As Dykmann further notes, "considering these critical perspectives, the fact that Latin American countries agreed on participating in this system might initially appear surprising" Dykmann, *Philanthropic Endeavors or the Exploitation of an Ideal?*, 15. That they did choose to participate in the OAS can be understood as motivated in part by their hopes for economic assistance, in part by the faith they placed in the formal commitment of the OAS to nonintervention. For more on American Cold War foreign policy in the postwar decades, see John Lewis Gaddis, *Strategies of Containment: A Critical Appraisal of Postwar American National Security Policy* (Oxford University Press, 1982); Thomas McCormick, *America's Half-Century: United States Foreign Policy in the Cold War* (Johns Hopkins University Press, 1989); Melvyn Leffler, *A Preponderance of Power: National Security, the Truman Administration, and the Cold War* (Stanford University Press, 1992).

81 Alwyn Freeman, "Current Notes: The First Meeting of the Inter-American Council of Jurists," 44 *American Journal of International Law* (1950), 382. See also Inter-American Juridical Committee, Report of the Inter-American Council of Jurists Concerning Resolution XXXI of the Bogota Conference.

82 Support was lacking on all sides. The United States, for its part, remained skeptical of international human rights obligations, and worried in particular that its systemically racist domestic policies would be singled out for criticism. Latin American states, for their part, were afraid rights might provide another tool of US interventionist imperialism. On the ongoing significance of the concerns over nonintervention in the period, see A. J. Thomas,

The catalyst for change came unexpectedly, in the form of two incidents of unrest in the Caribbean in the late 1950s. The first was occasioned by the authoritarian regime of Rafael Trujillo in the Dominican Republic. In 1958 democracy was restored in Venezuela, and President Rómulo Betancourt came to power. Venezuela's democratic transition was part of a wider democratic shift, which increased the number of states with elected governments in the region to approximately seventy-five percent. This democratic momentum was felt in the Dominican Republic as well, where calls for reform grew, soon receiving the support of Betancourt's Venezuela. Incensed, Trujillo lent his support to oppositional forces in Venezuela, and, after Betancourt complained to the OAS, attempted to have Betancourt assassinated by arranging the bombing of his motorcade, an attempt that only narrowly failed to achieve its aim. In response, OAS members voted to sever diplomatic relations with the Dominican Republic, and to impose economic sanctions.

The second catalyst for change came from Cuba. After several years of guerilla warfare, Castro's revolutionary forces gained the upper hand, resulting in Batista fleeing to the Dominican Republic on January 1, 1959. Within a week, Castro had assumed full control. Castro's new communist government set about asserting control with speed, suppressing Batista's supporters and instituting major economic reforms. The success of Castro's Communist revolution set off alarm bells across American capitals.

One effect of these events was to generate a willingness on the part of OAS member states to reassess their previously held position that the internal workings of states should be off limits to regional oversight, prompted by the recognition that serious rights violations were unlikely to stay confined within national borders, but might instead overflow those boundaries, leading to broader regional repercussions.[83] At the Fifth Meeting of

"Non-Intervention and Public Order in the Americas," 53 *Proceedings of the American Society of International Law* (1959), 72–80; M. Margaret Ball, "Issue for the Americas: Non-Intervention v. Human Rights and the Preservation of Democratic Institutions," 15 *International Organization* (1961), 21–37; John Dreier, *The Organization of American States and the Hemisphere Crisis* (Harper & Row, 1962); Ann Thomas and Aaron Thomas, *The Organization of American States* (Southern Methodist University Press, 1963); Jose Cabranes, "Human Rights and Non-Intervention in the Inter-American System," 65 *Michigan Law Review* (1967), 1147–82; Anna Schreiber, *The Inter-American Commission on Human Rights* (A. W. Sijthoff, 1970).

83 The Inter-American Peace Committee (a body created at the Second Meeting of Consultation of Ministers of Foreign Affairs in 1940) for instance observed at the time that interstate tensions had been aggravated by serious and widespread rights violations, in violation of the OAS Charter and the American Declaration.

Consultation of Ministers of Foreign Affairs of the American Republics, held in 1959 in Santiago, Chile, President Betancourt of Venezuela proposed that international human rights oversight no longer be regarded as an impermissible form of intervention in internal affairs. While the assembled foreign ministers were not willing to endorse this statement outright, the measures they adopted were supportive of such a sentiment, to such an extent that one close observer shortly thereafter declared that "The true beginnings of the regional human rights program may be found in the Fifth Meeting of Consultation of Ministers of Foreign Affairs of the American Republics, held in 1959."[84]

The "Declaration of Santiago" produced by the meeting emphasized not only the importance of human rights, but also the deeply intertwined nature of human rights and democracy.[85] Among other outcomes, the assembled ministers called upon the Inter-American Council of Jurists to take up the task of drafting a regional human rights convention, together with the statute of a court to supervise it.[86] More unexpectedly, a majority of the assembled ministers also supported the creation of an "Inter-American Commission on Human Rights." While the idea of a convention, to be overseen by a court, was the bolder vision, it continued to be imagined as a future goal toward which progress would gradually be made. The creation of a commission, by contrast, was potentially immediately achievable, and so, despite the weaker nature of such a body, it proved more contentious. Brazil, the Dominican Republic, Mexico, and

[84] Cabranes, "The Protection of Human Rights," 893.

[85] Among other things, the Declaration emphasized the rule of law, separation of powers, "control of legality of governmental acts by competent organs of the State," free elections and fixed terms, "system[s] of freedom for the individual and of social justice based on respect for fundamental rights," "effective judicial procedures" to protect rights, "freedom of the press, radio, and television, and, in general, freedom of information and expression, [which] are essential conditions for the existence of a democratic regime," and the progressive development of economic structures in order to "achieve just and humane living conditions" Declaration of Santiago, Chile, 1959, OAS, Fifth Meeting of Consultation of Ministers in Foreign Affairs. As the Minister of Foreign Affairs of Uruguay put it, the Santiago Declaration "was to democracy what the Bogota Declaration is to the rights of man." Following the declaration, there was discussion of a draft convention on democracy in the Americas; state resistance prevented the development of such a document however.

[86] The Council took to the task with relish, producing a draft convention the same year. No further progress was made on the issue until 1965, however. See Final Act of the Fourth Meeting of the IA Council of Jurists, Santiago, Chile, August 24–September 9, 1959, CIJ-43. The initial draft included social and economic rights, though it imagined a separate set of procedures for their oversight.

Uruguay all opposed the idea and voted against the resolution,[87] while the United States and Bolivia, expressing skepticism, abstained from the vote. The other member states of the OAS, however, with Venezuela in the lead, voted in favor, leading to the resolution's adoption.[88]

While agreement to create a commission was the most momentous achievement of the meeting, the resolution establishing it was anything but detailed. It went no further than providing that the Commission would be composed of seven members, and charged with the "promotion" of human rights. As one commentator put it, "the language of the resolution was brief to the point of making it appear that the act was almost an afterthought";[89] in the words of another, the creation of the Commission was essentially an "accident";[90] in the words of a third, the Commission was "a hasty improvisation … with no well-thought-out role or procedure."[91] In reality, the vagueness of the resolution was probably a sign that its supporters felt an urgent need to seize the moment, pushing through the creation of a commission while support for rights was high, aware that attempting to draft more precise language would in all likelihood draw out the process and allow support to diminish.

The following year, the Council of the OAS prepared a statute for the Commission, fleshing out the Commission's mandate.[92] The statute made clear that the Commission's fundamental responsibility was to oversee the rights laid out by the American Declaration. The initial draft prepared by the Council also stipulated that the Commission would have broad powers to consider individual complaints and to make recommendations.

87 The reasons for their resistance were varied. Uruguay, a strong rights supporter in general, opposed the creation of the Commission on the basis of the argument that it was illogical to create such a body prior to the preparation of a more specific, binding convention on human rights for the region. Venezuela countered this argument however by observing that, in contrast to the relatively developed legal system in Uruguay, other countries in the region were more in need of general encouragement than precise stipulations, and by stressing the importance of taking immediate steps, emphasizing that however imperfect such steps might be it was necessary to take advantage of the ongoing "democratic surge" in order "to strengthen everything that serves the purpose of making human rights respected." Quiroga, *Battle of Human Rights*, 68.

88 See Resolution VIII of the Fifth Meeting of Consultation of Ministers of Foreign Affairs, August 12–18, 1959, OAS Doc. DEA/Ser.C/II.5 at 4. The new Cuban administration was among those that voted in favor.

89 Sandifer, *Human Rights in the Inter-American System*, 516.

90 Cesar Sepulveda, "The Inter-American Commission on Human Rights," 12 *Israel Yearbook of Human Rights* (1982), 47.

91 Dreier, *The Organization of American States*, 132.

92 Statute of the Inter-American Commission, OEA/Ser. L/V/I.1.

While this position was supported by some countries, including Ecuador and El Salvador, others, with the United States in the lead, were opposed to granting the Commission such sweeping powers. Ultimately the opposition prevailed, leading to only inter-state complaints being unambiguously allowed.[93] Beyond that, the Commission was left with a vague, general mandate.[94]

The Commission's statute was also less than convincing on the issue of its independence. The Commission was declared an "autonomous entity" of the OAS, a vague designation that did little to assert the body's autonomy. While the Secretary General of the OAS was not formally in charge of the Commission, he was tasked with appointing the Commission's Executive Secretary and staff, and given the power to ask the Commission to consider particular issues. The Commission's budget, meanwhile, was to be fixed and annually reviewed by the Council of the OAS.[95]

As has so often occurred within the history of supranational human rights institutions, therefore, the Inter-American Commission's first moment was less than promising, as the Commission was given a weak

[93] The vote was 10–3 against the potential for individual complains, with 8 abstentions. *See* Consejo de La OEA, Acto de la Sesion Ordinaria Celebrada el 25 de Mayo de 1960, Serie del Consejo OEA/Ser.G/II C-a-371.

[94] Specifically, Article 9 of the Commission's original statute gave the Commission the powers:

a. To develop an awareness of human rights among the peoples of America;
b. To make recommendations to the Governments of the member states in general, if it considers such action advisable, for the adoption of progressive measures in favor of human rights within the framework of their domestic legislation and in accordance with their constitutional precepts, appropriate measures to further the faithful observance of those rights;
c. To prepare such studies or reports as it considers advisable in the performance of its duties;
d. To urge the Governments of the member states to supply it with information on the measures adopted by them in matters of human rights;
e. To serve the Organization of American States as an advisory body in respect of human rights.

[95] As one commentator noted at the time, "budgetary restrictions served as a non-statutory and perhaps the most significant limitation upon [the] powers [of the Commission], and figured strongly in the deliberations of the Council regarding the nature and powers of the Commission" Ronald Scheman, "The Inter-American Commission on Human Rights," 59 *American Journal of International Law* (1965), 336–7. Budgetary limitations were responsible, for instance, for the decision that the Commission would not meet for ten months a year as proposed, but rather for eight weeks.

mandate,[96] constrained independence, and limited financial support. No doubt many at the time would not have been surprised had the organization quickly faded into obscurity. This was not to be the Commission's fate, however. As had happened with the United Nations Human Rights Commission before it, as soon as the Inter-American Commission was created, communications began to pour in.[97] Unlike the United Nations Human Rights Commission, however, and despite its formally weak mandate, the Inter-American Commission decided to adopt a vigorous approach, and to develop a methodology for responding to the communications. While it had been denied the formal power to consider communications, the Commission had been granted mandates both to collect information and to make recommendations. At its first meeting, the Commission announced that it would bring these two mandates together, asserting both the ability to receive information concerning violations, and the ability to respond with recommendations of measures to be taken. At the same time, the Commission recognized that it did not have the power to make decisions on individual communications, thereby seeking to legitimize the procedure it was adopting by emphasizing the differences between that procedure and a more formal complaint process.[98]

Having laid out its understanding of its mandate, the Commission commenced "taking note" of petitions – accepting the submission of information, and, in a select set of cases, forwarding that information, with the authors' identities withheld, to the relevant governments in order to solicit an official response. Where it received a response, the Commission transmitted that information back to those who had submitted the communications.[99] Thus, as one commentator later put it, "the Commission

[96] As one commentator put it, the mandate of the Commission was so weak that "some members of the OAS may have supposed that in voting to create the Commission they had merely voted for the establishment of one more 'study group.'" Cabranes, "The Protection of Human Rights," 894.

[97] By 1964, the Commission had received more than 2,000 specific communications, as well as many more general communications. See Scheman, "The Inter-American Commission," 338.

[98] Int.-Am. Comm. H.R., Report of the Work Accomplished During Its First Session, October 3–28, 1960, OEA/Ser. L/V/II.1, Doc. 32. The Commission also asked that it be formally granted the power to consider complaints, albeit only relative to the most serious violations. Despite the Commission's attempt to distinguish its approach, many considered that it was in practice considering individual complaints in all but name. See Cabranes, "Human Rights and Non-Intervention," 1167–8, citing OAS, Annual Report of the Secretary-General to the Council of the Organization, OEA/Ser. D/III.13, Introduction (1961).

[99] For more, see Int.-Am. Comm. H.R., Report on the Work Accomplished During its Second Session, April 10–26, 1961, OEA/Ser.L/V/II.2, Doc. 24.

evolved from a study group into a supervisory organ by resorting to a broad interpretation of the norms governing its activities and by applying the theory of implied powers."[100]

In its early years the Commission devoted its attention to less powerful and politically connected states – including Cuba and the Dominican Republic, the original sources of concern for the states of the Americas, together with Haiti and Nicaragua. At its second session, in early 1961, having received 45 communications concerning Cuba, the Commission decided to request a report from Cuba on measures it was taking in respect of human rights.[101] At its third session, later in 1961, the Commission asked the government of the Dominican Republic for permission to conduct a human rights fact-finding trip. The Commission's strategy of focusing on less powerful and politically ostracized states proved successful, as despite the Commission's assertive reading of its mandate, neither powerful states nor the organs of the OAS raised objections.[102] Rather, there was general support for the Commission: at the Eighth Meeting of Consultation of Ministers of Foreign Affairs, held in Punta del Este, Uruguay, in January 1962, the Ministers approved a resolution affirming the Commission's ability to engage in such activities.[103] The Secretary-General of the OAS was also supportive.[104]

Three years later an opportunity came for the Commission to further demonstrate its value to the most influential states of the Americas. In

100 Quiroga, *Battle of Human Rights*, 89.

101 The Commission also mailed this request to all those who had submitted complaints, and made it public. The Commission's ability to adopt such an approach was aided by the fact that at the same time that the Commission's ability to receive individual complaints was eliminated from its mandate, a provision imposing limitations on the Commission's ability to publicly disseminate information was also removed, on the theory that it would no longer be necessary, with the ironic consequence that the informal route to case consideration the Commission had adopted was strengthened. See Scheman, "The Inter-American Commission," 340 n. 20.

102 As Quiroga later put it, "The OAS political organs, by not questioning these powers … tacitly agreed on their validity." Quiroga, *Battle of Human Rights*, 74.

103 The Eighth Meeting also saw Cuba expelled from the OAS after several years of concerted US pressure. Increasing support for human rights was doubtless in part due to the fact that such support provided cover and justification for the stance taken against Cuba. As one commentator later observed, "the Cuban case was for the inter-American system, not only and not mainly a problem of human rights, but a political problem of another sort. This notwithstanding, a significant number of the attacks on Cuba within the OAS were carried out at least nominally in the name of human rights and representative democracy." Quiroga, *Battle of Human Rights*, 186.

104 *See* Int.-Am. Comm. H.R., Report on the Work Accomplished During Its Sixth Session, April 16–May 8, 1963, OEA/Ser. L/V/II.7, Doc. 28.

December 1962, following the assassination of Trujillo in 1961, Juan Emilio Bosch Gaviño was elected in the Dominican Republic. After Gaviño attempted to implement democratic reforms, he was removed by a coup. The coup government was deeply unpopular, however, and in April 1965 a rebellion broke out. The United States government, fearful of a repeat of events in Cuba, responded promptly, sending in marines to set up an "international security zone," while the OAS issued a resolution calling on the combatants to end hostilities, leading to a ceasefire. On May 5 an OAS "Peace Force" arrived, and a second ceasefire was signed. The OAS Peace Force included a delegation from the Commission, tasked with supporting human rights during the transitional period. The Commission rose to this challenge with relish, distinguishing itself in the eyes of key regional players.[105] Later that year, the "Second Special Inter-American Conference" was convened. The assembled states, impressed by the Commission's role in the Dominican Republic, granted the Commission a formal mandate to consider individual petitions.[106] While the Commission's power was still limited – the resolution made clear that, after the Commission had issued its recommendations, its role would be over[107] – the resolution was a major victory for the Commission.

105 On Cabranes' account, the Commission:

> undertook a remarkable humanitarian effort to save the lives of innocent victims of the conflict, to safeguard the rights of persons held prisoner by both factions, to investigate charges of violations of human rights, … to mediate between contending groups in order to protect fundamental rights, [and even] to oversee and report on the conduct of the presidential election held in … June, 1966.

Cabranes, "The Protection of Human Rights," 895. See also OAS, Tenth Meeting of Consultation of Ministers of Foreign Affairs, Situation Regarding Human Rights in the Dominican Republic (Preliminary Report), OEA/Ser.L/V/II.12, Doc. 2 Rev. More broadly, United States and OAS intervention in the Dominican Republic did not follow the coup but rather the counter-coup aimed at restoring Gaviño to power, such that the fairness of the subsequent elections – in which the more conservative, right-wing candidate, Balaguer, was ultimately victorious, leading to a sustained period of further rights abuses – is open to serious question, casting doubt in turn on the broader implications of the Commission's involvement.

106 See Second Special Inter-American Conference, Rio de Janeiro, Brazil, November 17–30, 1965, OEA/Ser. C/I.13, Resolution XXII. The Resolution further stipulated that petitions might only be considered where domestic remedies had been exhausted and emphasized that particular attention should be given to certain rights.

107 While the matter could be referred on to the OAS, and often was, in practice the OAS never saw fit to discuss the Commission's findings. See Cecilia Medina Quiroga, "The Inter-American Commission on Human Rights and the Inter-American Court on Human Rights: Reflections on a Joint Venture," 12 *Human Rights Quarterly* (1990), 441.

Significantly, the Commission did not simply allow this new, more formal procedure to replace its already existing, less formal, flexible approach. Rather, it determined that it now had two powers, both the power to consider individual communications according to established procedures, with attention to the set of rights the OAS had designated as priorities, and the power to continue to "take cognizance" of communications, for the purpose of preparing more general reports. Meanwhile, the goodwill the Commission had generated in its brief period in existence was not yet exhausted. At the Third Special Inter-American Conference, held in Buenos Aires in February 1967, the Charter of the Organization of American States was amended in order to formally incorporate the Inter-American Commission.[108] Thus the Commission came to acquire a more solid institutional status, to complement and support its new and enhanced powers.

The second foundational moment of the Inter-American system, in sum, was concerned with the formation and establishment of the Inter-American Commission. This was a particularly prolonged "foundational moment," involving events stretching between 1959 and 1967. In that period the Commission was created, immediately adopted an assertive, activist approach to its mandate, and ultimately, perhaps surprisingly, received the grant of further powers together with a stronger institutional position through its incorporation as a formal organ of the OAS. The conditions of possibility for this evolution were initially set by events in Cuba and the Dominican Republic in the late 1950s, and the changing attitude to human rights in the region they engendered. Once created, the Commission benefited from its own savvy political maneuvering. More broadly, the period both saw regional inequalities in rights oversight, unsurprisingly in light of the stark power disparities in the Americas, and the gradual empowerment of an alternative rights institution, operating for a period in a significantly less-judicialized context.

[108] See Protocol of Amendment to the Charter of the Organization of American States, signed February 27, 1967, 21 UST 607, TIAS 6847, which entered into force February 27, 1970. Initially, this arrangement was imagined as temporary, expected to last only until the American Convention on Human Rights was ratified by all member states. To date, however, that is yet to occur. Later, the Commission argued that this incorporation had made the provisions of the American Declaration binding upon states – a position it suggested in the *Baby Boy Case* (Case No. 2141, Int.-Am. Comm. H.R. [March 6, 1981]) and the *Juvenile Death Penalty Case* (Case No. 9647, Int.-Am. Comm. H.R. [September 1987]), both of which concerned the United States. The United States, meanwhile, persistently contested such a position.

### *III.3 The American Convention and Court*

The good impression made by the Commission did not benefit the Commission alone. Rather, the second Special Inter-American Conference saw momentum toward the production of a binding rights convention reinvigorated as well. Chile and Uruguay took the lead, submitting new draft texts to be considered alongside the 1959 draft. While the assembled states were not ready to take any immediate steps, they did decide to refer the various drafts to the Inter-American Council of Jurists, which they charged with preparing a single text for consideration. The Council's consolidated draft, like the American Declaration, included extensive reference to social and economic rights. These references were removed in the next stage of consultations, however, on the recommendation of the Commission in particular.[109] The Commission's recommendations were strongly influenced by the example the European system had set, which, of course, had failed to incorporate social and economic rights.[110]

In mid-December 1966, the United Nations finally adopted the International Covenants on Economic, Social and Cultural Rights and on Civil and Political Rights. Five months thereafter, in May 1967, the OAS's Committee on Juridical-Political Affairs turned its attention to the new draft regional human rights convention. Given the recent progress on the global level, the Committee suggested that consideration of the draft American Convention should be delayed to give states the opportunity to consider whether or not it was necessary to go ahead with the development of a regional rights system, in view of international developments.[111] In light of the Committee's suggestion, the Council of Jurists sent out a questionnaire to member states, soliciting their opinions.[112] Two states, Argentina

[109] See Int.-Am. Comm. H.R., Opinion on the Draft Convention on Human Rights Approved by the IA Council of Jurists (Part Two), OEA/Ser.L/V/II.16, Doc. 8 Rev. (April 24, 1967).

[110] On the influence of the European model, see Thomas Buergenthal, "The European and Inter-American Human Rights Courts: Beneficial Interaction," in Mahoney et al. eds., *Protecting Human Rights*, 123–33.

[111] For more, see Cabranes, "The Protection of Human Rights."

[112] Specifically, the Council's questionnaire asked:

1. *Whether the governments of the American states ... wished to establish a single universal system of regulation of human rights; or whether on the contrary they contemplated the possibility of the coexistence and coordination of the worldwide and regional conventions on the same rights.*
2. *Whether, in the latter case, those governments consider the Inter-American Convention on Human Rights ... should be limited to establishing an Inter-American institutional*

and Brazil – both under military government at the time – seized this opportunity to declare their opposition to further work on a regional convention. Ten other states, however, including the United States, expressed their support for continuing work toward a regional system.[113]

The Secretariat of the Commission meanwhile produced a report that concluded that an autonomous regional convention would complement the international conventions. As that study put it:

> The need for, and the desirability of, a regional convention for the Americas are based on the existence of a body of American international law built up in accordance with the specific requirements of the countries of this hemisphere. That need and desirability also follow from the close relationship that exists between human rights and regional economic development and integration, in accordance with the statements of the Chiefs of State made at the meeting in Punta del Este.
>
> Consequently the Inter-American Convention on the Protection of Human Rights should be autonomous rather than complementary to the United Nations covenants, although it should indeed be coordinated with those covenants.[114]

The Council of Jurists therefore asked the Commission to prepare a new draft,[115] which was concluded in 1969. The draft included an extensive list

> *and procedural system for the protection of those rights that would include the Inter-American Commission on Human Rights and, eventually, an Inter-American Court of Human Rights.*

Council of the OAS, Report on a Consultation with the Member States Regarding the Draft Convention on Human Rights, submitted by the Committee on Juridical-Political Affairs, OEA/Ser.G/IV Rev. 3 (June 7, 1967).

113 The other supportive states were Bolivia, Chile, Colombia, Costa Rica, Ecuador, Guatemala, Mexico, Uruguay, and Venezuela. States' views were more fractured on what exactly the convention should include, with only five states – Ecuador, Guatemala, Venezuela, Colombia, and Costa Rica – supporting a convention that would create institutions, as well as guaranteeing substantive rights. Chile and Uruguay supported a convention that would create institutions but would not include new rights commitments, while the United States and Mexico did not take definitive positions on the question. See Goldman, "History and Action," 864. See also Cabranes, "The Protection of Human Rights," 903–4; Carlos Bauer, "The Observance of Human Rights and the Structure of the System for their Protection in the Western Hemisphere," 30 *American University Law Review* (1981), 18.

114 Int.-Am. Comm. H.R., Comparative Study of the United Nations Covenants on Civil and Political Rights and on Economic, Social and Cultural Rights and the Draft, OEA/Ser.L/II.19, Doc. 26 (1968).

115 See Consejo de la Organizacion de Estados Americanos, Serie del Consejo, Informe de la Comision de Asuntos Juridico-Politicos Referente al Proyecto de Convencion Sobre

of rights, together with references to a commission, to which individuals might bring complaints, as well as to a court. The draft convention ultimately produced was strongly influenced by the European system, which sent representatives to participate in the American Convention's drafting.[116] Later that year, the convention was adopted,[117] with its ambitious institutional architecture essentially intact.[118] The achievement represented by the adoption of the convention should not be underestimated; as many commentators have observed, the general atmosphere was less than favorable to such developments.[119] That such an inhospitable

Derechos Humanos, OEA/Ser.G/IV, Rev. 3 (June 13, 1968). The Council took such a decision "despite the failure of many American states to respond to either question and the obvious reluctance of many of those responding to support a separate system to protect substantive rights" Goldman, "History and Action," 865.

116 See Buergenthal, "The European and Inter-American Human Rights Courts," 124. Buergenthal notes however that "As a general proposition, it can be said that the European Convention played a more important role in shaping the institutions established by the American Convention than its substantive provisions" Ibid., 125. Among the most significant differences was Article 68, which in time helped the Court to develop a more assertive approach to remedies than that employed in the European system.

117 American Convention on Human Rights, opened for signature November 22, 1969, OASTS No. 36, entered into force 18 July 1978.

118 Among other features, the Convention granted the Court strong remedial powers, including the power to order individual as well as structural remedies, and specified that compensatory damages would be directly enforceable in national law. See ACHR, Articles 63(1), 68(2). The potential for noncompliance, naturally, remained a challenge, with the Convention specifying that noncompliance might be referred to the OAS General Assembly, but silent on steps the Assembly might then take. See Articles 65, 68(2).

119 See Cabranes, "Human Rights and Non-Intervention," 1167–82; Cabranes, "The Protection of Human Rights"; Carlos Bauer, "The Observance of Human Rights," 19. Cabranes' 1967 piece in particular, which took the European situation as a yardstick of comparison, was clear on the obstacles faced in the Americas: the fact that, unlike Europe, the Americas had not gone through a postwar reconstruction, and lacked a comparably deep recognition of the need to ensure democracy and rights in order to prevent future conflict; the fact that rights were less secured and respected, and judicial systems weaker, in the states of the Americas in comparison to Europe; the fact that Western Europe was more integrated, in terms of political and economic interdependence as well as the existence of common interests and ideals, while regional integration in the Americas was far weaker; the fact that there was a stronger culture of nonintervention in the Americas; and the fact that the United States posed a particular challenge, given its rights skepticism, its resistance to external oversight, and the wariness it provoked on the part of Latin American states. See Cabranes, "Human Rights and Non-Intervention," 1167–82. In his 1968 piece Cabranes further observed:

> The … draft convention embodies in one instrument many of the more far-reaching provisions of both the International Covenants and the European Convention. In this sense, it is the most ambitious multilateral convention on human rights of any

climate was overcome was largely due to the fact that some supportive institutions, in particular the Commission and the Council of Jurists of the OAS, already existed and were able to maintain pressure for further reforms.

While agreement on the American Convention represented a major success, the Convention did not receive a warm reception. The establishment of a military regime in Brazil in 1964, a few years before, was a sign of things to come,[120] as military governments were thereafter established in Argentina in 1966 (and again, after a brief period of civilian government, in 1976), in Peru in 1968, in Ecuador in 1972, and in Chile and Uruguay in 1973. These regimes were all of a broadly similar nature, giving pride of place to "national security" and "public order" concerns, which were enforced by extensive, interlocking sets of repressive measures.[121] It was hence some time before enough ratifications were received to bring the convention into force and the court into existence. While the Commission was somewhat protected by its entrenchment within the OAS structure, it too faced pushback, in part through the appointment of a number of more conservative commissioners.[122]

As the 1970s went on, impetus toward adoption of the Convention gathered strength. Momentum came from an unlikely source, given its traditional rights skepticism – the United States, which made a rapid

> prepared by an inter-governmental organization. And this may be why the draft convention has made so little progress in the nine years since its adoption by the Inter-American Council of Jurists in 1959 and why, in its present form, it appears to have little chance of success.

Cabranes, "The Protection of Human Rights," 900.

120 On the campaign against the dictatorship and rights violations in Brazil, see James Green, *We Cannot Remain Silent: Opposition to the Brazilian Military Dictatorship in the United States* (Duke University Press, 2010); Kelly, *Sovereign Emergencies*, Chapter 1.

121 As Dykmann has put it,

> During the 1960s, military strategists of the Brazilian Escola Superior da Guerra developed the Doctrine of National Security as a response to the guerilla threat … The doctrine constitutes an etatist ideology … This strategy, outlined by the Brazilian Gilberto Cuoto, regarded order and silence as the first duties of the citizen. If necessary, human rights too were required to be subordinated under this primacy. Accordingly, the Doctrine of National Security led to the declaration of states of emergency and siege and was used as a standardized justification for numerous human rights abuses. The state of siege often became the "permanent constitutional condition" in Latin America.

Dykmann, *Philanthropic Endeavors or the Exploitation of an Ideal?*, 27–8.

122 For more, see Forsythe, "Human Rights, The United States."

*volte-face* in its position on human rights under the Carter administration.[123] This new foreign policy was met with skepticism from other American states, suspicious of the United States' motives.[124] Despite such skepticism the push was effective: whereas by the end of 1977 only five states had ratified the convention,[125] seven more joined in 1978,[126] surpassing the eleven ratifications required in order for the Convention to enter into force.[127]

The success of the Convention was unfortunately timed, insofar as, while the Americas had largely been governed by elected officials when the Convention was negotiated, by the time the American Convention entered into force, in 1978, numerous states, including several of the region's most powerful, were under the control of military regimes.[128]

[123] For more on Carter's rights-based foreign policy, see David Schmitz and Vanessa Walker, "Jimmy Carter and the Foreign Policy of Human Rights: The Development of a Post-Cold War Foreign Policy," 28 *Diplomatic History* (2004), 113–44. On the increasing emphasis on human rights in the 1970s that underpinned this turn, in the United States and elsewhere, see Moyn, *Last Utopia*; Eckel and Moyn eds., *The Breakthrough*; Keys, *Reclaiming American Virtue*. See also Forsythe, "Human Rights and U.S. Foreign Policy," 439–41, where Forsythe observes that the new US position was driven in part by the legacy of Vietnam, and the public discrediting of the idea that fighting communism might lead to greater respect for rights. The rise of a new international rights practice in the period was demonstrated by the formation of an organization called "Helsinki Watch" in 1978, which grew rapidly, taking on the new name "Human Rights Watch" in 1988. For more, see Peter Slezkine, "From Helsinki to Human Rights Watch: How an American Cold War Monitoring Group Became an International Human Rights Institution," 5 *Humanity: International Journal of Human Rights, Humanitarianism, and Development* (2014), 345–70.

[124] For more, see L. Ronald Scheman, "The OAS and the Quest for International Cooperation: American Vision or Mirage," 13 *Case Western Reserve Journal of International Law* (1981), 83–105.

[125] Costa Rica ratified the Convention in 1970, Colombia in 1973, and Venezuela, Honduras, and Haiti in 1977.

[126] The states which ratified the convention in 1978 were the Dominican Republic, Guatemala, Panama, El Salvador, Peru, Grenada, and Jamaica.

[127] Ratifications continued in the following years. Bolivia and Nicaragua ratified the convention in 1979, followed by Mexico and Barbados in 1981, Argentina in 1984, Uruguay in 1985, Suriname in 1987, Paraguay in 1989, Chile in 1990, Trinidad and Tobago in 1991 (before its 1998 denunciation), Brazil in 1992, Dominica in 1993, and Ecuador in 1997. While Carter transmitted the American Convention (together with the ICCPR, the ICESCR, and the International Convention on the Elimination of All Forms of Racial Discrimination) to the Senate in 1978, it was not approved by the US Congress, and still has not been.

[128] As Goldman has put it,

> when the American Convention was being negotiated in the mid 1960s, most OAS member states, despite their pronounced institutional weaknesses, did have

The support of the United States, however, guaranteed the system a certain authority. Energy was added by the growing strength of the international human rights movement, consisting among others of many who had fled their home countries and ended up in the United States, who provided a powerful new source of energy for the regional human rights system.[129]

The most immediate institutional effect of the entry into force of the Convention was the further empowerment of the Commission, because, although its recommendations were still not binding, the Convention on which many of the Commission's judgments were based was.[130] The Commission was also given several new powers, including the power to "prepare such studies or reports as it considers advisable in the performance of its duties."[131] In addition to empowering the Commission, the entry into force of the Convention paved the way for the creation of the Court. Costa Rica – the host nation, seventy years earlier, of the Central American Court of Justice – played a key role by providing the Court

> nominally democratic and freely elected governments … by the time the American Convention entered into force in 1978, Argentina, Brazil, Bolivia, Chile, Peru, and Uruguay, as well as several Central American states, were ruled either by coupist military regimes or weak civilian governments under military tutelage.

Goldman, "History and Action," 871–2. As Buergenthal has noted, speaking on behalf of the Court's first set of judges:

> we … knew that the fact that the Convention entered into force at all in 1978 had less to do with the support by [Latin American] regimes for human rights, which many of them still violated on a massive scale at the time, and more with the pressure brought to bear on them by President Jimmy Carter.

Buergenthal, "The European and Inter-American Human Rights Courts," 126.

129 On the significance of the growing strength of rights organizations and networks in the Americas in the period, and of the role played by those who had been driven into exile in particular, see Sikkink, "Emergence, Evolution, and Effectiveness"; Keck and Sikkink, *Activists Beyond Borders*; Margaret Keck and Kathryn Sikkink, "Transnational Advocacy Networks in International and Regional Politics," 51 *International Social Science Journal* (1999), 89–101; Markarian, *Left in Transformation*.

130 With the passage of the Convention the Inter-American system acquired an unusual degree of formal complexity, as from that point forward, and unusually for international rights bodies, the Commission oversaw two different regimes, one concerning those states only governed by the nonbinding provisions of the American Declaration, and one concerning those governed not only by the Declaration but also by the Convention. In practice, the tendency was to collapse the difference between the substantive scope of the regimes, as happened for instance when the Commission invoked the Convention even before to it came into force.

131 ACHR, Article 41(c).

with both a home and financial support. The first task for the Court was the preparation of its statute. While, as one of the Court's first judges has recalled, this "provided a rare opportunity to enlarge the Court's powers, [and so] we drafted it accordingly,"[132] states made sure the Court would not be too powerful, rejecting both the Court's proposal that it be a full-time body and its proposed budget.[133] The first Inter-American Court convened on June 29, 1979, though it was several years before it passed its first full judgments. The Court's creation was marked by a tension that would prove enduring, between a strong institution with a substantial degree of internal independence, on the one hand, and extensive external political constraints, on the other.

## IV Africa

### *IV.1 The African Charter on Human and Peoples' Rights*

While the Atlantic Charter agreed by the United States and the United Kingdom during World War II emphasized the importance of the principle of self-determination, the British made it clear they did not intend to extend self-determination to their colonial subjects. Those subjects took a different position on the matter. In 1943 Nnamdi Azikiwe, a leader in the Nigerian nationalist movement and later the first president of independent Nigeria, presented a memorandum to the British government asking that the principles included in the Atlantic Charter be applied after the war to the African colonies, and prepared his own outline of rights that should be guaranteed to every colonial subject.[134]

132 Thomas Buergenthal, "Remembering the Early Years of the Inter-American Court of Human Rights," 37, *New York University Journal of International Law and Politics* (2005), 259–80, 263.

133 See ibid., 264. On the budget vote in particular Buergenthal observes:

> Despite the fact that we had been assured that we had the necessary votes, including the support of Sandinista Nicaragua, when it came to the actual vote, the Nicaraguan delegate did not respond to the roll call. He claimed later that he had fallen asleep. We never learned whether his sleep was motivated by diplomatic considerations or induced by altitude sickness.

Buergenthal, "The Inter-American Court," 233.

134 See Nnamdi Azikiwe, *The Atlantic Charter and British West Africa* (Delegation, 1943); Nnamdi Azikiwe, *Political Blueprint for Nigeria* (African Book Company, 1943). Carlos Rómulo of the Philippines, Kwame Nkrumah of Ghana, and Ferhat Abbas of Algeria all called for the Atlantic Charter's emphasis on self-determination to be given broader effect, as, later, did Nelson Mandela.

Azikiwe's document in turn gave birth to the "Freedom Charter," drawn up by Azikiwe's political party, the National Council for Nigeria and the Cameroons.[135]

Achieving self-determination in practice necessarily meant first throwing off colonial rule. Colonial rule had always been founded upon widespread and systematic rights violations;[136] as struggles for independence intensified, so did the intensity of colonial repression.[137] The success of independence struggles, leading to an increasing number of African states gaining their independence from the late 1950s on, was accordingly a prerequisite for rights improvement;[138] calls for greater respect for human rights were hence, unsurprisingly, closely connected to calls

[135] For more, see Bonny Ibhawoh, *Imperialism and Human Rights: Colonial Discourses of Rights and Liberties in African History* (State University of New York Press, 2007), Chapter 6. Prior to the war, the cause of decolonization was advanced in a number of fora, including, for instance, the "Pan-African Congress" meetings, organized by W. E. B. Du Bois and others, which emphasized issues faced by Africans and those of African dissent around the world, and called for a "Charter of Rights" for Africans that specifically emphasized the right to participate in government. Following on from the Pan-African Conference in 1900, the Pan-African Congress met in 1919, 1921, 1923, and 1927, and the Pan-African Federation was established in 1944, with an important fifth meeting of the Congress, organized by Trinidadian George Padmore and Ghanaian Kwame Nkrumah, following in 1945. For more, see Nnamdi Azikiwe, *Zik: A Selection from the Speeches of Nnamdi Azikiwe* (Cambridge University Press, 1961); W. E. B. Du Bois, *The World and Africa: An Inquiry into the Part which Africa has Played in World History* (Viking Press, 1965); Nnamdi Azikiwe, *My Odyssey: An Autobiography* (Praeger, 1970); Penny Von Eschen, *Race Against Empire: Black Americans and Anticolonialism, 1937–1957* (Cornell University Press, 1997); Klaus Benesch and Geneviève Fabre eds., *African Diasporas in the New and Old Worlds: Consciousness and Imagination* (Rodopi, 2004); Fitzroy Baptiste and Rupert Lewis eds., *George Padmore: Pan Africa Revolutionary* (Ian Randle, 2009); David Lewis, *W.E.B. du Bois: A Biography* (Holt, 2009); Adom Getachew, *Worldmaking after Empire: The Rise and Fall of Self-Determination* (Princeton University Press, 2019).

[136] A fact observed by the Declaration on the Granting of Independence to Colonial Countries and Peoples, approved as United Nations General Assembly Resolution 1514 on the December 14, 1960, which concisely observed that "The subjection of peoples to a foreign domination is a negation of fundamental human rights."

[137] For the relevance of decolonization struggles, and particularly the brutal repression employed by the French and British in Algeria and Kenya, to the development of human rights, see Fabian Klose, "'Source of Embarrassment': Human Rights, State of Emergency, and the Wars of Decolonization," in Hoffmann ed., *Human Rights in the Twentieth Century*, 237–57; Fabian Klose, *Human Rights in the Shadow of Colonial Violence* (University of Pennsylvania Press, 2013).

[138] As Du Bois put it, "The greatest single question is the ending of colonialism. For unless this is done, the world cannot be democratic." W. E. B. Du Bois, *The Amsterdam News* (August 19, 1944).

for decolonization.[139] On the formal level, the 1958 All African Peoples' Conference in Accra saw human rights receive prominent emphasis, as did the Conference of Independent States and the Conference of the Pan-African Movement of East and Central Africa.[140] Many newly independent countries went on to adopt strong bills of rights, moreover, which demonstrated the influence of the Universal Declaration and the European Convention. Nigeria's constitution in particular, drafted shortly before many others, served as an example for the later constitutions in countries such as Botswana, Kenya, Lesotho, Malawi, Sierra Leone, Eswatini, Uganda, and Zambia.[141]

139 For some considerations on rights rhetoric and decolonization struggles, see Bethwell A. Ogot, "Mau Mau and Nationhood: The Untold Story," in Eisha Stephen Atieno Odhiambo and John Lonsdale eds., *Mau Mau and Nationhood: Arms, Authority and Narration* (Ohio University Press, 2003), 8–36; Ullrich Lohrmann, *Voices from Tanganyika: Great Britain, the United Nations and the Decolonization of a Trust Territory, 1946–1961* (LIT Verlag, 2007); Andreas Eckert, "African Nationalists and Human Rights, 1940s–1970s," in Hoffmann ed., *Human Rights in the Twentieth Century*, 283–300. The 1955 Asian-African Conference in Bandung saw rights prominently emphasized; see Roland Burke, "'The Compelling Dialogue of Freedom': Human Rights at the Bandung Conference," 28 *Human Rights Quarterly* (2006), 961; Burke, *Decolonization*, Chapter 1. Meanwhile, as Simpson has observed relative to the British in particular,

> It cannot be said that the extension of the European Convention to the colonies played any direct role in encouraging decolonization … But indirectly respect for human rights … did play an important part. For it came to be accepted by a significant sector of British public opinion that the repression of colonial insurrections more or less inevitably led to violations of human rights and illiberal actions by colonial governments … Holding on to the colonies became, increasingly, morally unacceptable.

Simpson, *Human Rights and the End of Empire*, 1057.

140 For more on the conferences, and the soft war between Nasser and Nkrumah that lay behind them, see Robert Vitalis, "The Midnight Ride of Kwame Nkrumah and Other Fables of Bandung," 4 *Humanity: An International Journal of Human Rights, Humanitarianism and Development* (2013), 261–88.

141 For more, see Taslim Elias, "The New Constitution of Nigeria and the Protection of Human Rights and Fundamental Freedoms," 11 *Judicial Review* (1960), 30–46; Stanley Smith, *The New Commonwealth and its Constitutions* (Stevens & Sons, 1964); Taslim Elias, *Nigeria: Development of its Laws and Constitution* (Stevens & Sons, 1967), 165–7; Hastings Okoth-Ogendo, "National Implementation of International Responsibility: Some Thoughts on Human Rights in Africa," 10 *East African Law Journal* (1974), 1–16; Bello, "The African Charter"; Christof Heyns, "African Human Rights Law and the European Convention," 11 *South African Journal of Human Rights* (1995), 257. For a full account of the changing attitudes toward bills of rights held by departing British colonial administrators, and the influence of the European Convention on Human Rights in particular, see Charles Parkinson, *Bills of Rights and Decolonization: The Emergence of Domestic Human*

From the beginnings of decolonization momentum toward an African regional human rights system was driven forward by African jurists.[142] In the early 1960s, the International Commission of Jurists (hereinafter the "ICJ") organized a series of global conferences, calling for greater protection for the rule of law around the world.[143] It was a conference they organized in 1961 in Lagos that would have the most significant repercussions, constituting the first small step toward building the momentum necessary to establish an African regional human rights system.[144]

The Organisation of African Unity (hereinafter the "OAU") was established on May 25, 1963, in Addis Ababa.[145] The preamble of the Charter of the Organization declared that freedom, equality, justice, and dignity were essential objectives of the African people, while also emphasizing the importance of the Universal Declaration of Human Rights. Despite these affirmations, it was clear that the primary purpose of the OAU was not to advance human rights, but rather to support political unity across the continent and to unify African forces in support of the liberation struggles that still remained to be fought. As Murray put it, "any threats to human rights appeared to be reflected in the OAU Charter as coming from outside the continent, something which African unity may help to prevent. It was clear, therefore, that state sovereignty was sacrosanct."[146]

*Rights Instruments in Britain's Overseas Territories* (Oxford University Press, 2008). The Universal Declaration of Human Rights was also often looked to, and specifically referenced in the constitutions of Algeria, Burundi, Dahomey, Equatorial Africa, Gabon, Guinea, Mali, Mauritania, Niger, the Republic of Congo, Rwanda, Senegal, Somalia, Togo, and Zaire.

142 See Germain Baricako, "The African Charter and African Commission on Human and Peoples' Rights," in Evans and Murray eds., *The African Charter*, 1–19.

143 On the history of the ICJ, see Tolley, *The International Commission of Jurists*; Richard Pierre Claude, "The International Commission of Jurists: Global Advocates for Human Rights (Book Review)," 16 *Human Rights Quarterly* (1994), 576–8.

144 See ICJ, Report on the Proceedings of the African Conference on the Rule of Law, Lagos, Nigeria (January 3–7, 1961). The conference had almost two hundred participants, including ministers of justice such as Taslim Elias from Nigeria as well as other chief justices and prominent legal experts from some two dozen countries.

145 For more on the early history of the OAU, see Jon Woronoff, *Organizing African Unity* (Scarecrow, 1971); Elenga M'buyinga, *Pan-Africanism or Neo-Colonialism? The Bankruptcy of the OAU* (Zed, 1982).

146 Murray, *Human Rights in Africa*, 8. Mathews has pointed to the similar observation of Nyerere, writing

> As President Nyerere of Tanzania, one of the founding fathers of the OAU, has pointed out, the OAU Charter spoke for the African peoples still under colonial or racial domination, but once the countries emerged to nationhood, the Charter stood

The continuing existence of the apartheid regime in South Africa and the white settler regime in Zimbabwe, together with the refusal of the Portuguese to relinquish control over their colonies, provided clear injustices against which newly independent African states could rally and focus their efforts. African states' critiques of the various colonial regimes in the Southern African region combined emphases on self-determination, decolonization, and human rights. Following the International Court of Justice's decision in the South-West Africa cases in 1966,[147] which came as a major disappointment to third world states in general and African states in particular, those states exerted pressure for the creation of an ad hoc working group within the Commission on Human Rights that would focus on the Southern African situation as a whole. African states' condemnation of ongoing colonialism in Southern Africa found concrete expression in the 1969 Lusaka Manifesto, which among other things strongly emphasized human rights principles.[148]

> for the protection of their heads of state and served as a trade union which protected them. In other words, the OAU appears to be an institution of the African heads of state, by the heads of state and for the heads of state.

K. Mathews, "The Organization of African Unity," in Domenico Mazzeo ed., *African Regional Organizations* (Cambridge University Press, 1984), 79. As the states of the continent became comfortable in their newfound independence, an initial radicalism, which tended to emphasize the elimination of borders, was replaced by a general affirmation of the supremacy of the state over and against such movements. For more, see Murray, *Human Rights in Africa*, 9–14. As Umozurike put it, shortly before the African regional human rights system was created, "with regard to breaches of human rights, even of a grave nature such as genocide, the OAU has been bogged down by the domestic jurisdiction clause" Oji Umozurike, "The Domestic Jurisdiction Clause in the OAU Charter," 78 *African Affairs* (1979), 202.

147 South-West Africa Cases (Ethiopia v. South Africa; Liberia v. South Africa), Second Phase, International Court of Justice (July 18, 1966).

148 The Manifesto for instance began by stating "all men are equal, and have equal rights to human dignity and respect, regardless of colour, race, religion or sex ... all men have the right and the duty to participate as equal members of the society, in their own government." Lukasa Manifesto: A Policy Statement for Decolonization in Respect of Southern Africa, adopted by the OAU and UN, GA Res. 2505, UN Doc. A/PV.1815 (November 20, 1969). For more on the Manifesto, see N. M. Shamuyarira, "The Lusaka Manifesto Strategy of OAU States and its Consequences for the Freedom Struggle in Southern Africa," 2 *African Affairs* (1977). As Clapham has put it, however,

> In bringing their outrage to the attention of an external and especially Western audience ... African governments and other anti-apartheid campaigners both explicitly breached the frontiers of juridical sovereignty and raised issues relating to the treatment of individuals which could equally be raised with reference to their own

The adoption of the Convention on the Elimination of All Forms of Racial Discrimination in 1965 and of the international covenants in 1966 provided impetus and support to human rights advocates across the world.[149] Following adoption of the covenants, a series of seminars and conferences were organized by the UN in Dakar, which ultimately resulted in a 1967 proposal for the creation of an African regional human rights commission, a proposal that was supported at the UN Human Rights Commission by a number of African countries.[150] The Human Rights Commission took up the proposals, and requested that the Secretary-General take further steps to accomplish that end.[151] The following years saw a series of conferences across the continent, aimed at further bolstering support for a regional human rights system. The culmination of this series of conferences was a 1973 meeting in Dar es Salaam, at which twenty-three African states agreed on the idea of preparing a regional charter on human rights.[152]

> states. Once the human rights record of African-ruled states started to attract external attention, it was correspondingly harder to claim the protection of sovereign statehood.

Andrew Clapham, *Africa and the International System: The Politics of State Survival* (Cambridge University Press, 1996), 189.

149 For more on the role of third world states in supporting the development of the covenants, see Burke, *Decolonization*, Chapter 3; Burke, "Some Rights are More Equal"; Jensen, *Making International Human Rights*. On the drafting process of the covenants, see also Whelan and Donnelly, "The West, Economic and Social Rights."

150 Two resolutions proposing such an end were put forward, one by Senegal, Tanzania, Benin, and Congo-Brazzaville, the other by Nigeria. See Bello, "The African Charter," 24.

151 In particular, the General Assembly called on the Secretary General "to consider the possibility of arranging suitable regional seminars under the programmes of advisory services … where no regional commission on human rights exist at present" UN Doc. E/4475 (1968).

152 Prior to the Dar es Salaam conference, conferences were held in Cairo in 1969 and in Ethiopia in 1971. See Seminar on the Establishment of Regional Commissions on Human Rights with Special Reference to Africa, UN Doc. ST/TAO/HR/38, Cairo, Egypt (September 2–15, 1969); Report of the Conference of African Jurists on the African Legal Process and the Individual, UN Doc. E/CN/14/521, Addis Ababa, Ethiopia (April 19–23, 1971). 1969 also saw the adoption by the OAU of the Convention Governing the Specific Aspects of the Refugee Problem in Africa. For more, see Warren Weinstein, "Human Rights in Africa: A Long-Awaited Voice," 78 *Current History* (1980), 97–132. 1973 saw the adoption of the Convention on the Suppression and Punishment of the Crime of Apartheid. For more on the anti-apartheid struggle and its broader significance, see Thorn, *Anti-Apartheid*; Hostetter, *Movement Matters*; Anderson, "International Conscience"; Thorn, "The Meaning(s) of Solidarity"; Irwin, *Gordian Knot*; all the papers in the special 2014 edition of Radical History Review on *The Global Anti-Apartheid Movement;* and Skinner, "The Dynamics of Anti-Apartheid."

It was in the late 1970s, however, that all the conditions necessary for the creation of an African regional rights system finally came together. As noted earlier, the commencement of the Carter administration in 1977 saw US foreign policy become increasingly supportive of rights globally. Meanwhile, African-based pressure for the creation of a regional rights system resumed, through the efforts of Nigeria on the international level,[153] and through a major conference in Dakar in 1978, thanks in part to the urging of President Senghor, long a human rights supporter.

While this ongoing advocacy work was crucial, it is doubtful whether an African regional human rights system would have been put in place, had not several incidents of major political unrest and violence served to change the attitudes of several key African state toward such a venture. First, Uganda declared war on Tanzania on October 30, 1978, and sent troops into the Kagera border region with the intent of annexing it. Tanzania responded with force, quickly overwhelming the Ugandans and their Libyan allies. Tanzanian forces captured Kampala on April 10, 1979, after which President Amin fled the country.

Second, in April 1979, school children in the Central African Republic who had protested the expensive uniforms that they were forced to wear to school, which bore President Bokassa's image, and could only be purchased from a store owned by one of his wives, were arrested, tortured, and executed. The following month, Amnesty International released a powerful report on their torture and killing. The Amnesty Report was followed by a second report produced by French-speaking African countries, which reached a similar conclusion.[154] The French military subsequently intervened, removing President Bokassa and his associates from power.

Both events encouraged African leaders to rethink the value of a regional rights system. Events in the Central African Republic served as a powerful demonstration of the consequences that could flow from a failure to

[153] Among other efforts Nigeria sponsored a resolution at the UN Human Rights Commission that was adopted in 1978. *See* Res. 24, Human Rights Commission, UN Doc. E/CN.4/1292, 132.

[154] As Bello has put it,

> when the report of the enquiry was made known to the general public it engendered much public outcry and indignation. It produced such a sustained, unmitigated and tedious conglomeration of international revulsion that almost every African leader felt humiliated; and in spite of Bokassa's entrenched position in the Franco-African community, it was obvious the die was cast. The Emperor was forced out of office.

Bello, "The African Charter," 82.

take strong measures to address rights violations on the continent. The Ugandan invasion of Tanzania, meanwhile, demonstrated the manner in which, if ignored, brutal domestic regimes could create problems for their neighbors, revealing the flaw in the argument of those who suggested that human rights violations were purely a matter of national concern. Equally significant was the fact that the attack had come against Tanzania, which helped to make Tanzania's influential president, Julius Nyerere, a strong advocate for a regional rights system.[155]

Whatever the factors which helped to change state leaders' minds,[156] when Senghor advanced a resolution within the OAU calling for the creation of a group of experts tasked with preparing a draft regional rights charter in 1979, it was unanimously adopted.[157] At the end of 1979, the new expert group convened in Dakar.[158] A working draft was prepared for the group by Kéba M'Baye, a Senegalese jurist then president of the ICJ, supported by Ibrahima Fall and Mohamadou M'Backe. The draft Charter drew on several sources,[159] but was ultimately a fairly conventional rights document. On the institutional side, while some had hoped there might be support for the creation of a court, the drafters instead preferred to opt for a commission.[160] Although the initial proposal was that the commission

155 Tanzania in fact presented its war against Amin in part as a reaction to Amin's rights violations within Uganda. At the 16th OAU summit, in 1979, Tanzania followed up on this newfound faith in the international human rights project by urging member states to sign existing international human rights instruments. See 16th Summit Conference: Ugandan Invasion Issue and its Implications, 16 *Africa Research Bulletin: Political Social and Cultural Series*, 5329–30 (1979).

156 For a powerfully argued alternative account of the factors that led to agreement on the African Charter, see Kufuor, *The African Human Rights System*.

157 See Decision 115 (XVI), Rev. 1, OAU, AHG/115 (1979).

158 See Meeting of Experts for the Preparation of the draft African Charter of Human and Peoples' Rights, Dakar, Senegal, OAU Doc. CAB/LEG/67/draft Rpt. 11 (November 28–December 8, 1979). The group consisted of twenty experts.

159 Sources relied upon included the International Covenant on Civil and Political Rights and the American Convention on Human Rights. A draft document produced at a UN seminar in Liberia a few months earlier provided some guidance on the question of how the system's institutional architecture might be set up. See Seminar on the Establishment of Regional Commissions on Human Rights with Special Reference to Africa, UN Doc. ST/HR/SER.A/4, Monrovia, Liberia (September 10–21, 1979); Viljoen, "The Travaux Préparatoires," 315.

160 The possibility of creating a Court was quickly written off, because it was generally understood that states would not accept such a major step. Article 66 of the Charter, which contemplated that the Charter might in time be complemented by new "special protocols or agreements," made clear that the Charter's more rights-supportive drafters were taking a long-term perspective, hoping to achieve further progress in due course. As M'Baye, one

be granted a clear mandate to receive individual petitions, this clarity was diluted over the course of the meeting, replaced by a much more obscure reference to the commission's ability to receive not only state communications but also "other communications," which became the wording of the final text.

While a first draft was achieved with minimal effort, obtaining state consent was more challenging. A first attempt to obtain OAU approval for the Charter took place at a meeting of government experts in Ethiopia in March 1980; the experts did not look kindly on the venture, however. After this failure the rights-supportive Secretary-General of the OAU, Edem Kodjo, adopted another tack, urging President Dawda Jawara of the Gambia to host a ministerial meeting in Banjul where he might encourage states to support the new project. While the ministers who assembled in Banjul ultimately signaled their consent to a portion of the draft – eleven of the proposed articles to be exact – they called for the rest to be reconsidered, criticizing it both for "not taking into account certain African beliefs, and containing ideas that were too capitalist."[161] A second ministerial meeting in Banjul was, therefore, arranged for January 1981. At that meeting the assembled parties worked together to revise the text, ultimately achieving a final document to which all were willing to consent. On the substantive side, the most notable inclusion within the document were a set of "peoples' rights," speaking to a more radical, expansive vision of human rights that has come to be closely associated with the "African" rights vision.[162] On the institutional side, the changes produced were more

of the chief proponents of a strong African human rights system and chief drafter of the Charter, put it,

> Conscious of having drafted a useful statement which, however, requires to be perfected, the authors of the Charter envisaged provisions concerning its amendment and revision. The Charter constitutes what the African states were able to accept in 1981 and was therefore only a stage. It is to be hoped that it can be improved at a later date. The provision concerning additions which may be added to it is in response to this objective.

Cited in Raymond Sock, "The Case for an African Court on Human and Peoples' Rights: From a Concept to a Draft Protocol Over 33 Years," *African Topics* (March/April 1994).

161 See Baricako, "The African Charter," 7; Report of the Rapporteur, CAB/LEG/67/3 draft Rapt (11) (June, 1980).

162 These articles drew upon a longer tradition, in and through which third world states had pushed back against the international economic and legal order. For more, see Inclusion in the International Covenant or Covenants on Human Rights of an Article Relating to the Right of Peoples to Self-Determination, GA Res. A/Res/545 (VI) (February

notable for limiting the independence of the system in many ways, as a number of political checks and controls were introduced.[163]

Having obtained consensus in the ministerial meeting at Banjul, the draft now had to overcome the potentially more challenging hurdle of the Committee of Ministers of the OAU. The Committee of Ministers raised a number of questions: they were concerned that the Charter was vague and that conflicts could arise over interpretation; that the Charter did not make clear that heads of state would have the power of interpretation; that the Charter would conflict with the principle of nonintervention and with domestic legal orders; and that the Charter did not protect certain important rights, or sufficiently enumerate duties.[164] Despite the concerns they expressed, however, the Committee of Ministers referred the draft to the OAU Assembly without amendment.

5, 1952); The Right to Exploit Freely Natural Wealth and Resources, GA Res. 626 (VII) (December 21, 1952); United Nations Declaration on Permanent Sovereignty over Natural Resources, GA Res. 1803 (XVII) (December 14, 1962); Oji Umozurike, *Self-Determination in International Law* (Archon, 1972); Declaration on the Establishment of a New International Economic Order, GA Res. 3201 (S-VI) (May 1, 1974); Charter of Economic Rights and Duties of States, GA Res. 3281 (XIX) (December 12, 1974); Mohammed Bedjaoui, *Towards a New International Economic Order* (Holmes & Meier, 1979); Kamal Hossain ed., *Legal Aspects of the New International Economic Order* (Bloomsbury, 1980). For more recent developments within and reflections on this tradition, see Report of the Secretary-General, Progressive Development of the Principles and Norms of International Law Relating to a New International Economic Order, UN Doc. A/39/504/Add.1 (October 23, 1984); Kamal Hossain and Subrata Roy Chowdhury eds., *Permanent Sovereignty Over Natural Resources* (Palgrave, 1984); Mark Ellis, "The New International Economic Order: The Debate over the Legal Effects of General Assembly Resolutions Revisited," 15 *California Western International Law Journal* (1985), 647–704; Mohammed Bedjaoui ed., *International Law: Achievements and Prospects* (Martinus Nijhoff, 1992); Nico Schrijver, *Sovereignty over Natural Resources: Balancing Rights and Duties* (Cambridge University Press, 1997); Sundhya Pahuja, *Decolonising International Law: Development, Economic Growth and the Politics of Universality* (Cambridge University Press, 2011). In 1986, the idea of a right to development achieved recognition as a United Nations Declaration (GA Res. 41/128 [December 4, 1986]). For more on the right to development specifically, see Keba M'Baye, "Droits de l'homme et pays en développment," in René-Jean Dupuy ed., *Humanité et droit international* (Pedone, 1991), 211–22; Daniel Whelan, "'Under the Aegis of Man': The Right to Development and the Origins of the New International Economic Order," 6 *Humanity: An International Journal of Human Rights, Humanitarianism and Development* (2015), 93–108; Julia Dehm, "Highlighting Inequalities in the Histories of Human Rights: Contestations Over Justice, Needs and Rights in the 1970s," 31 *Leiden Journal of International Law* (2018), 871–95.

163 For more, see Viljoen, "The Travaux Préparatoires," 324.

164 See OAU Doc. CM/Plen. Draft Rapt. Rpt. (XXXVII), 60–1 (1981); OAU Diary No. 6 (June 21, 1981).

As with the OAU's Committee of Ministers, achieving the support of the Assembly of the OAU proved a surprisingly easy hurdle to surmount: the draft was approved by the Assembly, without substantive amendment, in June 1981.[165] As Viljoen has put it, highlighting the strange lack of attention garnered by the occasion,

> During its Eighteenth Session, on 17 June 1981 in Nairobi, the Assembly adopted the African Charter. This date, now celebrated as a decisive moment for human rights promotion in Africa, passed almost unnoticed at the Assembly session and in contemporaneous press reports, government feed-back and other discussions immediately thereafter. The proposal for the Charter's adoption was postponed until midnight of the last day of the meeting. At that stage, President Jawara of the Gambia urged the adoption of the Charter. Perhaps motivated by the late hour and fatigue after days of deliberations, the heads of states present adopted it without debate. No formal vote was even taken on the matter.[166]

Whether states had paid attention or not, as of 1981 the African Charter was officially adopted and open for signature. As noted earlier, on a substantive level the Charter included not only a range of rights protections commonly found within the other regional and international treaties on civil and political rights (together with a number of "duties" which were generally understood as claw-back clauses but which have yet to be extensively interpreted or invoked), but also a number of novel "peoples' rights," including the rights to self-determination, to free disposal of wealth and natural resources, to economic, social, and cultural development, to national and international peace and security, and to a generally satisfactory environment.[167]

On an institutional level, the Charter's central accomplishment was to establish the "African Commission on Human and Peoples' Rights." As with the European and Inter-American Commissions, the understanding was that the African Commission's decisions would be nonbinding. In addition, the Charter gave the Secretary-General of the OAU a quasi-supervisory role in relation to the Commission, thanks to their power to appoint the Secretary and to set the budget of the Commission. The Charter also placed strong emphasis on friendly settlement, and only allowed the Commission's decisions to be made public where a majority of OAU member states so approved.

165 See OAU doc CAB/LEG/67/3/Rev.5.

166 Viljoen, "The Travaux Préparatoires," 315.

167 See Articles 20–24 of the Charter.

With respect to the subjects the Commission might address and the procedures through which its attention might be called to a matter, the Charter included several rather ambiguous provisions. In the first place, the Charter established a special procedure for addressing serious or massive rights violations, through which the Commission might refer such situations to the OAU – a body whose past record did not inspire great confidence. As with the other regional systems, the African Charter also laid out a process by which inter-state complaints might be submitted. Debates over the treatment of individual complaints, meanwhile, produced the curious language of Article 55 of the Charter referred to earlier, which provided that, in addition to the communications from state parties, the Commission might also hear "communications other than those of state parties." While the intent of the drafters may have been to foreclose the possibility of individual communications, in the end this language was anything but clear, leaving the door to individual complaints open, should the Commission be inclined to interpret its mandate assertively.

The African Charter entered into force in 1986, following ratification by a majority of the member states of the OAU.[168] While some early ratifiers were comparatively progressive states, others were major rights violators, signifying that for many states ratification of the Charter was seen as a claim to political legitimacy rather than a sincere commitment to rights protection and advancement. The first African Commission was composed in 1987; it commenced its work gradually, as explored in the following section.

### *IV.2 The African Court*

The idea of an African regional rights court had been floated during the 1961 Lagos conference, only to recede in subsequent years, with state representatives disguising their unwillingness to countenance a binding judicial oversight mechanism behind the claim that "African culture frowned

[168] Mali ratified in 1981; Guinea, Liberia, Senegal, Togo, and Congo in 1982; Tunisia, Gambia, Nigeria, Rwanda, and Sierra Leone in 1983; Zambia, Tanzania, Egypt, and Burkina Faso in 1984; Somalia and Guinea-Bissau in 1985; and Benin, Sudan, Gabon, Equatorial Guinea, the Central African Republic, the Sahrawi Arab Democratic Republic, Uganda, Sao Tome and Principe, Zimbabwe, Comoros, Mauritania, Botswana, Niger, Libya, and Chad in 1986, bringing the total number of states parties up to 32 by the end of the year. Algeria, Cape Verde, and the Democratic Republic of the Congo ratified in 1987, Ghana, Mozambique, Cameroon, Burundi, and Malawi in 1989, Angola in 1990, Djibouti in 1991, Cote d'Ivoire, Kenya, Lesotho, Madagascar, Seychelles, Mauritius, and Namibia in 1992, Swaziland in 1995, South Africa in 1996, Ethiopia in 1998, and Eritrea in 1999.

upon litigation."[169] The idea of creating an African court of human rights began to gather steam in the post-Cold War period, however. A judicial colloquium on the potential creation of an African Court was held in 1990 in Banjul. In 1993, the Secretary-General of the OAU, Salim Ahmed Salim, declared that "The time has come to begin discussions for the establishment of an African Court of Human Rights." The idea of an African court of human rights also began to attract substantial attention in the literature, with scholars debating the relative merits of relying on a court or developing the Commission, and, if a court was created, how the two might interact.[170] Civil society in particular played a key role in pushing for a court. Some one-hundred and forty NGOs were registered with the Commission by the end of 1994, with Commission sessions providing an ideal setting in which advocates could come together to organize joint efforts in support of the creation of additional regional rights mechanisms. Momentum also came from a wave of democratic transitions within African countries, most dramatically those that transformed the southern African region.[171] As one commentator put it,

> In the face of unprecedented democratic changes in Africa and the emergence of popular grassroots movements as promising engines of change and catalysts for state accountability, those who once advocated a gradualist approach became increasingly convinced of the urgency of establishing a regional human rights court.[172]

As with the lead up to the creation of the Commission, the ICJ, now headed by Adama Dieng, played a crucial role in spearheading the efforts aimed at the creation of a court. The ICJ commissioned a legal expert to produce a draft protocol in 1993, which was discussed at a meeting of African and regional NGOs. The text was developed with the assistance of the OAU's legal division and the Commission, and the resulting document submitted

[169] See Udombana, "Towards the African Court."

[170] See, e.g., Sock, "Case for an African Court"; Chidi Odinkalu, "Courting the Court," *African Topics* (March/April 1994), 11; Ankumah, *African Commission*, 194–8.

[171] Other countries in the region also underwent transitions toward more democratic governance in the period. Elections and transition to civilian governance occurred for instance in Benin in 1991 and in Mali in 1992. In Tanzania, opposition parties were legalized in 1992, and the first multiparty elections occurred in 1995.

[172] Udombana, "Towards the African Court," 77. For more on such a theme, see Claude Welch, "The African Commission on Human and Peoples' Rights: A Five-Year Report and Assessment," 14 *Human Rights Quarterly* (1992), 47 n. 21; H. Kwasi Prempeh, "Africa's 'Constitutionalism Revival': False Start or New Dawn?," 5 *International Journal of Constitutional Law* (2007), 469–506.

to the OAU in early 1994. The OAU then called on the Secretary-General to convene a meeting of experts to consider the matter. In 1995 that meeting was convened in Cape Town.

The Cape Town meeting resulted in the production of a new, more authoritative draft protocol. The Cape Town draft was ambitious, granting individuals direct access to the court. At the next meeting to consider the text, however, which took place in Mauritania in April 1997, several steps were taken to make the draft more palatable to states, including the introduction of a limitation on who might access the court: under the new draft, only the Commission or states would be able to bring claims to the court as a matter of right. This limitation was qualified by one potential exception, however: individuals and NGOs would be allowed to access the court directly, should a state submit an optional declaration allowing such access.[173] A third meeting in Addis Ababa in December 1997, in which state representatives were also included, confirmed the approach adopted.[174]

The Protocol establishing the African Court on Human and Peoples' Rights was adopted by the Council of Ministers of the OAU in February 1998, and approved by the Assembly in June. The OAU adopted a more supportive stance relative to rights issues generally in the period as well. In 1999 OAU member states committed to the "Grand Bay (Mauritius) Declaration and Plan of Action" as well as the "Algiers Declaration," both of which recognized the importance of human rights and aimed at the fuller incorporation of rights into the OAU's work.[175] These steps were

[173] See Article 34(6) of the final text. For further commentary on the text, see Mutua, "The African Human Rights Court," 355; Udombana, "Towards the African Court," 99–100; Viljoen, "A Human Rights Court for Africa," 39–40.

[174] For more, see Udombana, "Towards the African Court."

[175] In addition, from 1999 on a series of regional conferences focusing on security, stability, development, and cooperation took place, in which rights concerns were once again highlighted, incorporating a pledge by states to

> promulgate constitutions with Bills of Rights, free and fair elections, separation of powers, multiparty systems, free expression, independent judiciary, popular participation, civilian authority, protection of human rights, establishment of African Court on Human and Peoples' Rights, improve good governance, promote and protect rights and welfare of the African child.

See Draft Memorandum of Understanding on Security, Stability, Development and Cooperation. The process also saw states commit to the ratification and implementation of human rights instruments, to taking measures oriented toward the achievement of democratic, rights-respecting systems, to setting up domestic human rights institutions, and to support for rights on the regional level. For more, see Murray, *Human Rights in Africa*, 28–30.

followed by an even more significant transformation, as in 2000 the constitutive act of the African Union (hereafter the "AU") was adopted, leading to the creation of the AU in 2002. The constitutive act highlighted the importance of human rights several times, leading commentators to opine that the AU would likely provide much stronger support for human rights than the OAU had done.[176] Exactly how the existing human rights system would relate to the AU was left open, however.[177]

Along with the creation of the AU came plans for an African Court of Justice, oriented toward enabling greater regional integration, particularly with respect to economic issues. Seeing that an African Court on Human and Peoples' Rights was soon to be created, the office of the legal counsel of the AU suggested the two courts should be merged, arguing that such an approach made both logistical and financial sense.[178] Initially this plan was resisted, on the grounds that it would add unnecessary complexity to the system. Meanwhile, ratifications of the Protocol establishing the African Court continued; sixteen states had submitted their ratifications by the end of 2003, leading to the Protocol formally coming into effect in January 2004.[179]

Shortly after the Protocol establishing the African Court of Human and Peoples' Rights came into effect, President Obasanjo of Nigeria, at the time the chairperson of the Assembly of the AU, suggested that the

176 See Frans Viljoen and Evarist Baimu, "Courts for Africa: Considering the Co-Existence of the African Court on Human and Peoples' Rights and the African Court of Justice," 22 *Netherlands Quarterly of Human Rights* (2004), 241–67; Gino Naldi, "The African Union and the Regional Human Rights System," in Evans and Murray eds., *The African Charter*, 20–48.

177 Coordination between the two bodies would unsurprisingly prove a problem in practice. See Murray, *Human Rights in Africa*, 33–4, 69–70; Amnesty International, *Organization of African Unity: Making Human Rights a Reality for Africans* (1998).

178 For reflections on the merits of such a merger from the period, see Viljoen and Baimu, "Courts for Africa," 252.

179 Burkina Faso and Senegal ratified in 1998; Gambia in 1999; Gabon and Mali in 2000; Uganda in 2001; South Africa in 2002; and Algeria, Burundi, Comoros, Cote d'Ivoire, Lesotho, Libya, Mauritius, Rwanda, and Togo in 2003. Ghana, Kenya, Mozambique, Niger, and Nigeria ratified in 2004, Mauritania in 2005, Tanzania in 2006, Tunisia in 2007, Malawi in 2008, Congo in 2011, Benin in 2012, the Arab Sahrawi Republic and Cameroon in 2015, and Chad in 2016, bringing the total number of ratifications up to thirty as of the end of 2018. The high number of ratifications received in the initial years in which the Protocol was open for signature testified to the progressive optimism of the period, an optimism not only mirrored but in fact exceeded by African states' enthusiasm for the International Criminal Court, which twenty-six African states had signed up to the jurisdiction of as of the end of 2004.

previously mooted and rejected merger should take place after all, taking observers and jurists by surprise.[180] One immediate consequence of that decision was a delay in the formation of the African Court of Human and Peoples' Rights. The Court was eventually established in 2006, in Arusha, Tanzania, in the complex in which the International Criminal Tribunal for Rwanda previously sat. The complications created by the plan for a combined court, meanwhile, were addressed through the drafting of a new "Protocol on the Statute of the African Court of Justice and Human and Peoples' Rights," agreed in 2008. The new protocol imagined two courts, with two different sets of judges, who would share the same facilities, a compromise between the suggestions of single and dual court advocates.[181]

Even this did not mark the end of the process of institutional reshaping, however. In 2009 the AU Assembly decided to grant the "African Court" additional jurisdiction over war crimes.[182] This move was prompted in part by a desire on the part of some African states to preempt prosecutions of African leaders conducted by non-African actors, and was widely criticized by international criminal law advocates as evincing a desire to shield leaders from vigorous prosecution.[183] At the same time, the idea of granting the African Court criminal jurisdiction also received support

180 In the words of one pair of commentators the remarks of Obasanjo "surprised officials of the AU Commission, and advisors to President Obasanjo denied any prior knowledge. Despite the legal uncertainty of this proposal, the Assembly proceeded to adopt a decision" Ibrahima Kane and Ahmed Motala, "The Creation of a New African Court of Justice and Human Rights," in Evans and Murray eds., *The African Charter*, 409–10. As Kane and Motala further put it, by deciding on merger the AU Assembly "not only undermine[d] its own previous decision but also point[ed] to a failure to consider the legal and political implications of such a decision." Ibid., 413.

181 For commentary on the new protocol, see Kane and Motala, "Creation of a New African Court," 432; Dan Juma, "Lost (or Found) in Transition? The Anatomy of the New African Court of Justice and Human Rights," 13 *Max Planck Yearbook of United Nations Law* (2009), 287–94. The new protocol requires fifteen ratification to come into effect.

182 *See* AU Decision 213 (XII).

183 For some criticisms, including criticisms focused on procedural issues, see Chacha Murungu, "Towards a Criminal Chamber in the African Court of Justice and Human Rights," 9 *Journal of International Criminal Justice* (2011), 1067–88; Gino Naldi and Konstantinos Magliveras, "The African Court of Justice and Human Rights: A Judicial Curate's Egg," 9 *International Organizations Law Review* (2012), 440–46; Max Du Plessis, *Implications of the AU Decision to Give the African Court Jurisdiction over International Crimes* (Institute for Security Studies, 2012); Letter on behalf of 49 civil society organizations to Justice Ministers and Attorneys General of African states parties to the ICC (May 3, 2012), available at: www.hrw.org/sites/default/files/related_material/Letter_on_African_Court_May_2012.pdf; Ademola Abass, "Prosecuting International Crimes in Africa: Rationale, Prospects and Challenges," 24 *European Journal of International Law* (2013), 933–46.

from some rights advocates, who believed that, whatever its motivations, the creation of such a court would serve to promote international criminal law norms and advance the fight against impunity.[184]

After several years' delay in June 2014 the "Malabo Protocol," which granted the expanded African Court of Justice and Human and Peoples' Rights criminal jurisdiction, was adopted by the AU.[185] When fifteen states have ratified this new protocol, a new body, the African Court of Justice and Human and Peoples' Rights, will come into being, composed of three chambers. Following adoption of this protocol many rights advocates who previously resisted expansion of the Court's powers switched tacks, advocating for the removal of the provision immunizing heads of state, while otherwise supporting the protocol's expansion of international criminal jurisdiction.[186]

The rapid creation of the African Court testifies to the fertile climate for rights and regional institutions that existed in Africa in the 1990s and early 2000s.[187] That fertile climate somewhat diminished over the 2010s, however, as explored further later.

[184] In support of the Court's criminal jurisdiction, see Don Deya, "Is the African Court Worth the Wait," All Africa (March 22, 2012), available at: https://allafrica.com/stories/201203221081.html, pointing out that the idea was initially developed by the Group of African Experts, and resisted by AU member states. As Van Schaack has put it, relative to the existence of divergent views, "The emergence of this fatal flaw [i.e. sovereign immunity – discussed later], and the mixed motives behind the entire project, have left proponents of international justice efforts torn between their instinct to support the development of indigenous justice mechanisms and their fealty to evenhanded accountability." Beth Van Schaack, "Immunity before the African Court of Justice & Human & Peoples Rights – The Potential Outlier," Just Security (July 10, 2014), available at: www.justsecurity.org/12732/immunity-african-court-justice-human-peoples-rights-the-potential-outlier/.

[185] See AU Decision 529 (XXIII).

[186] For more, see Beth Van Schaack, "Immunity"; Beth Van Schaack, "Statement Regarding Immunity for Sitting Officials Before the Expanded African Court of Justice and Human Rights," Human Rights Watch (November 13, 2014).

[187] African receptivity to supranational judicial institutions could also be seen in the development of several subregional bodies in the period, including the East African Court of Justice and the ECOWAS Court of Justice. Individuals were given the right to submit complaints to the latter through a 2005 protocol, since which the ECOWAS Court has gained a reputation as a strong voice on rights issues. See Supplementary Protocol Amending the Protocol relating to the Community Court of Justice, ECOWAS Doc. A/SP.1/01/05 (January 19, 2005), Art. 4 (amending Arts. 10(c) & (d)). A regional tribunal was created in Southern Africa as well, the Southern African Development Community Tribunal; following a string of decisions challenging Zimbabwe's decision to redistribute land belonging to white farmers (Campbell v. Zimbabwe, Case No 2/2008, SADC (T) (November 28, 2008); Tembani v. Zimbabwe, Case No. 7/2008 SADC (T) (June 5, 2009); Gondo and others v. Zimbabwe, Case No. 5/2008, SADC (December 2010)), the tribunal had its ability to consider individual complaints stripped.

## V Conclusion

This chapter has explored the European, Inter-American, and African regional human rights systems' different foundational moments. Foundational moments are important for the simple reason that they provide the initial impetus setting international institutions on their paths, exerting significant influence on their subsequent activities. In considering "foundational moments," it is necessary to recognize that the notion is internally complex, however. Each regional human rights system had an initial moment of foundation. Just how much was determined in that initial moment, however, varies, as the experience of the Inter-American system demonstrates – "foundations" may be extended in time. Even when a system's initial formation is relatively complete, moreover, nothing is set in stone, as key elements of a system can always be reformed and reconsidered through inter-state agreement, or through gradual evolution and reorientation over time. Above and beyond considerations of the extent to which a system's foundation was consolidated or extended, foundational moments are important because they reveal different visions and imaginations of human rights work, produced and shaped by the political opportunities and constraints inherent in particular historical contexts. The following discussion considers such issues in broader comparative perspective, in order to highlight the manner in which the systems' varying foundational moments have helped to produce enduring differences.

### *V.1 Europe*

To a greater degree than either of the other two regional systems considered here, the European human rights system was more or less comprehensively put in place through the initial drafting process that led to agreement on the Convention in 1950. To be sure, rights supporters were initially disappointed, given that both the right to individual petition and the jurisdiction of a court were made optional. Before long, however, both had been accepted by enough states to bring individual complaints and the court into operation. As such, no further major treaty revision was necessary, and even when Protocol 11 refounded the system, its function was to perfect the original vision of the system, rather than to complement one mechanism with another.

The fact that the creation of the European system was more consolidated suggests, if anything, the greater importance of its moment of creation relative to its subsequent evolution. What were the key coordinates of that creation? The first, as with much of the modern global human rights system, was the end of World War II. In addition to providing the necessary political space for rights advancement, the wartime context provided a dramatic illustration of the sorts of regimes and policies human rights work was to be targeted against. In the first place, therefore, the European system was established with an eye to attempting to ensure that the member states of the Council of Europe never again descend into a state of authoritarianism in which core civil and political rights, and human dignity, might be trampled.

While the horrors of the war provided important initial impetus toward the creation of the European human rights system, the systems' founders had much more immediate challenges in mind as well – in particular, the challenges posed by the Soviet Union. Opposition to the Soviet Union, and the desire to produce a text that would help to accentuate the differences between Western and Eastern Europe, helped to sway the drafters toward an emphasis on civil and political rights as well. In addition, that opposition helped to shape the system in a more general way, making one broader purpose of the system from the beginning its publicity role on behalf of the higher rights standards, and from an internal perspective the higher standard of "civilization," of Europeans.[188]

In addition, the system's creation at a time when numerous founding states, including the United Kingdom, France, and Belgium, all possessed colonial empires, also impacted its nature. This was directly reflected in the clause stipulating that the Convention would only apply in colonial territories by way of special declaration, and entrenched by the Commission's lackluster response to British colonial rights violations in Cyprus. The European human rights system's colonial limitations helped to reinforce the system's exclusionary logic as well, underscoring that a dual standard was being established, with one set of rules to be applied to Europeans, another to those under the control of European powers abroad.[189]

Finally, it is important to recognize that the European system was created by states with relatively sophisticated and well-established domestic legal systems. This led to a concern on the part of member states with ensuring that the language of the Convention was relatively sharp and

[188] For a similar point, see Duranti, *The Conservative Human Rights Revolution*, 210.

[189] See European Consultative Assembly, Second Session of the Consultative Assembly (August 7–28, 1950), reprinted in *Collected edition of the "Travaux Préparatoires" of the ECHR* (statement of Leopold Senghor); Bates, *Evolution of the European Convention on Human Rights*, 94.

clear, aimed at the protection of standards that, while they might be presented as general rights guarantees, had relatively readily discernable implications. The greater attention of European states to such details – to a significant extent, a sign of the fact that they took the Convention more seriously, thanks not least to the fact that it was a binding document – helped to curb some of the more progressive tendencies that might otherwise have found their way into the document.[190] It was also closely linked to European states' strong belief in the superiority of judicial institutions, an emphasis that was reconfirmed and entrenched through the system's redesign in the 1990s.

In sum, the European system's initial founding moment had a number of characteristics that set it apart from the initial founding moments in the other systems. It was consolidated, giving the system a more unitary, concentrated character. Convention drafters elevated the importance of civil and political rights over social and economic rights, limiting the Convention's scope. The Convention, and the broader human rights project it was to spearhead, was defined in substantial part as on behalf of Western Europeans and against the Soviet Union, providing the European rights vision with a certain exceptional, regionally limited character, that was reinforced by the limits placed on the Convention's applicability to colonial territories (where severe rights violations were taking place). Finally, the European Convention was established in the context of states that, comparatively speaking, paid enhanced attention to compliance with their domestic legal obligations, leading to an emphasis on the importance of carefully and narrowly defined standards.

### *V.2 The Americas*

In contrast to the European system, the Inter-American system had multiple foundations. Three moments were particularly important. First, there was the drafting of the American Declaration of the Rights and Duties of Man, following World War II. Second, there was the decision to create the Inter-American Commission at the end of the 1950s. Third, was the drafting of the American Convention on Human Rights in the 1960s, leading to the creation of the Court in the 1970s. Above and beyond the specifics of each of these moments, this long-drawn-out process helped to shape the system as a whole, as such a prolonged "foundation" could not help but emphasize the naturalness and virtues of an evolutionary approach

190 On this factor, see Simpson, *Human Rights and the End of Empire*, 655–93.

to regional rights work, while the generation of two separate core documents, and a more complex regime, in effect required the recognition of a looser, more multifaceted, multilevel approach.

The system's initial moment differed from that in Europe as well. Unlike in Europe, drafters in the Americas opted in the end for a declaration, rather than a binding document. Thanks in part to the different regional composition of views on rights in the Americas, the declaration included not only civil and political rights, but also social and economic rights.[191] This inclusion was also facilitated by the fact that a nonbinding document was produced, which made the assembled state parties more comfortable including looser, more generalist statements of rights protections therein. The result of the first founding moment in the Inter-American system, therefore, was the creation of a system loosely committed to broad, progressive principles, a very different sort of initial position than that generated in the European system.

The system's next moment also had no European analogue, though it closely paralleled an important early moment in the African system. While there was initial resistance to the creation of any form of rights oversight mechanism in Americans, that resistance was overcome following two crises in the Caribbean: the crisis generated by Trujillo's attempts to assassinate President Betancourt, and the crisis generated by the success of Castro's communist revolution in Cuba. These crises helped weaken American states' preexisting resistance to regional human rights oversight. In addition, the fact that the Inter-American Commission was set up in the wake of and in response to these crises gave it a mandate from the beginning to respond to serious, big picture political challenges, establishing a different model of rights work from that which developed in the European system. This broad mandate was enabled not only by the regional unrest that preceded the Commission's creation, but also by the fact the Commission was a body with nonbinding powers, authorized to oversee a nonbinding declaration, reducing states' incentives to mount strong resistance.

The Inter-American system's final foundational moment came through the process of agreement on the American Convention on Human Rights. The drafting of the Convention was initially supported by the

[191] An inclusion enabled, as suggested earlier, by the strong emphasis on social and economic rights in the region that had been kicked off by their inclusion in the 1917 Constitution of Mexico, which was emulated by several other states in the following decades. See Grandin, "The Liberal Tradition in the Americas."

same momentum that led to creation of the Commission, and further encouraged by the positive impression the Commission made during its early years. The American Convention was more similar to the European Convention than the American Declaration. The fact that the Convention did not replace but rather complemented the Declaration, however, and the fact that its agreement came late in the day, after the Commission had already set about its work, meant that rather than being understood as narrowing the system's focus, it was understood as granting additional powers and force.

The background political context in the region was key to the Inter-American system's founding as well. While there was some variation over time, certain factors remained fairly consistent, including the severe nature of the rights violations in many states in the region, the existence of national legal systems that were less resourced and respected than those in Western Europe, and the caution of many states toward the regional project generally, thanks to their historic struggles against external intervention. Taken together, these factors reinforced the trends highlighted earlier toward the development of a looser system, that would adopt a bigger-picture and less jurisprudentially focused mode of work.

In sum, the Inter-American human rights system's extended foundation set it on a different path from that followed by the European system. The American Declaration was a broad and ambitious document, the scope of which was enabled by the fact that no one expected it to be immediately operationalized. Following regional political crises, a Commission was rapidly created, and given a broad and vague mandate to oversee the Declaration and to report on rights violations in the hemisphere, including big picture violations of the sort that had led to the Commission's creation. The result was the formation of a loose, flexible system, empowered to adopt a broad lens, which quickly established its ability to deploy a range of experimental approaches. When the Convention was added to this system, it did not serve to reorient it so much as to give greater force to the mode of rights work already adopted.

### *V.3 Africa*

The African system's founding was less drawn out than that of the Inter-American system, more extended than that of the European. Essentially, the African system was founded in two moments. The first, and the most important, was the preparation of the African Charter on Human and Peoples' Rights. After independence, African states were reluctant to create a regional human rights mechanism, fearing its potential to interfere with their domestic jurisdictions. In the late 1970s, however, unrest in the Central African Republic and Uganda led to disruptive cross-border incidents, causing several important African states to reconsider their positions. When the Charter was prepared and the Commission established, therefore, it was from the beginning understood that its role would include responding to wide-scale violations.[192]

Substantively, the African Charter is perhaps best known, and rightly so, for its inclusion of the innovative category of "peoples' rights."[193] The inclusion of such a category drew from African states' desire to emphasize the importance of the lessons they had learned through their struggles against colonialism, as the category of peoples' rights emphasized both the centrality of national political sovereignty in general, as well as the importance of economic sovereignty in particular.[194] Functionally, inclusion of the category of peoples' rights further emphasized the virtues and validity of adopting a big-picture approach to rights violations. As in the Inter-American system, the fact the Charter was to be overseen by a Commission with nonbinding powers helped facilitate the system's adoption of a broad approach as well.

The African system's second foundational moment came with agreement on the Protocol to the African Charter on Human and Peoples' Rights on the Establishment of the African Court on Human and Peoples' Rights. The Protocol did not include a new conventional text, only a new oversight body. Perhaps the most notable innovation of the Protocol, in comparison to similar institutions in the other regional systems, was a provision allowing states to submit declarations enabling rights claims concerning them to be brought directly before the Court, bypassing the Commission.[195] In addition to facilitating the advancement of cases in general, this provision set up the African Court in a more independent position relative to the African Commission, providing more space for the two institutions to evolve down different paths.

The background context in the region provided a final key component of the African system's foundation. Serious and widespread rights

[192] For the reflection of this point of emphasis in the Charter, see African Charter on Human and Peoples' Rights, OAU Doc. CAB/LEG/67/3 rev. 5, 21 I.L.M. 58 (1982), Art. 58.

[193] See ibid., Arts. 19–24.

[194] See ibid., Arts. 19–22.

[195] See OAU, Protocol to the African Charter on Human and Peoples' Rights on the Establishment of an African Court on Human and Peoples' Rights (June 10, 1998), Art. 5(3).

violations, against a backdrop of states in which legal power was weakly established, formed a constant backdrop to the system's formation. This had the consequence, as in the Americas, of reinforcing other factors involved in the system's formation, pushing the system to adopt a broad, loose, and flexible approach, and one that would allow for prioritization of the worst abuses.

In sum, the African system's formation was defined by several mutually supportive factors. The system's creation in the wake of serious and widespread rights abuses made attention to such serious situations a priority from the beginning. African states' historical experience with colonialism led them to emphasize the importance of "peoples' rights," a category designed to recognize the importance of both political and more structural, economic sovereignty. The emphasis on serious violations and the rights of collectives, together with persistent state concern with overly powerful supranational oversight, required and were enabled by the adoption of a looser, less formalized oversight system. While the Commission was eventually complemented by a Court, as in the Americas the Court inherited much of the Commission's more holistic approach to rights adjudication.

# 3

# Struggles

## I Introduction

The conditions in which the various regional human rights systems were formed constitute one key source of the differentiation among the systems' understandings of rights work, and modes of functioning, today. Focusing on those historical moments and conditions alone does not present a full picture of the forces that have driven the evolution of the systems, however, and that have led them to assume their contemporary shapes. Rather, in order to have a fuller picture, it is also necessary to consider the manner in which the systems have evolved gradually over time in response to the conditions they have encountered. Of course, some of the forces to which the systems have been responsive, in the course of such gradual processes of evolution, have been the same as those that shaped their founding – including in particular in terms of the need to ensure prominent state parties are not too seriously aggrieved. In addition, however, and lost in rights histories that focus only on background processes of inter-state treaty negotiation, human rights institutions have been shaped by the sorts of rights violations they have confronted. The types of rights violations confronted by each of the systems have not been the same, nor has each system had an unchanging experience over time. As such, it is necessary to trace these different experiences and encounters and their impact in order to obtain a fuller understanding of the approach to human rights work that has developed in each of the systems.

## II Europe

### *II.1 The Triumph of the Individual Complainant*

One of the first struggles in the European system was fought on what may have appeared a relatively small stage, pertaining primarily to a procedural issue, but would have major implications in the years to come. In the same period in which the Commission was refusing to adopt an assertive stance on Greece's communication concerning the United Kingdom's actions in Cyprus, steps were being taken toward a system in which individual claimants would be given a more central role. The initial contours of that relationship were fleshed out in the first case referred by the Commission to the Court, *Lawless v. Ireland,* which concerned a member of the Irish Republican Army, Gerard Richard Lawless, who in 1957 was detained indefinitely under Ireland's emergency legislation.

The ultimate substantive result of the case was disappointing for rights advocates, as the Court found no violations. Along the way, however, several issues pertaining to the relationship between the Commission and the Court, and between individual claimants and both bodies, had to be resolved. At the heart of the contention was the question of whether individuals should be allowed to assume an equal posture to that of states on the international level.[1] The issue was not only symbolic: if individuals were granted a more significant place within proceedings, the ability of individuals to bring forward and control their claims would be facilitated as well, expanding individuals' ability to make use of the system.

Prior to *Lawless,* it was unclear whether claimants would have any procedural role should a case be referred by the Commission to the Court, or even if they would be informed of the Commission's decisions. Two days before referring *Lawless* to the Court, the Commission introduced a new rule into its rules of procedure, however, stipulating that applicants would be informed of the results of their cases, and allowing applicants to submit observations that the Commission might utilize before the Court, should it choose to do so. While the Irish government objected, it was for the Court to decide, and the Court supported the Commission's position.[2]

[1] Judge Maridakis's dissent, in which he expressed his fear that the system was moving in such a direction, emphasized the importance of this step.

[2] As the Court put it,

> in any democratic society, within the meaning of the Preamble and the other clauses of the Convention, proceedings before the judiciary should be conducted in the presence of the parties and in public …
>
> The Court must bear in mind its duty to safeguard the interests of the individual, who may not be a Party to any court proceedings … the whole of the proceedings in the Court, as laid down by the Convention and the Rules of Court, are upon issues which concern the individual applicant … it is in the interests of the proper administration of justice that the Court should have knowledge of and, if need be, take into consideration, the applicant's point of view … the Commission … as the defender of the public interest, is entitled of its own accord, even if it does not share them, to make known the applicant's views to the Court as a means of throwing light on the points at issue.

While the step taken in *Lawless* was a small one, it was the first step down a path the system would continue to follow. As time went on, the Court granted individuals an increasingly prominent role in proceedings before it. Thus, for instance, while applicants' lawyers were not allowed to address the Court directly in its early years, the Court allowed them to begin attending its hearings, and to speak to the Commission's delegates during breaks. In the 1971 *Vagrancy* case,[3] the Court determined that the Commission might rely on the assistance of any person of its choosing in making its presentation to the Court, allowing claimants' lawyers the opportunity to address the Court directly, albeit in a roundabout manner. While initially claimants' lawyers were only allowed to make brief presentations, by the end of the decade they had become in practice, if still not officially, the representatives of applicants' cases before the Court.[4]

While a *modus operandi* was thus reached, individuals had not yet received full, formal recognition. From 1974 on the Court began pushing for the adoption of a new optional protocol, to put individuals squarely in charge of their own cases.[5] With time, some state representatives came to support such reforms as well – believing, not without reason, that they would be better off arguing directly against claimants, rather than against the Commission.[6] Despite such pressure, formal progress remained impossible throughout the 1970s and 1980s. Instead, therefore, the Court continued to take small steps to improve the procedural situation of individuals in practice, squarely recognizing for instance that individual claimants were the parties before it in its 1982

Lawless v. Ireland, App. No. 332/57, Eur. Ct. H.R., Preliminary Objections 1, at 13, 17 (November 14, 1960). For more, see Arthur Robertson, "The First Case Before the European Court of Human Rights: Lawless v. The Government of Ireland," 36 *British Yearbook of International Law* (1960), 343–53.

[3] De Wilde, Ooms and Versyp v. Belgium, App. Nos. 2832/66, 2835/66, & 2899/66, Eur. Ct. H.R. (June 18, 1971).

[4] For more, see Paul Mahoney, "Developments in the Procedure of the European Court of Human Rights: The Revised Rules of the Court," 3 *Yearbook of European Law* (1983), 127–8.

[5] See Opinion of the Eur. Ct. H.R. on the draft short- and medium-term program for the Council of Europe in the general field of human rights, doc CDH (74) 30, paras. 12–17, cited in Mahoney, "Developments," 132 n. 33. The extent to which the tide was with them can be seen in the comments of Judge van de Meersch, who describing the existing situation, in which individuals did not play a central role, as "abnormal and shocking." See Fifth ECHR Colloquy, Frankfurt 1980, Oral Intervention at 69, quoted in Bates, *Evolution of the European Convention*, 404 n. 86.

[6] For more, see Mahoney, "Developments," 130–1.

Rules of Procedure.[7] In 1990, Protocol 9, which sought to amend the Convention to allow individuals to refer cases from the Commission to the Court directly, was opened for signature.[8] Ultimately, Protocol 9 was superseded by the broader reforms included in Protocol 11, which finally established the place of the individual, and the right of individual petition, as one of the pillars of the system, as highlighted earlier. While the final reform came via inter-state action, it was a reform prepared and driven by a momentum long underway at the level of the Commission and the Court's rules of procedure.

### *II.2 The Gradual Development of Jurisprudential Standards*

As observed in the previous chapter, an early decision by the European Commission created a clear division between inter-state cases, which it was understood could take more of a big picture, systemic form, and individual cases, which were expected to be more tightly focused. While the Commission heard a number of inter-state cases over the years, the volume of such cases received was quickly swamped by the number of cases received from individual complaints. In its early years, the Commission rejected the vast majority of such cases as inadmissible, motivated by fear that moving too quickly might lead to political challenges.[9] Where it did decide cases, the Commission demonstrated reluctance to refer those cases to the Court: while the Commission referred two cases in 1960,[10] it

[7] The new rules granted applicants other powers as well, including the ability to request interim measures, to ask for the confidentiality of certain documents to be maintained, to request special measures of evidential acquisition, and to submit claims for just satisfaction. See ibid., and Peter Muchlinski, "The Status of the Individual under the ECHR and Contemporary International Law," 34 *International and Comparative Law Quarterly* (1985), 376–82.

[8] The explanatory report to Protocol 9 was explicit as to the reason such a change was needed, observing that the existing failure to recognize individuals explicitly as parties "could today be regarded as inconsistent with the spirit of the Convention, not to mention compatibility with domestic-law procedures in States Parties." Explanatory Note to Protocol 9, para. 12. For more on the background to Protocol 9, see Turk, "The European Ministerial Conference," 653.

[9] On the Commission's attempt to pursue a cooperative rather than an antagonistic relationship with states in its early years, see Anthony McNulty, "The Operation and Effectiveness of the ECHR," 3 *University of San Francisco Law Review* (1969), 228–43. One early exception to the Commission's reluctance.

[10] One of these was *De Becker v. Belgium* (App. No. 214/56, Eur. Ct. H.R. (March 27, 1962)). The case was important both in terms of the Commission's and the Court's calls on Belgium to change its laws, and in terms of the Commission's rejection of Belgium's challenge to its

forwarded no more over the course of the following five years, leading to substantial friction.[11] The Commission overcame its reluctance in the mid-1960s, however, from which point on the number of cases it submitted to the Court increased year-on-year for decades to come.

Already in the cases decided in this period, key aspects of the European system's approach began to take shape. Among the European Court's important early judgments was the "Belgian Linguistics" case.[12] The case concerned a challenge by French-speaking Belgians concerning the lack of French-language educational opportunities in Belgium. Both the Commission and the Court found that Belgium's approach violated the Convention, though they presented their holdings in cautious, limited form, allowing Belgium to claim compliance while adopting reforms far short of those the claimants desired. Above and beyond its substantive outcomes, and more centrally for present purposes, the case was important due to the procedural approach the Court adopted. In the first place, the Court stipulated that its approach would be guided by "the principles which may be extracted from the legal practice of a large number of democratic states."[13] This brief formula suggested what has since then come to be known as the "European consensus" approach – the idea that the European human rights system should be guided, in developing its human rights jurisprudence, by existing, gradually developing standards within European states. In addition, the Court articulated a particular approach to remedies – as it put it, it would:

> assume the role of the competent national authorities, for it would thereby lose sight of the subsidiary nature of the international machinery

jurisdiction *ratione temporis*, on the grounds that the harm in question constituted a "continuing violation."

[11] The Commission's reluctance to refer cases was criticized by Rolin, at that point a judge on the Court, in a public speech in 1965. Judge Rolin was further critical of the Commission's tendency to play a dispute resolution role, rather than acting more along the lines of a court. Other judges, as well as the Court's registrar, made similar points. For more, see Henri Rolin, "Has the European Court of Human Rights a Future?," 11 *Howard Law Journal* (1965), 442; Hermann Mosler, "The Protection of Human Rights by International Legal Procedure," 52 *Georgetown Law Journal* (1964), 800–24; Rolv Ryssdal, "The Future of the European Court of Human Rights," Lecture (1990); Phedon Vegleris, "Twenty Years' Experience of the Convention and Future Prospects," Third ECHR Colloquy 388 (Brussels, 1970); Hermann Mosler, "Turning a Page of History," in Mahoney et al. eds., *Protecting Human Rights*, 228; Madsen, "Legal Diplomacy"; Bates, *Evolution of the European Convention*, 213–15.

[12] App. Nos. 1474/62, 1677/62, 1691/62, 1769/63, 1994/63, & 2126/64, Eur. Ct. H.R., Merits, "The Law" (July 23, 1968).

[13] Ibid., para. 10.

> of collective enforcement established by the Convention. The national authorities remain free to choose the measures which they consider appropriate in those matters which are governed by the Convention. Review by the Court concerns only the conformity of those measures with the requirements of the Convention.[14]

This formula, which has come to be referred to in shorthand as the principle of "subsidiary," has consistently been articulated and rearticulated since, and has become central to the European system's approach. What purpose does this formula serve? It is important to observe that it is rendered necessary, in the first place, by the fact that the European Convention is a binding document, and that the Court's rulings in any particular case are binding. As such, the Court could, if it so desired, pose a potent challenge to states, calling on them with the force of law to adjust their domestic legal frameworks. Should it do so, however, the Court would subject itself to serious risk of blowback. As such, the Court faced and faces a quandary: how to remain faithful to its mandate to ensure the protection of Convention rights, while minimizing pushback from state parties. It is on the basis of this structural situation that the idea of subsidiarity becomes valuable, offering, as it does, a rhetorical means through which to minimize the otherwise potentially overly confrontational nature of the Court's judgments.

Already from the *Belgian Linguistics* case, in other words, several of the key coordinates of the European system's approach to human rights work were set. What was it about the *Belgian Linguistics* case, and/or the broader context in which it was considered, that pushed the court in such a direction? In the first place, it was significant that the case concerned a matter of national sensitivity. In addition, and with the benefit of comparative insight, a number of broader background factors may also be identified as having been important: the system was operating in a context in which the international human rights project was still relatively nascent, such that international rights jurisprudence remained (comparatively) thin; the system was operating in the context of a set of nations in which the rule of law was relatively advanced, meaning a substantial pool of national jurisprudential examples could be drawn upon; and the system was operating in the context of a set of states which, it could be presumed, would accord its holdings and judgments a high degree of attention. The first two factors help to explain the system's emphasis on the European

[14] Ibid.

consensus approach; the fact the case concerned a matter of national significance and the fact Belgium could be expected to take the Court's judgment fairly seriously help to explain the Court's emphasis on the principle of subsidiary.

As the 1960s went on, the Commission began receiving growing numbers of submissions, approximately five hundred a year by the end of the decade, numbers which appeared substantial at the time, even though they appear minuscule in comparison to the system's contemporary caseload. The Commission only allowed a few cases past the admissibility stage, however. Many of the cases that were considered in those years concerned procedural rules pertaining to detention,[15] in response to which both the Commission and the Court deployed what might be described as a "leveling up" approach, gradually pushing states in the direction of higher standards. The Court generally confined itself to finding violations of the Convention, without stipulating precise remedial measures that should be taken, with the exception that it began to ask states to provide "just satisfaction," in the form of monetary payments to wronged parties.[16]

As the 1960s ended and the 1970s began, the European system found itself bolstered by the growing strength of popular support for human rights.[17] The number of submissions to the system continued to rise, testifying to the increasing familiarity of lawyers with the system.[18] The early to

[15] The system's early and persistent receipt of numerous cases concerning detainee rights makes sense, insofar as detainees are among the populations most likely to be represented by lawyers.

[16] See Neumeister v. Austria, App. No. 1936/63, Eur. Ct. H.R. (May 7, 1974).

[17] For Madsen, this new support rested both on the development of a new and more progressive cultural movement in the West, and a new emphasis on social justice lawyering. See Madsen, "Protracted Institutionalization of the Strasbourg Court," 59. Moyn traces the development more directly to a decline in leftist potential and political energy; see Moyn, *Last Utopia*. See also Stuart Scheingold, *The Politics of Rights: Lawyers, Public Policy, and Political Change* (2nd edn University of Michigan Press, 2004); Eckel and Moyn eds., *The Breakthrough*; Eckel, "The International League for the Rights of Man"; Keys, *Reclaiming American Virtue*. As several have pointed out, while human rights organizations had been around since before World War I, they grew in strength dramatically from the 1970s on. Thus for example while Amnesty International was founded in 1961, it expanded and grew in prominence over the course of the 1970s, as demonstrated by its receipt of the Nobel Prize in 1977. See Powers, *Against Oblivion*; Powers, *Like Water on Stone*; Buchanan, "'The Truth Will Set You Free'"; Hopgood, *Keepers of the Flame*.

[18] As one commentator has put it,

> The dynamics of the Convention changed … when British lawyers at the end of the 1960s and in the 1970s discovered the Convention. They realized that the Commission's report and the Court's judgment could be a valuable tool in

mid-1970s saw the Council of Europe bolstered by greater participation by Italy, Switzerland, and France,[19] the return to the fold of Greece following the fall of the military government in 1974, and the additions of a democratizing Portugal, in 1976, and Spain, in 1977. A thaw in the Cold War and increasing momentum toward European unity also helped bolster the strength of the system.

In this newly rights-receptive context the European system gained new self-confidence, helping to pave the way for a series of key judgments passed in the 1970s that fleshed out what remains the dominant European approach to human rights. The Court's first such key decision was *Golder v. United Kingdom.*[20] Golder was a prisoner who had sought to consult with his solicitor because he wanted to initiate a legal action against a prison guard; the prison authorities, however, had refused to allow such a consultation to take place. The Commission found that in refusing to allow Golder to meet with his solicitor, the United Kingdom had violated Article 6(1) of the Convention, guaranteeing the right of access to a court.[21] Unsatisfied with this result, and optimistic the Court would overturn it, the United Kingdom referred the case to the Court.

In their arguments before the Court, the British presented two central arguments as to why the Commission's position was mistaken. More narrowly, they argued that Article 6(1) should only apply once a matter was before a judge, and not to limitations on the ability of prisoners to consult

> implementing their clients' rights in the domestic sphere. With their polished, at times brilliant presentations in often spectacular cases, they drew the attention of other lawyers to the Strasbourg complaints system.

Mark Villiger, "Comment," in Wolfrum and Deutsch eds., *European Court of Human Rights*, 22.

19 Italy accepted individual petitions and the Court's jurisdiction; Switzerland ratified the Convention for the first time, and immediately accepted individual petitions and the Court's jurisdiction; and France accepted the Court's jurisdiction, though it continued to resist the right of individual petition until 1981.

20 App. No. 4451/70, Eur. Ct. H.R. (February 21, 1975).

21 Article 6(1) of the 1950 version of the European Convention read:

> In the determination of his civil rights and obligations or of any criminal charge against him, everyone is entitled to a fair and public hearing within a reasonable time by an independent and impartial tribunal established by law. Judgment shall be pronounced publicly but the press and public may be excluded from all or part of the trial in the interests of morals, public order or national security in a democratic society, where the interests of juveniles or the protection of the private life of the parties so require, or to the extent strictly necessary in the opinion of the court in special circumstances where publicity would prejudice the interests of justice.

with lawyers. More expansively, they presented an argument pertaining to how Convention rights should be interpreted, contending that the Commission had inappropriately expanded the scope of the Convention by going above and beyond state parties' understandings of their obligations at the time the Convention was agreed. In response, the Commission contended that far from being unreasonable, its interpretation of the Convention was necessary in order to avoid a reading that would render the Convention's rights guarantees ineffective in practice. In doing so, the Commission suggested that it was interpreting the text in accordance with the object and purpose of the Convention.

The British sent a large delegation to present their case to the Court, emphasizing how seriously they took the case, and attempting to subtly (or not so subtly) suggest, as they had done previously, the potentially serious consequences should the Court rule against them. On the basis of the system's past record, they had good reason to be confident in the effectiveness of such an approach. The 1970s were a different time, however, in which human rights bodies had greater freedom to maneuver. In this new context, the Court was unafraid to support the Commission's position, finding that Article 6(1) had been violated by the United Kingdom's refusal to let Golder consult with his lawyer, an important precedent in its own right. More fundamental still, in terms of the case's impact on the European approach to human rights more broadly, was the Court's affirmation of the Commission's approach to the matter: in deciding in agreement with the Commission and against the United Kingdom, the Court could not help but rule on the arguments surrounding interpretation that had been put forward, holding, in effect, that the broad, holistic approach employed by the Commission had been the appropriate one, as opposed to the narrower approach advocated by the United Kingdom. To this day, *Golder* stands for the principle of progressive interpretation.[22]

The Court's next major judgment came in the 1978 decision *Tyrer v. United Kingdom*.[23] *Tyrer* concerned the use of corporal punishment on children, which the Court found a rights violation, on the basis that it constituted a form of degrading treatment. More broadly, like *Golder, Tyrer*

[22] The Court reiterated the appropriateness of a progressive approach to interpretation in other decisions in the period, including *Kjeldsen, Busk Madsen & Pedersen v. Denmark* (App. Nos. 5095/71, 5920/72, & 5926/72, Eur. Ct. H.R. (December 7, 1976)) and *Ireland v. United Kingdom* (App. No. 5310/71, Eur. Ct. H.R. (January 18, 1978)).

[23] App. No. 5856/72, Eur. Ct. H.R. (April 25, 1978).

was significant on the basis of the approach to interpretation the Court enunciated. As the Court put it:

> The Convention is a living instrument which, as the Commission rightly stressed, must be interpreted in the light of present-day conditions. In the case now before it the Court cannot but be influenced by the developments and commonly accepted standards in the penal policy of the member States of the Council of Europe in this field.[24]

The approach articulated by the Court in *Tyrer* confirmed the emphasis on progressive interpretation in *Golder*, expressed now in the even more vital terms that the Convention should be understood as a "living instrument." *Tyrer* went a step further as well, linking the emphasis on purposive progressive interpretation of the Convention with the need to ensure the Convention might be interpreted in accordance with "developments" and "commonly accepted standards" in the opinions and approaches adopted within European states.[25] As well as helping to justify and substantiate the Court's approach to progressive interpretation, this reliance on European "standards" served another purpose as well. By interweaving its own case law with the laws, standards, and jurisprudence of the various states of Europe, the European Court took a subtle yet significant step toward establishing a more constitutional position for itself. Now, even though formally particular decisions would only apply to the countries against which they were rendered, the fact that those decisions were part of "commonly accepted standards" suggested they should be understood as more widely generalizable, the system's ongoing emphasis on subsidiarity notwithstanding.

Rounding off the flowering of the Court's standard-setting jurisprudence were three decisions issued in 1979. First came *Sunday Times v. United Kingdom*.[26] The case concerned the *Sunday Times'* intent to publish an article highlighting a link between thalidomide, a drug manufactured by the Distillers company, and birth defects. In response, the Distillers company obtained a court order, upheld by the House of Lords, prohibiting publication of the article, on the basis that publication would interfere with ongoing litigation concerning the issue. In the face of this

[24] Ibid., para. 38.

[25] The Court's determination to use *Tyrer* to cement a more progressive approach was highlighted by the fact that while Tyrer himself, the youth on whose behalf the case was brought, expressed a desire to drop the case, the Court insisted on proceeding with its consideration regardless, making clear that its concern was as much with setting standards as with individuated justice.

[26] App. No. 6538/74, Eur. Ct. H.R. (April 26, 1979).

prohibition, the lawyers for the *Sunday Times* decided to bring the matter to the European Commission, which referred the case to the Court.

In its *Sunday Times* decision, the Court explicitly rejected adoption of a deferential "rationality" mode of review, opting instead to employ "a less discretionary power of appreciation."[27] Employing this stricter approach, the Court found that the prohibition of publication had not been a proportionate response to the aims the British courts sought to achieve, emphasizing along the way the importance of freedom of expression and the clear public concern in the subject matter at hand.[28] This judgment was important in its own right, setting a strong standard relative to the protection of freedom of expression, and insofar as it saw the Court directly countermanding a decision of the highest judicial body in the United Kingdom.[29] Procedurally, it was important in that it saw the Court injecting a greater degree of flexibility into its "margin of appreciation" approach, which could now be broadened at times, when necessary in order to avoid confrontation, or narrowed, as it was in *Sunday Times*, when the Court desired to adopt a firmer position. Most important, however, was the fact the Court did decide to adopt the narrower standard in this instance, a decision that helped to cement the image and understanding of the Court, both in its own eyes and those of the broader community of interested parties, as the ultimate arbiter of appropriate standards – in short, as a body akin to a constitutional court for Europe, at least as far as the relevant rights standards were concerned.

The second key 1979 decision of the Court was *Marckx v. Belgium*.[30] In its judgment, the Court found that Belgian law, which failed to recognize

[27] Ibid., para. 59.

[28] The judgment in *Sunday Times* built on the judgment three years earlier in *Handyside v. United Kingdom* (App. No. 5493/72, Eur. Ct. H.R. (December 7, 1976)). In that case the Court had not found a violation of the Convention. In order to distinguish *Sunday Times*, therefore, the Court observed that a wider margin of appreciation had been justified in *Handyside* due to the fact that *Handyside* concerned legislation on morality.

[29] The fact that the case concerned freedom of expression, a right already well-recognized on the international level, doubtless helped encourage the Court's adoption of a forceful decision in *Sunday Times*. The language of the Court's judgment in *Sunday Times*, which has been frequently cited, conveyed the importance of that right in the Court's estimation: "Freedom of expression constitutes one of the essential foundations of a democratic society … it is applicable not only to information or ideas that are favorably received or regarded as inoffensive or as a matter of indifference, but also to those that offend, shock or disturb the State or any sector of the population …" Sunday Times v. United Kingdom, App. No. 6538/74, Eur. Ct. H.R. (April 26, 1979), para. 65.

[30] App. No. 6833/74, Eur. Ct. H.R. (June 13, 1979).

an automatic legal bond between unmarried mothers and their children, and granted the children of unmarried mothers lesser inheritance rights, violated the Convention guarantees of the rights to private life, family life, and property, as well as the prohibition on discrimination. The broader significance of the case stemmed from the nature of the obligations the Court indicated states were bound to enforce – as the Court put it, "in addition to … primarily negative undertaking[s], [the Convention] may [imply] positive obligations" as well.[31] *Marckx* thus stood for the fact that, in addition to being required to refrain from infringing rights, states' conformity with the Convention required positive measures, including the adoption of rights-respecting legal structures. *Marckx* thus further reinforced the necessity of interpreting the Convention in a progressive manner, as well as the Court's constitutional role in that process, while dramatically expanding the strength and scope of the subject matter over which the Court would have jurisdiction.[32]

The third key 1979 decision was *Airey v. Ireland*.[33] The lawyer for the applicants was Mary Robinson – future President of Ireland and High Commissioner for Human Rights – acting on behalf of an Irish woman who was attempting to obtain an official order of separation from her alcoholic and abusive husband, but was prevented from doing so by the high fees that had to be paid in order to bring such an action in Ireland. The European Court found a violation of Article 6(1) of the Convention guaranteeing the right to a fair trial, and required that Ireland provide an accessible avenue through which individuals might obtain separation orders. While *Airey* did not advance any dramatically new standard, its combined emphasis on access to justice, positive obligations, and the need for progressive interpretation, along with its specific suggestion for structural reform on the national level, represented a high-water mark in the European system's willingness to adopt a forceful, progressive vision of its rights mandate.

[31] Ibid., para. 31.

[32] *Marckx* also helped to open up the system's approach to standing and "victimhood," making access to the system easier and enhancing the system's constitutional role even further. While the Belgian government argued that the applicants had not been directly harmed and that therefore the case represented a challenge "*in abstracto*," the Court found that the applicants could be considered victims, and that in general individuals could "contend that a law violates their rights by itself, in the absence of an individual measure of implementation, if they run the risk of being directly affected by it" Ibid., para. 27.

[33] App. No. 6289/73, Eur. Ct. H.R. (October 9, 1979), paras. 24–8.

While the substantive jurisprudence of the European human rights system has expanded enormously in numerous different areas since, the decisions made in the 1970s, and earlier, were key to the broader delineation of the system's approach, in a manner that has had enduring relevance ever since. At the center of that approach was the constitutional vision, and the idea that the unique function and role of the European system would be the task of articulating and expanding rights jurisprudence, the better to build rights-respecting legal orders in future. Allied to this broader project were the ideas of a progressive approach, a "living" convention and the idea of "European consensus," all of which both justified and promoted that progressive vision, as well as the ideas of a flexible margin of appreciation and the doctrine of subsidiarity, which helped the system to calibrate its response, in order to avoid overly severe confrontations and the concordant political damage. Underpinning all such developments was a more fundamental shift still, as the European Court took over from the Commission at the vanguard of the system.

The development of such a new understanding and approach did not occur in a vacuum. Rather, it was the product of the circumstances in which the European system found itself – ensconced in Western Europe, surrounded by states in which standards were (comparatively) high, and in which judicial actors and decisions possessed particular weight and authority. It was the product, too, of the carefully delimited set of rights enumerated in the European Convention – selected because they were at least relatively amenable to individualized determination – as well as of the Commission's decision to link bigger-picture claims of rights violation to the inter-state path. Far from the norm, such circumstances were in fact relatively unique; even in Europe, they would not hold.

### *II.3 Institutional Pressure and Reform*

The European Court proved remarkably successful at the task of gradual jurisprudential expansion it set for itself, playing a leading role in developing detailed standards flowing from the civil, political, and due process rights enumerated by the Convention. For decades, the European system was able to proceed self-confidently on the basis of its success in these terms. With the fall of the Soviet Union these standards had yet more utility, since, as the Council of Europe expanded to the East, and with the help of institutions such as the Venice Commission, they could be extended into new terrain. As discussed in the previous chapter, the system's self-confidence in its own success, together with the energy injected by enthusiastic new Eastern European members,[34] helped enable its transformation into a fully judicialized system in the 1990s.

Inherent in several distinct ways in the European system's successes, however, were grounds for the challenges it would soon face. In addition to broader support for judicialization as such, the reform of the 1980s and 1990s, discussed in the previous chapter, were driven in significant part by the increasing caseload of the system. While those reforms helped the system achieve efficiency gains, those gains were not commensurate with the rapidity with which submissions were increasing.[35] In the 1960s, the Commission registered 3,662 applications and declared 49 admissible; in the 1970s those numbers were up to 4,492 and 163 respectively; and in the 1980s to 7,085 and 455. Between 1990 and the abolition of the Commission in 1998, the Commission registered 29,117 applications and declared 4,253 admissible. This pace increased further in the following years: between 1998 and 2004, the Court allocated 120,642 applications to decision-making bodies and declared 4,717 cases admissible.

What drove this constant increase? The territorial expansion of the Council of Europe played a significant role. Beyond that, however, the system was also a victim of its own success in that the more influential and the better known the system became, the more the volume of submissions increased. The further jurisprudence extended, moreover, the more grounds there were on which to submit complaints. Had every state in the Council of Europe brought its domestic system fully and immediately into compliance with its Convention obligations, of course, this would not have posed much of a problem, as there would have been little ground for complaint and significant grounds not to hear such cases as were submitted. In several areas, however, whether due to lack of will or lack of capacity, rights violations persisted even after the Court had called on the state in question to bring them to an end. In such contexts, complaints continued to pour into the Court.

[34] On the energy injected into the system by its expansion to include the states of Eastern Europe, see Wojciech Sadurski, "Partnering with Strasbourg: Constitutionalization of the European Court of Human Rights, the Accession of Central and East European States to the Council of Europe and the Idea of Pilot Judgments," 9 *Human Rights Law Review* (2009), 397–453.

[35] As one commentator has put it, "Within eight months of Protocol 11 coming into effect on November 1, 1998, the President of the Court, Luzius Wildhaber, admitted that the system was 'under pressure.' A year later he urged states to appoint a committee to consider further major reforms in order to avert 'asphyxiation' by the ever-increasing backlog of applications." Alastair Mowbray, "Proposals for reform of the European Court of Human Rights," *Public Law* (2002), 252–64.

The new system was thus under two simultaneous pressures. First, its ever-increasing caseload pressured the Court to find new and more efficient ways of disposing of cases. Second, as the Court's jurisprudence grew and expanded, attention inevitably shifted to achieving the successful implementation of that jurisprudence – a much harder aim to achieve.

The pressure on the system to ensure effective implementation of its judgments led to three interrelated developments. First, the system's traditional reluctance to take a strong approach to remedial awards gradually began to break down. Thus in the *Hentrich* case, for example, the Court "timidly ... suggest[ed] that the best way of reparation would be to restore the assets taken ... to their former owners."[36] The Court also began to employ a similar approach in a number of cases concerning the right to property, where it went beyond its traditional declaratory statements and orders for just satisfaction by suggesting restitution and/or compensation as appropriate remedial measures as well.[37] Similarly, while the Court had traditionally been reluctant to offer monetary awards in the case of unreasonably prolonged procedural delays, that reluctance gradually broke down too.

By 2004, this jurisprudence advanced another step, thanks to the Court's decisions in *Assanidze v. Georgia*[38] and *Ilascu v. Moldova and Russia*[39] in particular. *Assanidze* concerned the ongoing detention of the former mayor of a town in the Ajarian region of Georgia, after the Supreme Court acquitted him of the charges brought against him. *Ilascu* concerned two political dissidents arrested in the Transdnestr area of Moldova, detained without due process. In both cases the Court went further than it had traditionally done by ordering the release of the detainees.[40]

36 Christian Tomuschat, "Just Satisfaction under Article 50 of the European Convention on Human Rights," in Mahoney et al. eds., *Protecting Human Rights*, 1412.

37 See Philip Leach, "Beyond the Bug River: A New Dawn for Redress before the European Court of Human Rights?," 2 *European Human Rights Law Review* (2005), 148, 151–4; Valerio Colandrea, "On the Power of the European Court of Human Rights to Order Specific Non-Monetary Measures: Some Remarks in Light of the *Assanidze, Broniowski and Sejdovic Cases*," 7 *Human Rights Law Review* (2007), 398–9.

38 App. No. 71503/01, Eur. Ct. H.R. (April 8, 2004).

39 App. No. 48787/99, Eur. Ct. H.R. (July 8, 2004).

40 As the Court put it in *Assanidze*,

> As regards the measures which the Georgian State must take ... the Court reiterates that its judgments are essentially declaratory ...
>
> However, by its very nature, the violation found in the instant case does not leave any real choice as to the measures required to remedy it.
>
> In these conditions, considering the particular circumstances of the case and the urgent need to put an end to the violation[s] ... the Court considers that the respondent State must secure the applicant's release at the earliest possible date.

Among other factors, the Court was doubtless emboldened by the fact that *Assanidze* and *Ilascu* concerned Georgia and Moldova and Russia respectively, states with records of serious, consistent rights violations, which lacked the political clout within the Council of Europe held by the system's longer-term Western European member states.

Second, the Court's jurisprudence evolved relative to the need for more systemic responses to structural violations. In *Bottazzi v. Italy*, concerning the length of judicial processes in Italy, the Court pronounced that it had found:

> an accumulation of identical breaches which are sufficiently numerous to amount not merely to isolated incidents. Such breaches reflect a continuing situation that has not yet been remedied and in respect of which litigants have no domestic remedy. This accumulation of breaches accordingly constitutes a practice that is incompatible with the Convention.[41]

The following year, the Court considered another case against Italy, this time pertaining to the placement of two children in a children's home, the proprietors of which had been found guilty of sexual abuse. Perhaps emboldened by the shocking nature of the underlying claim, the Court used its decision in *Scozzari and Giunta v. Italy*[42] to develop a new approach to remedies. It labeled this approach "*restitutio in integrum,*" holding that, in cases in which the rights violation in question was found to be due to an ongoing, underlying systemic violation, the state would be required not only to provide compensation, but also to remedy the situation that gave rise to the violations in question.[43]

Assanidze v. Georgia, App. No. 71503/01, Eur. Ct. H.R. (April 8, 2004), paras. 202–3. As this brief excerpt from the Court's judgment attests, the continuing nature of the violation was key in prompting the Court to suggest a stronger remedy. For more on this point, see Colandrea, "Power of the European Court." For more on the Court's power to issue non-monetary relief generally, see Ingrid Nifosi-Sutton, "The Power of the European Court of Human Rights to Order Specific Non-Monetary Relief: A Critical Appraisal from a Right to Health Perspective," 23 *Harvard Human Rights Journal* (2010), 51–74.

41 Bottazzi v. Italy, App. No. 34884/97, Eur. Ct. H.R. (July 28, 1999), para. 22. See also Messina v. Italy, App. No. 25498/94, Eur. Ct. H.R. (September 28, 2000).

42 App. Nos. 39221/98 & 41963/98, Eur. Ct. H.R. (July 13, 2000).

43 As Gattini has put it, in *Scozzari* the Court "[made] the point that the means chosen by the Respondent State to comply with the judgment must be compatible with the conclusions set out in the judgment itself." Gattini, "Mass Claims," 278. For more on the concept of *restitutio in integrum,* see Loukis Loucaides, "Reparation for Violations of Human Rights under the European Convention and *restitutio in integrum,*" 2 *European Human Rights Law Review* (2008), 182–92.

The third area in which the Court's jurisprudence evolved concerned Article 13 of the Convention, the article guaranteeing the right to a remedy. Key here were a series of decisions beginning with *Aksoy v. Turkey*,[44] in which the Court emphasized states' obligations to conduct thorough and effective investigations in cases of arguable claims of rights violation, a standard augmented by *Çakici v. Turkey*, in which the Court suggested that a remedial avenue should be provided wherever an "arguable complaint" of a Convention violation existed.[45] In *Kudla v. Poland*,[46] meanwhile, the Court found the excessive length of proceedings in Poland gave rise not only to a violation of Article 6(1), on the right to a fair trial, but also to a violation of Article 13. While on one level a technical distinction, the implication was in another sense more profound, as attested to by the substantial attention both the judgment and Judge Casadevall's dissent thereto devoted to the matter. The implication, in essence, was not only that prolonged proceedings were in violation of the Convention and must therefore be reformed, but also that states must establish national remedial procedures through which individuals might be able to bring effective claims aimed at producing such reform. In short, as Judge Casadevall put it, the judgment aimed to "confront the State with their responsibilities, in accordance with the subsidiarity principle,"[47] by suggesting, albeit in a roundabout way, that states were obliged to embed the Convention within their national legal systems.[48]

44 See Aksoy v. Turkey, App. No. 21987/93, Eur. Ct. H.R. (December 18, 1996); Aydin v. Turkey, App. No. 23178/94, Eur. Ct. H.R. (September 25, 1997); Kaya v. Turkey, App. No. 22729/93, Eur. Ct. H.R. (February 19, 1998); Ergi v. Turkey, App. No. 23818/94, Eur. Ct. H.R. (July 28, 1998); and Assenow and others v. Bulgaria, App. No. 24760/94, Eur. Ct. H.R. (October 28, 1998), as well later cases such as Anguelova v. Bulgaria, App. No. 38361/97, Eur. Ct. H.R. (June 13, 2002); Suheyla Aydin v. Turkey, App. No. 25660/94, Eur. Ct. H.R. (May 24, 2005); and Cobzaru v. Romania, App. No. 48254/99, Eur. Ct. H.R. (July 26, 2007).

45 App. No. 23657/94, Eur. Ct. H.R. (July 8, 1999), para. 112. *See also* Camenzind v. Switzerland, App. No. 21353/93, Eur. Ct. H.R. (December 16, 1997). For more, see Jochen Frowein, "Art. 13 as a Growing Pillar of Convention Law," in Mahoney et al. eds., *Protecting Human Rights*, 550.

46 App. No. 30210/96, Eur. Ct. H.R. (October 26, 2000).

47 Ibid., partial dissent, para. 5.

48 For more, see ibid., paras. 147, 151–52, 154–56. See also Conka v. Belgium, App. No. 51564/99, Eur. Ct. H.R. (February 5, 2002), which referred to Article 13 as protecting "one of the fundamental principles of a democratic society" (para. 83); and Anguelova v. Bulgaria, App. No. 38361/97, Eur. Ct. H.R. (June 13, 2002), para. 161. See also the discussion in Laurence Helfer, "Redesigning the European Court of Human Rights: Embeddedness as a Deep Structural Principle of the European Human Rights Regime," 19 *EJIL* (2008), 125–59.

All three sets of cases – those expanding the Court's remedial orders, those articulating the idea of *restitutio in integrum*, and those developing the Court's Article 13 jurisprudence – represented different ways in which the Court was attempting to grapple with the challenges involved in making the Convention system more immediately effective on the national level. At the same time, the system was also attempting to deal with its increasing unmanageable caseload. The system's most concerted efforts to address the caseload challenge came in the form of proposed procedural reforms. First came Protocol 14,[49] which enabled the quick filtering out of cases in which no "significant disadvantage" had been demonstrated, allowed admissibility determinations to be made by a single judge in the majority of cases, and provided for a summary procedure in cases of repeat applications.[50] Protocol 14 was immediately criticized, both for

[49] The process that led to Protocol 14 began with a European Ministerial Conference in Rome in November 2000, which urged the Committee of Ministers to "identify without delay the most urgent measures to be taken to assist the Court in fulfilling its functions" and to "initiate, as soon as possible, a thorough study of the different possibilities and options with a view to ensuring the effectiveness of the Court in the light of this new situation." European Ministerial Conference of Human Rights (Rome, 3–4 November 2000), Resolution I, para. 18. The following years saw extensive debates and the consideration of numerous different proposals. See Report of the Evaluation Group to the Committee of Ministers on the European Court of Human Rights, EG Court (2001)1 (September 27, 2001); CDDH, Interim Report of the CDDH to be Submitted to the Committee of Ministers, "Guaranteeing the Long-Term Effectiveness of the European Court of Human Rights," CDDH(2002)016 Addendum (October 14, 2002); CDDH, "Report of the Reflection Group on the Reinforcement of the Human Rights Protection Mechanism," CDDH-GDR(2002)012 (December 12, 2002); CDDH, "Guaranteeing the Long-Term Effectiveness of the European Court of Human Rights – Addendum to the Final Report Containing CDDH Proposals (Long Version)," CDDH(2003)006 Addendum Final (April 9, 2003); and see Greer, *The European Convention on Human Rights*, 143 and Christina Hioureas, "Behind the Scenes of Protocol No. 14: Politics in Reforming the European Court of Human Rights," 2 *Berkeley Journal of International Law* (2006), 718–57. Protocol 14 was adopted on May 12th, 2004.

[50] Protocol 14 also created new rules aimed at strengthening the enforcement of judgments, including allowing the Committee of Ministers to seek interpretation from the Court where the holding was not clear, and allowing the Committee to bring infringement proceedings before the Court. While the adoption of such rules indicated an intent to strengthen enforcement, by leaving enforcement primarily in the Committee's hands Protocol 14 did little to address the underlying need to create a more independent and dynamic enforcement system. For more on this issue, see Andrea Gattini, "Mass Claims at the European Court of Human Rights," in Breitenmoser et al. eds., *Human Rights*, 288. For a recent call to grant the Court an expanded role in overseeing implementation, see Helen Keller and Cedric Marti, "Reconceptualizing Implementation: The Judicialization of the Execution of the European Court of Human Rights' Judgments," 26 *European Journal of International Law* (2016), 829–50.

having done too little to address systemic violations, and for having introduced controversial new criteria through which to exclude cases.[51]

Another effort to resolve the problem of multiple complaints addressing the same underlying issue was that of the "pilot judgment procedure." The pilot judgment procedure was first formally proposed in a 2003 paper prepared by the Court.[52] Protocol 14 saw no reference to the procedure, as the proposal to include such a reference was rejected by the Steering Committee that drafted the protocol, due to the contentiousness of the idea.[53] At the same time, however, the Steering Committee suggested the Court itself might introduce such a procedure of its own accord within the existing Conventional framework, and the Committee of Ministers adopted a resolution calling for the same.[54]

[51] See Marie-Aude Beernaert, "Protocol 14 and New Strasbourg Procedures: Towards Greater Efficiency? And at What Price?," 5 *European Human Rights Law Review* (2004), 544–57; Steven Greer, "Protocol 14 and the Future of the European Court of Human Rights," *Public Law* (2005), 83–106; Greer, *The European Convention on Human Rights*, 136. For a general review of Protocol 14, see Lucius Caflisch, "The Reform of the European Court of Human Rights: Protocol No. 14 and Beyond," 6 *Human Rights Law Review* (2006), 403–15.

[52] See Position Paper of the European Court of Human Rights on Proposals for Reform of the European Convention on Human Rights and Other Measures, as set out in the Report of the Steering Committee for Human Rights of April 4, 2003. See also Leach et al., *Responding to Systemic Human Rights Violations*, 9–10; Response of the Court to the Steering Committee for Human Rights, Interim Activity Report, Doc. CDDH-GDR (2004) 001 (February 2, 2004), para. 24, referring to Eur. Ct. H.R. Position Paper, Doc. CDDH-GDR (2003) 024 (September 12, 2003).

[53] As Gattini noted shortly thereafter,

> the concept of actual or potential mass claims has not yet entered into the language of the European Convention on Human Rights. If it would, it could disturb many, because the simple utterance of "mass claims" inevitably evokes the concept of mass violations, a circumstance that we usually dismiss as wholly unrealistic in the democracies of the Contracting Parties of the ECHR.

Gattini, "Mass Claims," 273. The caution of Protocol 14's drafters was also illustrated by their response to a proposal, supported by the Parliamentary Assembly, that the Commissioner for Human Rights be given the power to lodge applications with the system in cases revealing "a pattern of violations of a trans-national or systemic character" (Explanatory Report to Protocol 14, para. 86). As Gattini observed, "the majority in the Steering Committee considered that such a proposal would be a 'major departure' from the current system of the Convention, introducing a sort of *actio popularis*." Gattini, "Mass Claims," 288, citing Martin Eaton and Jeroen Schokkenbroeck, "Reforming the Human Rights Protection System Established by the European Convention on Human Rights," 26 *Human Rights Law Journal* (2005), 12. The Commissioner was instead granted the ability to submit written comments and to take part in hearings.

[54] See Committee of Ministers, Res(2004)3 on judgments revealing an underlying systemic problem, adopted May 12, 2004; Luzius Wildhaber, "Pilot Judgments in Cases of Structural

The pilot judgment procedure was put into effect for the first time in *Broniowski v. Poland*.[55] *Broniowski* concerned tens of thousands of claimants who lost their property when the Eastern border of Poland was demarcated at the end of World War II. While Poland had taken some positive steps, adequate compensation had not been delivered. The European Court, therefore, decided to deploy the pilot judgment procedure, which involved suspending consideration of the vast bulk of the cases dealing with the matter before it, and hearing instead a representative "pilot" case. In its decision the Court underscored the "systemic" nature of the situation before it, and called on Poland to create a comprehensive scheme to address that situation and to provide redress to all the claimants.[56]

In the years following *Broniowski* the Court issued several more pilot judgments and "quasi-pilot judgments,"[57] in cases concerning seizure of

or Systemic Problems," in Wolfrum and Deutsch eds., *European Court of Human Rights*, 70. See also Committee of Ministers, Rec 6 2004, para. 13, calling on the Court:

I. as far as possible, to identify, in its judgments finding a violation of the Convention, what it considers to be an underlying systemic problem and the source of this problem, in particular when it is likely to give rise to numerous applications, so as to assist states in finding the appropriate solution and the Committee of Ministers in supervising the execution of judgments;
II. to specially notify any judgment containing indications of the existence of a systemic problem and of the source of this problem not only to the state concerned and to the Committee of Ministers, but also to the Parliamentary Assembly, to the Secretary General of the Council of Europe and to the Council of Europe Commissioner for Human Rights, and to highlight such judgments in an appropriate manner in the database of the Court.

The language of the resolution proposed that the Court's suggestions should be presented as an attempt "to assist states in finding the appropriate solution," thus leaving the Court deprived, as before, of clear power to require specific structural changes. A summit convened in Warsaw in May 2005, moreover, with the aim of reflecting on the challenges facing the system, ultimately called for the setting up of a "Group of Wise Persons," in order to produce recommendations for further reforms. Among the reforms this group recommended was as extensive a use of the pilot judgment procedure as possible. See Report of the Group of Wise Persons to the Committee of Ministers (November 15, 2006), para. 105. This point of emphasis was reinforced in 2006 by amendments the Committee of Ministers made to its rules of procedure, which prioritized supervision of such cases. See Rules of the Committee of Ministers for the Supervision of the Execution of Judgments and of the Terms of Friendly Settlements, adopted May 10, 2006, Rule 4, para. 1.

[55] App. No. 31443/96, Eur. Ct. H.R (June 22, 2004).

[56] See ibid., paras. 193–4, operative paras. 3–4.

[57] "Quasi-pilot judgments" are decisions in which the Court does not formally deploy the pilot judgment procedure, but nonetheless identifies a systemic problem.

property,[58] rent ceilings,[59] foreign currency holdings,[60] domestic judicial procedures,[61] unduly delayed national proceedings,[62] the enforcement of domestic judgments,[63] pretrial detention,[64] conditions of detention,[65]

[58] See, e.g., Xenides-Arestis v. Turkey, App. No. 46347/99, Eur. Ct. H.R (December 22, 2005); Driza v. Albania, App. No. 33771/02, Eur. Ct. H.R. (November 13, 2007); Viasu v. Romania, App. No. 75951/01, Eur. Ct. H.R. (December 9, 2008); Katz v. Romania, App. No. 29739/03, Eur. Ct. H.R. (January 20, 2009); Maria Atanasiu and others v. Romania, App. Nos. 30767/05 & 33800/06, Eur. Ct. H.R. (October 12, 2010); Manushaqe Puto and others v. Albania, App. Nos. 604/07, 43628/07, 46684/07, & 34770/09, Eur. Ct. H.R. (July 31, 2012); M.C. and others v. Italy, App. No. 5376/11, Eur. Ct. H.R. (September 3, 2013); Alisic and others v. Bosnia and Herzegovina, Croatia, "the former Yugoslav Republic of Macedonia," Serbia and Slovenia, App. No. 60642/08, Eur. Ct. H.R. (July 16, 2014).

[59] See Hutten-Czapska v. Poland, App. No. 35014/97, Eur. Ct. H.R. (June 19, 2006).

[60] See Suljagic v. Bosnia and Herzegovina, App. No. 27912/02, Eur. Ct. H.R. (June 20, 2006).

[61] See, e.g., Sejdovic v. Italy, App. No. 56581/00, Eur. Ct. H.R (November 10, 2004) (concerning trial *in absentia*); Ocalan v. Turkey, App. No. 46221/99, Eur. Ct. H.R (May 12, 2005) (concerning a flawed domestic trial); Ramirez Sanchez v. France, App. No. 59450/00, Eur. Ct. H.R. (July 4, 2006) (concerning the lack of appropriate avenues of appeal through which Mr. Sanchez, a Venezuelan citizen infamous for carrying out a number of terrorist attacks, might challenge his solitary confinement).

[62] See, e.g., Lukenda v. Slovenia, App. No. 23032/02, Eur. Ct. H.R (October 6, 2005). See also Scordino v. Italy (No 1), App. No. 36813/97, Eur. Ct. H.R (March 29, 2006) (a case following up on the 1999 *Bottazzi v. Italy* judgment); Ramadhi v. Albania, App. No. 38222/02, Eur. Ct. H.R (November 13, 2007); Faimblat v. Romania, App. No. 23066/02, Eur. Ct. H.R (January 13, 2009); Rumpf v. Germany, App. No. 46344/06, Eur. Ct. H.R. (September 2, 2010); Athanasiou and others v. Greece, App. No. 36546/10, Eur. Ct. H.R. (December 21, 2010); Dimitrov and Hamanov v. Bulgaria, App. Nos. 48059/06 & 2708/09, Eur. Ct. H.R. (May 10, 2011), Finger v. Bulgaria, App. No. 37346/05, Eur. Ct. H.R. (May 10, 2011), Ummuhan Kaplan v. Turkey, App. No. 24240/07, Eur. Ct. H.R. (March 20, 2012); Michelioudakis v. Greece, App. No. 54447/10, Eur. Ct. H.R. (April 3, 2012); Glykantzi v. Greece, App. No. 40150/09, Eur. Ct. H.R. (October 30, 2012); Rutkowski and other v. Poland, App. Nos. 72287/10, 13927/11, & 46187/11, Eur. Ct. H.R. (July 7, 2015); Gazso v. Hungary, App. No. 48322/12, Eur. Ct. H.R. (July 16, 2015).

[63] See, e.g., Burdov v. Russia, App. No. 33509/04, Eur. Ct. H.R. (January 15, 2009); Olaru and others v. Moldova, App. Nos. 476/07, 22539/05, 17911/08, & 13136/07, Eur. Ct. H.R. (November 15, 2009); Yuriy Nikolayevich Ivanov v. Ukraine, App. No. 40450/04, Eur. Ct. H.R. (January 15, 2010); Gerasimov and others v. Russia, App. Nos. 29920/05, 3553/06, 18876/10, 61186/10, 21176/11, 36112/11, 36426/11, 40841/11, 45381/11, 55929/11, & 60822/11, Eur. Ct. H.R. (July 1, 2014).

[64] See, e.g., Kauczor v. Poland, App. No. 45219/06, Eur. Ct. H.R. (February 3, 2009).

[65] See, e.g., Dybeku v. Albania, App. No. 41153/06, Eur. Ct. H.R. (December 18, 2007); Slawomir Musial v. Poland, App. No. 28300/06, Eur. Ct. H.R. (January 20, 2009); Ananyev and others v. Russia, App. Nos. 42525/07 & 60800, Eur. Ct. H.R. (January 10, 2012); Torreggiani and others v. Italy, App. Nos. 43517/09, 46882/09, 55400/09, 57875/09, 613535/09, 35315/10, & 37818/10, Eur. Ct. H.R. (January 8, 2013); Neshkov and others v. Bulgaria, App. Nos. 36925/10, 21487/12, 72893/12, 73196/12, 77718/12, & 9717/13, Eur. Ct. H.R. (January 27, 2015); Varga and others v. Hungary, App. Nos. 14097/12, 45135/12, 73712/12, 34001/13, 44055/13, & 64586/13, Eur. Ct. H.R. (March 10, 2015).

freedom of expression[66] and the stripping of residence rights.[67] The Court also increasingly used the threat of the pilot judgment procedure to prompt preemptive action. Thus, for instance, in *Nachova,* which concerned discrimination against the Roma population in Bulgaria, the Court emphasized that its decision constituted "a last warning," indicating that if Bulgaria did not comply with the judgment, it might have to implement the pilot judgment approach.[68]

While the Court was thus willing to deploy the more systemic approach represented by the pilot judgment or quasi-pilot judgment approach more frequently, it never formalized the criteria that would trigger the use of such an approach, preferring to maintain its discretion as to whether to employ that approach or not.[69] In numerous cases

66 See Manole and others v. Moldova, App. No. 13936/02, Eur. Ct. H.R. (September 17, 2009).

67 See Kuric and others v. Slovenia, App. No. 26828/06, Eur. Ct. H.R. (July 13, 2010); Kuric and others v. Slovenia, App. No. 26828/06, Eur. Ct. H.R. (June 26, 2012).

68 See Gattini, "Mass Claims," 284. *Nachova and others v. Bulgaria* (App. Nos. 43577/98 & 43579/98, Eur. Ct. H.R. (July 6, 2005)) was also important insofar as it addressed systemic discrimination, and saw the Court adopt a more flexible approach to evidential matters. The Court stipulated that the approach taken would be one in which "there are no procedural barriers to the admissibility of evidence or pre-determined formulae for its assessment" and in which the Court would proceed with "free evaluation of all evidence, including such inferences as may flow from the facts and the parties' submissions," so that "proof may follow from the coexistence of sufficiently strong, clear and concordant inferences or of similar unrebutted presumptions of fact." The Court went on by observing that

> Moreover, the level of persuasion necessary for reaching a particular conclusion and, in this connection, the distribution of the burden of proof are intrinsically linked to the specificity of the facts, the nature of the allegation made and the Convention right at stake …
>
> in certain circumstances, where the events lie wholly, or in large part, within the exclusive knowledge of the authorities, as in the case of the death of a person within their control in custody, the burden of proof may be regarded as resting on the authorities to provide a satisfactory and convincing explanation of, in particular, the causes of the detained person's death (see Salman v. Turkey [GC], no. 21986/93, § 100, ECHR 2000-VII). The Grand Chamber cannot exclude the possibility that in certain cases of alleged discrimination it may require the respondent Government to disprove an arguable allegation of discrimination and – if they fail to do so – find a violation of Article 14 of the Convention on that basis.

Ibid., paras. 147, 157. See also D.H. and others v. The Czech Republic, App. No. 57325/00, Eur. Ct. H.R. (November 13, 2007), paras. 176–80.

69 In general, the Court was always careful to consider the political situation before deciding to apply the pilot judgment procedure, with Court personnel often reaching out to states behind the scenes to test how such an approach might be received. See Leach et al., *Responding to Systemic Human Rights Violations*, 35–7. On the Court's caution in

in which the Court might have emphasized the presence of systemic issues, it did not do so, including for instance in *Matko v. Slovenia*,[70] concerning Slovenian authorities' failure to investigate a complaint against the police; *Tysiac v. Poland*,[71] concerning refusal to allow an abortion; *Baczkowski v. Poland*,[72] concerning LGBT rights; and *Silih v. Slovenia*,[73] concerning failure to investigate medical negligence. Similarly, the Court made a point of addressing cases concerning major violations committed in the context of conflict – notably in southeastern Turkey and Chechnya – individually.[74]

general, see also Jochen Frowein, "The Binding Force of ECHR Judgments and its Limits," in Breitenmoser et al. eds., *Human Rights*, 261–70. The Court's discretion has extended to its post-decision handling of pilot judgment decisions as well. In 2017, the Court took the dramatic step of transferring responsibility relative to the broader issues considered in *Burmych and others v. Ukraine* (App. Nos. 46852/13 et al., Eur. Ct. H.R. (October 12, 2017)), a case concerning the nonexecution of national judgments, to the Committee of Ministers, following Ukraine's failure to comply with the Court's pilot judgment against it. The decision was sharply contested, with ten judges joining in the ruling while seven were opposed. For more, see Eur. Ct. H.R., "Strike-out and Transmission to the Committee of Ministers of More than 12,000 Ukrainian Cases," Press Release (October 12, 2017); Eline Kindt, "Non-Execution of a Pilot Judgment: ECtHR Passes the Buck to the Committee of Ministers in Burmych and Others v. Ukraine," *Strasbourg Observers Blog* (October 26, 2017).

70 App. No. 43393/98, Eur. Ct. H.R. (November 2, 2006).

71 App. No. 5410/03, Eur. Ct. H.R. (March 20, 2007).

72 App. No. 1543/06, Eur. Ct. H.R. (May 3, 2007).

73 App. No. 71463/01, Eur. Ct. H.R. (April 9, 2009).

74 See Leach et al., *Responding to Systemic Human Rights Violations*, 163–4. For details and criticism with regard to the cases concerning Chechnya, see Philip Leach, "The Chechen Conflict: Analysing the Oversight of the European Court of Human Rights," 6 *European Human Rights Law Review* (2008), 732–61; Kirill Koroteev, "Legal Remedies for Human Rights Violations in the Armed Conflict in Chechnya: The Approach of the European Court of Human Rights in Context," 1 *Journal of International Humanitarian Legal Studies* (2010), 275–303; for details as to the cases concerning Turkey see Aisling Reidy, Francoise Hampson, and Kevin Boyle, "Gross Violations of Human Rights: Invoking the European Convention on Human Rights in the Case of Turkey," 15 *Netherlands Quarterly of Human Rights* (1997), 161–73. The Turkish cases did help to push the system toward a more direct approach to fact-finding and a more flexible approach to evidence, important developments in their own right on the path toward a more systemic approach. See Helfer, "Redesigning the European Court," 142–4. For general criticism of the system's approach to entrenched situations of widespread violation, see Oren Gross, "'Once More unto the Breach': The Systemic Failure of Applying the European Convention on Human Rights to Entrenched Emergencies," 23 *Yale Journal of International Law* (1998), 437–45. The court's resistance to adopting a more systemic approach in such a context did not go totally unchallenged, as some commentators began to call on the system for more consistency and the adoption of stronger measures, including potentially the replacement of the pilot judgment approach by a class action procedure. See Gattini, "Mass Claims," 291; Greer and Wildhaber, "Revisiting the Debate."

While utilization of the pilot judgment procedure helped the Court to handle a portion of its caseload more expeditiously, it was not enough to offset the continuing increase in submissions. Protocol 14 entered into force in 2010, allowing for the efficiency-enhancing measures it authorized to be put into effect. Protocol 14's authorization of the summary exclusion of cases proved particularly effective in clearing the Court's backlog. A substantial number of pending applications remained, however.[75] The extent to which the Court was making progress was further questionable, however, insofar as the period saw the Court devoting the bulk of its attention to excluding cases considered not well-founded, rather than focusing on its backlog of more serious cases.[76]

In 2012 a major conference was organized in Brighton, at which those who hoped to strengthen the Court mingled with those who hoped to trim back its powers.[77] The Declaration produced by the conference[78] included several recommendations. Most centrally, the declaration emphasized the importance of subsidiarity, an appealingly vague concept, that could mean both (1) that states would have the upper hand, and (2) that states would be obliged to do more to ensure the advancement of the Convention. This emphasis was further reinforced in the following years

75 As of October 2017, the Court had 64,650 pending applications. See Elisabeth Lambert Abdelgawad, "The Practice of the European Court of Human Rights When Striking Out Applications," 36 *Netherlands Quarterly of Human Rights* (2018), 7 nt. 1.

76 See Mikael Rask Madsen, "Rebalancing European Human Rights: Has the Brighton Declaration Engendered a New Deal on Human Rights in Europe?," *iCourts Working Paper Series* No. 100 (June 2017), 14–5. The late 2000s also saw the Court adopt a prioritization policy, which highlighted the importance of cases raising urgent matters, violations having particularly widespread or systematic effect, and "core rights" violations of Articles 2, 3, 4, and 5(1). See Eur. Ct. H.R., The Court's Priority Policy. Manifestly inadmissible applications were, naturally, deemed the least important; hence it was ironic that much of the system's energies would end up focused on this category of cases.

77 For more on the conference and its effects, see Madsen, "Rebalancing European Human Rights." Among those who were not pleased with the system at the time was the United Kingdom. In 2010, the Court issued a decision in *Greens and M.T. v. the United Kingdom* (App. Nos. 60041/08 & 60054/08, Eur. Ct. H.R. (November 23, 2010)), in which it found UK legislation preventing prisoners from voting in violation of the Convention. The decision met a sharp response from the UK's Conservative government, however, which refused to comply with the Court's judgment, instead launching a series of strident attacks on the Court in the British press. For more on resistance to the European Court in the early 2010s, see Sarah Lambrecht, "Reforms to Lessen the Influence of the European Court of Human Rights: A Successful Strategy?," 21 *European Public Law* (2015), 257–83.

78 See Eur. Ct. H.R., High Level Conference on the Future of the European Court of Human Rights: Brighton Declaration (2012).

through the drafting of two new protocols, Protocol 15 and Protocol 16,[79] as well as by the Court's widely observed "procedural turn,"[80] a phrase coined to describe the Court's increasing deference to state decisions. Meetings similar to that at Brighton have continued to take place since, producing similar outcome documents, including for instance the 2018 "Copenhagen Declaration."[81]

The growing strength of national governments in relation to the system, demonstrated by the system's increasing emphasis on "subsidiarity," could be seen elsewhere as well. While momentum toward bringing the European Union within the European Conventional system began to gather in the late 2000s, that momentum ground to a halt in December 2014, following a decision by the Court of Justice of the European Union that essentially constituted a refusal by that court to subordinate itself to the European Court of Human Rights.[82] An increasingly powerful and emboldened Russia presented a further thorn in the side of the Court,[83] on top of which the rise of right-wing, anti-European and rights-skeptical political parties across Europe from the late 2000s on presented further challenges.

79 Among other things, Protocol 15 added a reference to subsidiarity and the doctrine of the margin of appreciation to the preamble of the Convention, shortened the time limit within which cases might be submitted to the Court, and removed a preexisting limitation on the Court's ability to reject cases found not to involve any significant disadvantage. Protocol 15 had not yet entered into force as of the end of 2018. Protocol 16 allowed the highest level of national courts to request the European Court to provide them with advisory opinions on questions pertaining to the Convention. Protocol 16 entered into force in August 2018.

80 See Oddný Mjöll Arnardóttir, "The 'Procedural Turn' under the European Convention on Human Rights and Presumptions of Convention Compliance," 15 *International Journal of Constitutional Law* (2017), 9–35; Janneke Gerards and Eva Brems eds., *Procedural Review in European Fundamental Rights Cases* (Cambridge University Press, 2017).

81 For more on the Copenhagen Declaration see the series of posts on the European Human Rights Blog between February and April 2018.

82 See Opinion 2/13, Court of Justice of the European Union (December 18, 2014).

83 Russia's challenge to the system has taken many forms. On the jurisprudential side, the European Court issued a major judgment concerning Russia in 2014 (OAO Neftyanaya Kompaniya Yukos v. Russia, App. No. 14902/04, Eur. Ct. H.R. (July 31, 2014)), in which it awarded $1.86 billion to Yukos shareholders. In response, the Duma passed a new law, allowing European Court judgments to be declared impossible to implement. This law was then applied both to the Yukos ruling and to *Anchugov and Gladkov* (App. Nos. 11157/04 & 15162/05, Eur. Ct. H.R. (July 4, 2013)), which had challenged Russia's restriction of prisoners' voting rights. For more on Russia and the Court, see René Provost, "Teetering on the Edge of Legal Nihilism: Russia and the Evolving European Human Rights Regime," 37 *Human Rights Quarterly* (2015), 289–340; Madsen, "The Challenging Authority," 167–72; Lauri Malksoo and Wolfgang Benedek eds., *Russia and the European Court of Human Rights: The Strasbourg Effect* (Cambridge University Press, 2018).

In sum, the European rights project took a particular shape in the 1970s. Most overarchingly, the system adopted as its primary purpose the gradual advancement of jurisprudential standards, a project it understood as best advanced through the development of a powerful international judicial body. By the 1990s and 2000s, that project had been extraordinarily successful, leading to the development of an extensive and detailed body of human rights standards, that could serve as a model not only for Europe but around the world, and to the creation of a fully judicialized system, as explored in the previous chapter. The system's success coincided with new challenges, however, in terms of increasing caseload, encounters with more serious rights violations in states such as Russia, Turkey, and Ukraine, and noncompliance with numerous judgments. Since then, the system has attempted to grapple with these challenges in numerous ways. The adoption of a new, more systemic approach has proven enduringly challenging for the European system, however, not least because of the conflict between such an approach and its traditional mode of operating.

## III The Americas

### *III.1 The Adoption of an Assertive Approach*

The Inter-American system was formed in very different conditions from the European system. As laid out in the previous chapter, from its formation the Inter-American Commission embarked down an assertive path, expanding its powers through creative interpretation, while carefully focusing its efforts on the regions' less politically powerful and important states, in order to minimize resistance. The difficulty of the system's task increased in the 1970s, as authoritarianism and repression increased in the region. Despite such challenges, the Commission remained committed to the gradual expansion of its powers. A key component of the Commission's experimental development of its powers came through its ongoing emphasis what it termed "general" as opposed to "individual" cases. Key to the development of this distinction was a communication concerning the military dictatorship in Brazil.[84] The communication attempted to highlight the violations committed by the Brazilian state from a broad and holistic perspective. Initially, the Commission was uncertain how to deal with such a complaint: should it consider the case as it was, in broad and systemic form, or alternatively should it force the applicants to

[84] Comm. No. 1684, Int.-Am. Comm. H.R. (June 25, 1970).

break up the application into numerous discrete complaints? Ultimately, under the leadership of Commissioner Sandifer, the Commission opted for the more holistic approach, accepting the case under its broader, more flexible "taking cognizance" power.[85]

In addition to recognizing systemic complaints under its "taking cognizance" power, the Commission started to develop other means of responding to serious, widespread, and systematic instances of violation as well. In particular, the Commission asserted its power to commence investigations into serious violations on its own initiative, where it deemed such investigations necessary, as well as a concomitant power to conduct country visits.[86] As time went forward, these practices assumed priority in the Commission's workload, in preference to the consideration of individual communications, due to the Commission's sense that such approaches provided a better means with which to address the most serious and extensive human rights violations.[87]

[85] As Quiroga would later observe,

> The direction given by the Commission to its powers … shows that although the Commission was attempting to create within the inter-American system a mechanism to deal with individual petitions, the attempt was actually, consciously or unconsciously, directed at finding a way to be able to give priority attention to the most serious violations of human rights occurring in the continent. The right of individual petition was the door that opened the way for the Commission to examine the general situation of human rights in states where gross violations were apparently being committed.

Quiroga, *Battle of Human Rights*, 316.

[86] See Int.-Am. Comm. H.R., Handbook of Existing Rules Pertaining to Human Rights, OEA/Ser.L/V/II.50, Doc. 6 (1980), Article 23(3); Quiroga, "Inter-American Commission."

[87] A similar movement was also underway on the international level at the time. Momentum in such a direction could be seen in the adoption of Resolution 1235 (XLII) by the Human Rights Commission's Sub-Commission on the Prevention of Discrimination and Protection of Minorities, which highlighted the concept of "consistent patterns of human rights violation," observing such violations in South Africa, South West Africa, Southern Rhodesia, Angola, Mozambique, Guinea Bissau, Greece, and Haiti. *See* Resolution 1235 (XLII) on Violation of Human Rights and Fundamental Freedoms, including policies of racial discrimination, segregation, and apartheid, E/4393 (June 6, 1967). Debate on this matter in fact led to ECOSOC adopting a resolution allowing complaints to be submitted to the sub-commission in cases of "consistent pattern of gross and reliably attested violations." See Resolution 1503 (XLVIII), Procedures for dealing with communications relating to violations of Human Rights, E/4832-/Add. 1 (May 27, 1970); Theresa Gonzales, "The Political Sources of Procedural Debates in the United Nations: Structural Impediments to Implementation of Human Rights," 13 *International Law and Policy* (1981), 427–72. The procedure was made confidential, however, and the sub-commission in question was a political, inter-state one, rather than an independent body, sharply limiting its effectiveness. For further discussion, see Quiroga, *Battle of Human Rights*, 7–10.

A prominent example of increasing repression in the period, as well as of the sort of approach the Commission would assume in response, came in the form of the overthrow of the Chilean government of Salvador Allende by a coup, on September 11, 1973. The months that followed saw the commission of widespread and systematic human rights violations that captured the attention of the world. Complaints from Amnesty International and the ICJ arrived at the Commission immediately after the coup, followed by a flood of further communications in the days, months, and years that followed. In response, the Commission decided to visit Chile in 1974. The Commission's presence in Chile led to the submission of hundreds of further communications, on top of which the Commission pursued its own fact-finding endeavors. At the end of its visit, the Commission composed a broad list of recommendations, which it made public in a concluding press release. The Commission also prepared a report, which flatly observed that "the [new] regime instituted in Chile" had, since its foundation, been involved in the commission of numerous "extremely serious violations of human rights," which it documented in detail.[88]

[88] See Report on the Status of Human Rights in Chile, findings of "on the spot" Observations in the Republic of Chile (July 22–August 2, 1974), OEA/Ser. L/V/II.34, Doc. 21 (October 25, 1974). Despite the fact that the Convention had not yet come into effect, the Commission found a creative way to give it some effect in its report, by observing that

> With respect to American International law – which is the normative system that the Commission must take primarily into account – it must be understood that, in the absence of conventional standards in force in this area, the "most accepted doctrine" is that which is set forth in the American Convention on Human Rights.

Ibid.

Events in Greece six years earlier, considered by the European Commission in the *First Greek Case*, had already brought the issue of torture to the forefront of the international community's attention, resulting in the launching of a major campaign by Amnesty International in 1972. See Keys, "Anti-Torture Politics." The European Commission's ongoing consideration of the topic in *Ireland v. United Kingdom*, concerning a British security operation in Northern Ireland, was also important. The coup and its aftermath in Chile brought further attention to this subject, which found international crystallization in the form of a 1975 United Nations resolution on torture, and later the 1984 United Nations Convention Against Torture. *See* UN Res. 3452 (XXX) (December 9, 1975); United Nations Convention Against Torture, UNTS 1465 (Opened for signature December 10, 1984; entry into effect June 26, 1987). The situation in Chile also sparked other global human rights developments. Together with the situation in Greece, it helped spur the incorporation of rights concerns in US foreign policy, thanks in particular to the pioneering energies of Donald Fraser, a Democratic Congressman from Minnesota. Steps taken included a series of amendments to the Foreign Assistance Act, beginning with the 1972 Hays Amendment, cutting off aid to Greece (though in practice Nixon took advantage of a national security exception in the law), and passage of the Arms Export Control Act. For more on this turn in American law, see Stephen Cohen, "Conditioning U.S. Assistance on Human

The Commission continued to be flooded with complaints concerning Chile after publication of its report, with approximately a thousand separate communications on its docket in 1975.[89] In the years to come, and at the request of the OAS, the Commission continued to issue broad follow-up reports on the situation in Chile.[90] Thereafter, the Commission adjusted

Rights Practices," 76 *American Journal of International Law* (1982), 246–79; Paul Albert, "The Undermining of the Legal Standards for Human Rights Violations in United States Foreign Policy: The Case of 'Improvement' in Guatemala," 14 *Columbia Human Rights Law Review* (1983), 231–74; Richard Nash, "Certifying Human Rights: Military Assistance to El Salvador and the International Security and Development Cooperation Act of 1981," 14 *Columbia Human Rights Law Review* (1983), 275–310; Tanya Broder and Bernard Lambek, "Military Aid to Guatemala: The Failure of U.S. Human Rights Legislation," 13 *Yale Journal of International Law* (1988), 111–45. In Europe too, the coup in Chile spurred a number of states, such as the United Kingdom, Germany, Italy, the Netherlands, and Norway to cut off various forms of support. The United Nations Commission on Human Rights meanwhile commissioned several major reports on the situation; *see* Report of the Ad Hoc Working Group to Inquire into the Present Situation of Human Rights in Chile, U.N. Doc. E/CN.4/1188 (February 4, 1976); Study of the Impact of Foreign Economic Aid and Assistance on respect for Human Rights in Chile, United Nations Commission on Human Rights, Sub-Commission on Prevention of Discrimination and Protection of Minorities, U.N. Doc. E/CN.4/Sub.2/412 (July 20, 1978). On the importance of the campaign against Chile to the development of human rights work generally, see Eckel, "'Under a Magnifying Glass'"; Patrick William Kelly, "The Chilean Coup and the Origins of Transnational Human Rights Activism," 8 *Journal of Global History* (2013), 165–86; Kelly, *Sovereign Emergencies*.

89 The Commission continued to receive complaints concerning other states as well, of course. In 1974, the Commission issued a ruling in the case of *Amalia Rada et al. v. Bolivia* (Case No. 1757, Int.-Am. Comm. H.R. (June 3, 1974)), in which it observed numerous violations by Bolivia relative to the arbitrary arrest of several women, and urged Bolivia to "adopt the measures necessary so that violations of the right to protection from arbitrary arrest and the right to due process of law in relation to the persons whose names appear above will immediately cease" and to "order an investigation" to determine the fate of three of the applicants. In 1975 the Commission issued a similar holding in its combined rulings on Cases 1702, 1748, and 1755, which concerned Guatemala (Int.-Am. Comm. H.R. (August 12, 1975)). Such holdings demonstrated the Commission's willingness to issue remedies of an expansive nature; at the same time, the Commission's holdings were still quite broad and vague, limiting their practical force.

90 The Commission's 1976 follow-up report on Chile was the first report of the Commission ever considered by the General Assembly of the OAS. As Quiroga has observed,

> From [1976] on an increasing interest in the situation of human rights in the Americas could be observed. The sheer number of pages dedicated to the discussion of the reports in the First Committee of the General Assembly and the number of references to human rights in the plenary meetings demonstrated the importance attached to the problem by all parties. This did not mean that the number of governments with a positive attitude towards human rights had increased, or that the debates had evolved towards a more meaningful attitude in the General Assembly. It meant, rather, that the topic of human rights touched an extremely sensitive point for most of the American governments.

Quiroga, *Battle of Human Rights*, 157.

its approach, including its review of the situation in Chile in a separate section of its annual report, a practice it continued from 1977 to 1980.

In 1979, the Commission undertook a trip to Argentina, which followed the model set by the Chilean mission. Thousands of complaints were submitted, resulting in a report forcefully condemning the rights violations committed by the Argentinian government. Argentina was more powerful than Chile, however, and when the Commission attempted to include a separate section within its annual report highlighting the human rights situation in Argentina, it was met with an immediate backlash so forceful that it temporarily decided to exclude such sections from its annual reports.[91] Instead, the Commission found another way to address the issue: in the following years, it utilized its power to "prepare such studies or reports as it considers advisable in the performance of its duties" both to report in depth on the rights situation in particular countries, and to explore particular rights issues on a more focused basis.[92] In the early 1980s in particular, the Commission demonstrated a preference for addressing the region's rights violations through systemic reports rather than through individual case review.[93]

[91] The Commission resumed the practice in 1984, after the tension had died down.

[92] For further discussion of the manner in which the Commission creatively expanded its role in this period, see Farer, "The Rise of the Inter-American Human Rights Regime," 520–2. Other important components of the Convention relative to the Commission included the fact that it established the right of petition to the Commission in liberal terms, and its generally positive approach to the publication of Commission reports. See ACHR, Articles 44, 50–1. The Convention's provisions on independence fell short of what rights advocates would have desired, however, by stipulating that the secretariat of the Commission would be considered formally a part of the OAS's general secretariat, and by preserving the Secretary General's power to appoint the Executive Secretary of the Commission's secretariat. For more, see Robert Norris, "The New Statute of the Inter-American Commission on Human Rights," 1 *Human Rights Law Journal* (1980), 379–83; Veronica Gomez, "The Interaction between the Political Actors of the OAS, the Commission and the Court," in David Harris and Stephen Livingstone eds., *The Inter-American System of Human Rights* (Clarendon Press, 1998), 204–5.

[93] In the 1983 *Cases of Disappeared Persons in Chile* and *Cases of Disappeared Persons in Argentina*, for instance, the Commission noted that it had received large numbers of complaints from each country, in response to which, while it affirmed the responsibility of the governments involved for human rights violations, it also observed that it would "suspend consideration of the individual cases of disappeared persons" while "reserv[ing] the right to reopen processing of cases in which new important evidence appears" *Cases of Disappeared Persons in Chile*, Res. No. 11/83, Int.-Am. Comm. H.R. (July 1, 1983), operative para. 4. The holding in the *Cases of Disappearance of Persons in Guatemala* in 1986 was similar. Meanwhile, a fourth assertive report relative to the human rights situation in Chile was issued by the Commission in 1985.

The authoritarian climate prevailing in the Americas when the Court was formed did not dissipate with the Court's creation. Rather, the next major change in the political situation came with the replacement of Carter by Reagan, who reversed Carter's substantive emphasis on rights as a component of foreign policy, though without abandoning the use of high-flying rights rhetoric to condemn the United States' perceived enemies, a rhetoric which was combined with the provision of extensive financing and support to many of the region's worst rights violators.[94] The shift in US foreign policy had an effect on regional rights work, leading the Commission to scale back its advocacy in the early 1980s. Whether due to political tentativeness or another reason – for instance institutional rivalry or simply the practical challenge posed by the fact that submitting cases required an already overstretched Commission to engage in a new and technically demanding task – the Commission did not submit any cases to the Court during the Court's first seven years of existence, from 1979 to 1985.

The tension between the two bodies was dramatically demonstrated by the case of *Viviana Gallardo*. The case concerned the murder of Gallardo and the wounding of two others by a member of the Costa Rican civil guard, while Gallardo and the others were detained on charges of having carried out terrorist attacks. Costa Rica, ever a supporter of the Court, took the highly unusual step of referring the case against itself in 1981. The Court determined that it was inappropriate for the matter to come before it directly; rather, the Commission should serve as reviewer of first instance.[95] In 1983, two years after the Court referred the case to the Commission, the Commission found the matter inadmissible. While it

[94] For more, see Forsythe, "Human Rights and U.S. Foreign Policy," 441–3; Goldman, "History and Action," 872. On the longer-term history of the United States' support for right-wing authoritarian military regimes in Latin America, see David Schmitz, *Thank God They're on Our Side: The United States and Right-Wing Dictatorships, 1921–1965* (University of North Carolina Press, 1999); Lesley Gill, *The School of the Americas: Military Training and Political Violence in the Americas* (Duke University Press, 2004); David Schmitz, *The United States and Right-Wing Dictatorships, 1965–1989* (Cambridge University Press, 2006); Greg Grandin, *Empire's Workshop: Latin America, the United States and the Rise of the New Imperialism* (Holt, 2006); Stephen Rabe, *The Killing Zone: The United States Wages Cold War in Latin America* (Oxford University Press, 2012).

[95] The Court reasoned that this was appropriate both in order to bring in the concerned victims, and in order to promote the possibility of friendly settlement. In the Matter of Viviana Gallardo et al., Int.-Am. Ct. H.R., Advisory Opinion No. G 101/81 (November 13, 1981), paras. 23–5.

might have referred this decision to the Court, the Commission did not do so, to the Court's clear frustration.[96]

While it refused to consider the *Viviana Gallardo* case, the Commission did take its first tentative steps toward a closer relationship with the Court by twice sending the Court requests for advisory opinions. The second and more significant of these requests pertained to whether a state might adopt a law imposing the death penalty after its acceptance of the American Convention. While the Commission put its question as a general one, it was clear from the context that the request for an advisory opinion concerned a complaint against Guatemala ongoing before the Commission. This was procedurally questionable, given that Guatemala had not accepted the jurisdiction of the Court. The Court deemed the referral reasonable, however, and found imposition of the death penalty to run contrary to the Convention.[97] Rather than objecting, Guatemala complied with the Court and the Commission's recommendations, suspending application of the death penalty in the relevant cases.

The Court was dissatisfied, however, with only receiving occasional requests for advisory opinions from the Commission, and its judges increasingly frustrated by their inability to play a more active role.[98] Things came to a head in the Stephen Schmidt case. Mr. Schmidt was an

[96] One judge went so far as to chastise the Commission in the context of the Court's subsequent judgment removing the matter from its docket. See In the Matter of Viviana Gallardo et al., Int.-Am. Ct. H.R., Advisory Opinion No. G 101/81 (September 8, 1983), Piza dissent.

[97] See Restrictions to the Death Penalty (Arts 4(2) and 4(4) American Convention on Human Rights), Int.-Am. Ct. H.R., Advisory Opinion OC-3/83 (September 8, 1983).

[98] On criticism of the Commission's nonreferral of cases, see Jane Peddicord, "The American Convention on Human Rights: Potential Defects and Remedies," 19 *Texas International Law Journal* (1984), 139–59; Farer, "The Rise of the Inter-American Human Rights Regime." As for the Court, in addition to Piza's statement, referenced in note 96, Buergenthal, another of the Court's judges, wrote in 1982:

> If the Commission were to resort to the Court's advisory and contentious jurisdiction, and do so in a judicious and creative manner, it could play an important role in strengthening the institutional framework and constitutional legitimacy of the entire inter-American human rights system. That the system urgently needs to be reinforced and that it would greatly benefit, particularly now, from judicial reaffirmation of its constitutional legitimacy can hardly be doubted.
>
> The Commission, more than any other OAS organ, has the legal authority and professional competence to lead this effort. Whether it also has the necessary wisdom to do so remains to be seen.

Buergenthal, "The Inter-American Court," 245.

American who had been working as a journalist in Costa Rica, without possessing the journalistic license required by Costa Rican law. In a contested decision, the Commission narrowly concluded that Costa Rica's journalistic licensing requirement did not violate Costa Rica's regional rights obligations.[99] Given that the case concerned a novel, important issue of jurisprudence, the Court expected the Commission to refer it on for their consideration; the Commission, however, declined to do so. Once again, however, Costa Rica stepped forward on the Court's behalf, requesting an advisory opinion from the Court on the matter, despite the fact the case had already resulted in a holding favorable to Costa Rica. In its advisory decision,[100] the Court found that the Commission's decision had been mistaken, and that the Costa Rican requirement that journalists be licensed did indeed violate the American Convention. Along the way, the Court delivered a strong rebuke to the Commission, observing that:

> It is implicit in the functions that the Convention assigns to the Commission and to the Court that certain cases should be referred by the former to the Court … The Schmidt case clearly falls into this category. The controversial legal issues it raised had not been previously considered by the Court; the domestic proceedings in Costa Rica produced conflicting judicial decisions; the Commission itself was not able to arrive at a unanimous decision on the relevant legal issues; and its subject is a matter of special importance to the hemisphere because several states have adopted laws similar to that of Costa Rica.[101]

Shortly thereafter, the Commission began referring cases to the Court. In 1986 it referred three cases – *Velásquez Rodríguez, Godinez Cruz,* and *Fairen-Grabi and Solis-Corrales*.[102] All three concerned widespread and serious violations committed in Honduras, including forced disappearance. Starved of cases for many years, the Court was eager to seize its opportunity. The Court's early decisions were groundbreaking, setting important precedents in the areas of forced disappearance, the duty to investigate, burden of proof and admissibility that remain influential

[99] Int.-Am. Comm. H.R., Annual Report 1984–5, Res. 17/84, OEA/Ser.L/V/II.66 Doc. 10 Rev. 1, at 51–77 (1985).

[100] Compulsory Membership in an Association Prescribed by Law for the Practice of Journalism (Arts 13 and 29), Int.-Am. Ct. H.R., Advisory Opinion OC-5/85 (November 13, 1985).

[101] Ibid., para 25.

[102] Velásquez Rodríguez v. Honduras, App. No. 7920, Int.-Am. Ct. H.R. (July 29, 1988); Saul Godinez Cruz v. Honduras, App. No. 8097, Int.-Am. Ct. H.R. (January 20, 1989); Francisco Fairen-Grabi and Yolanda Solis-Corrales v. Honduras, App. No. 7951, Int.-Am. Ct. H.R. (March 15, 1989). The three cases were selected from among a larger caseload of similar cases.

to the present day. In all three cases the Court found numerous violations of the Convention and ordered Honduras to pay reparations to the next-of-kin of the victims. Through their assertive tone and content, the Honduras cases established the Court from the beginning as a forceful and powerful actor, willing to push back directly against the most serious rights violations occurring in the hemisphere.

Shortly after the Court's first judgments the Cold War ended, opening up substantial space for the advancement of human rights institutions in the Americas as elsewhere around the world. In the following years the Commission and the Court developed their body of jurisprudence, building on the assertive momentum *Velásquez Rodríguez* had imparted. Central to the development of the system's approach was the use to which it put the cases of widespread and serious violations that formed the core of its docket. In the 1980s and 1990s many countries in the region transitioned toward more democratic governance, with civilian governments assuming power in Ecuador in 1979, in Argentina in 1983, in Brazil and Uruguay in 1985, and in Chile in 1989. In the 1990s, the Inter-American human rights system was therefore able to begin to address the legacy of authoritarian governance and the mass rights violations authoritarian governments had committed. The presence of new, more democratic governments in many countries in the region provided the Inter-American system with a key source of political support as it sought to tackle abuses committed by previous regimes. As the system was now able to contemplate past abuses and present transitional efforts side-by-side, moreover, it was able to devote increasing attention not only to the original violations, but also to transitional processes, which it endeavored to support.

Key early rulings concerning authoritarian legacies came in the form of a pair of decisions issued by the Commission in 1992, *Alicia Consuelo Herrera et al.* and *Hugo Leonardo de los Santos Mendoza et al.*,[103] which concerned the amnesties that had been put in place following the democratic transitions in Argentina and Uruguay. In both cases, the Commission found that the amnesties violated the states' obligations to guarantee the rights to a fair trial and to judicial protection, which, the Commission held, required that the states undertake investigations into serious crimes. Both holdings

[103] Alicia Consuelo Herrera et al. v. Argentina, App. Nos. 10.147, 10.181, 10.240, 10.262, 10.309, & 10.311, Int.-Am. Comm. H.R. (October 2, 1992) and Hugo Leonardo de los Santos Mendoza et al. v. Uruguay, App. Nos. 10.029, 10.036, 10.145, 10.305, 10.373, 10.374, & 10.375, Int.-Am. Comm. H.R. (October 2, 1992).

concluded with a recommendation that the states "adopt the measures necessary to clarify the facts and identify those responsible for the human rights violations that occurred during the past military dictatorship,"[104] emphasizing the need not only for accountability, but also for the establishment of an accurate historical record.

A few years later, the Commission was called upon to confront the amnesty that had been declared in Chile. The Commission addressed the issue twice, first in *Meneses et al. v. Chile,*[105] in 1996, and then again in *Alfonso Rene Chanfreau et al. v. Chile,*[106] in 1998. The Commission's holding in *Alfonso Rene Chanfreau* was particularly confident: while supranational rights bodies were typically cautious in terms of their recommendations, suggesting rather than directly calling for national-level legal reforms, in *Alfonso Rene Chanfreau* the Commission adopted a bolder line, calling directly on Chile to amend its amnesty law.[107]

Another important case in the period, that could be considered both part and parcel of the system's broader turn to transitional justice as well as the start of a new emphasis on marginalized communities, saw the system turn its attention to grave rights violations in Suriname. *Aloeboetoe v. Suriname* concerned the massacre of several members of an Afro-Surinamese community in 1987. The Court's judgment was notable not for its finding of violations, which were plainly apparent, but rather for its approach to remedies.[108] Rather than following the European system's approach, emphasizing "declaratory remedies" (i.e., the issuance of a judgment finding a violation) and potentially ordering a largely symbolic cash payment, the Court took a more expansive approach, ordering Suriname to ensure adequate education and healthcare in Gujaba and to establish

104 *Alicia Consuelo Herrera,* Recommendations para. 3; *Hugo Leonardo de los Santos Mendoza,* Recommendations para. 3.

105 App. Nos. 11.228, 11.229, 11.231, & 11.282 et al., Int.-Am. Comm. H.R. (October 15, 1996).

106 App. Nos. 11.505 et al., Int.-Am. Comm. H.R. (April 7, 1998).

107 Specifically, the Commission recommended:

> that the State of Chile adjust its domestic legislation by derogating Decree-Law 2191 enacted in 1978, in order to comply with the provisions of the American Convention on Human Rights, in order that the human rights violations of the military de facto government may be investigated and the perpetrators may be identified, their responsibility established and that they may be effectively punished, thus guaranteeing for the victims and their families the right to justice.

Ibid., para. 109.

108 See Aloeboetoe v. Suriname, App. No. 10.150, Int.-Am. Ct. H.R., Reparations and Costs (September 10, 1993).

a trust fund for the victims' relatives.[109] Between them, these remedial orders represented a step away from a purely individuated response and toward a more systemic one, imagining the violation in question to reside not merely in the past massacre alone, but also in the underlying situation of structural inequality that had enabled it and that persisted.

Alongside these more dramatic holdings, a number of Court cases from the period were notable for what might seem more insignificant, formalistic reasons, but which all contributed to the expansive approach the Court was developing. *Blake v. Guatemala*, which concerned forced disappearance, was notable for a preliminary holding: while the violation had occurred before Guatemala had accepted the jurisdiction of the Court, the Court found it could nonetheless consider it, as, in its judgment, the harm constituted a "continuing violation."[110] While the idea of "continuing violations" was not novel, application of the concept in the context of forced disappearances represented an extension of the underlying idea, potentially enabling the further extension of the concept in the years to come.

Around the same time, in a series of cases in the mid-1990s the Court was confronted with the question of whether or not it could pass judgment on laws in particular countries, even when they had not been enforced.

[109] In doing so, *Aloeboetoe* helped to initiate the practice of increasingly detailed and expansive remedial judgments. As one observer has noted,

> The Aloeboetoe ruling marked a level of remedial activism that would not be even approximated for another five years in Inter-American case law. A study of the few cases from the period indicates that Aloeboetoe's generous non-monetary reparations are hardly representative of the Court's general approach.

Key to the adoption of such a generous approach, it seems, was:

> an unprecedented visit made by the Court's Deputy Secretary to Suriname. It was decided that the Deputy Secretary "would travel to Suriname in order to gather additional information regarding the economic, financial, and banking situation of the country [and to] visit the village of Gujaba to obtain data that would enable the Court to deliver a judgment taking into account the prevailing conditions" … This personal visit likely occasioned a more sympathetic and generous approach to remedies in the case.

Antkowiak, "Remedial Approaches to Human Rights Violations," 366. The progressive nature of the call for the creation of a trust fund was somewhat limited by the fact that the Court called for the trust-fund to be managed by a foundation, rather than by the community itself. See Ariel Dulitzky, "When Afro-Descendants Became 'Tribal Peoples': The Inter-American Human Rights System and Rural Black Communities," 15 *UCLA Journal of International Law and Foreign Affairs* (2010), 29–81.

[110] See Blake v. Guatemala, App No. 11.219, Int.-Am. Ct. H.R., Preliminary Objections (July 2, 1996).

The Court's initial answer was no; in a series of dissents, however, Judge Trindade suggested the answer should be yes, along the way highlighting that laws should not be thought of as activated only when actively employed, but rather that they should be thought of as having continuous effects.[111] Trindade's approach was ultimately endorsed by the Court in *Suarez Rosero v. Ecuador*, in which the Court found that a certain provision of the Ecuadorian Penal Code "violates *per se* Article 2 of the American Convention, whether or not it was enforced in the instant case."[112]

On one level, such developments were formalistic, pertaining to questions of jurisdiction, rather than to the Court's substantive law. On another level, the system's approach could be seen to be changing with the Court's recognition of a more expansive notion of continuing violations and of the idea that laws alone might violate human rights even when they were not actively applied. Through these opinions, the Court gradually expanded the frame in which it viewed the field of human rights, moving away from a more concrete and atomistic vision, in which human rights violations might be defined by a specific time and space, and viewed as exceptions to the norm, toward of vision of violations as ongoing states of affairs, extended in time, because violations might be continuous, as well as in space, because laws, by their very existence, could be understood to violate the rights of all individuals or at the very least a distinct subset of individuals within a particular polity. The Court, in short, was moving away from an individualistic notion of human rights and human rights violations toward a more structural and systemic vision, in which rights violations could be understood as interwoven into the fabric of law and policy and as extending over time.

The progressive trend in the Inter-American system's approach as it developed from the late 1980s had a high point in 2001. As one observer has noted, "The Court unleashed a barrage of reparations judgments in

[111] See El Amparo v. Venezuela, App. No. 10.602, Int.-Am. Ct. H.R., Reparations, Trindade dissent, paras. 2–3, 5, 7, 10 (September 14, 1996); El Amparo v. Venezuela, App. No. 10.602, Int.-Am. Ct. H.R., Interpretation of Reparations, Trindade dissent, paras. 22–3 (April 16, 1997); Genie Lacoyo v. Nicaragua, App. No. 10.792, Int.-Am. Ct. H.R., Application for Review, Trindade dissent, paras. 9, 27 (September 13, 1997). In making this argument, Trindade drew on the more expansive understanding of the nature of rights violations underpinning the idea of continuing violations.

[112] App. No. 11.273, Int.-Am. Ct. H.R., Merits, para. 98 (November 12, 1997). See also Cancado Trindade, "The Inter-American Court of Human Rights at a Crossroads: Current Challenges and Its Emerging Case-Law on the Eve of the New Century," in Mahoney et al. eds., *Protecting Human Rights* (Heymann, 2000), 182.

2001, ten in total, nearly doubling its jurisprudence on the subject."[113] The significance of the year to the development of the system's approach can be seen from three key decisions. First, there was *Olmedo Bustos et al. v. Chile*.[114] The case concerned debates over the appropriate manner in which to deal with controversial film material in Chile. The Cinematographic Council of Chile had allowed the film "The Last Temptation of Christ" to be shown, subject to a restricted viewership classification. Following appeal by concerned Christian citizens, however, the Supreme Court of Chile ultimately confirmed a lower-court ruling prohibiting the film. The matter was then brought to the Commission. The central significance of the Commission's 1998 holding was not that it suggested Chile's Supreme Court's decision had violated the right to freedom of expression, though that was significant in its own right. Rather, the most significant part of the decision was the remedy the Commission proposed, as it called upon Chile not only to alter its law, but also to amend its constitution. The Court was not ultimately called upon to go quite as far, as Chile had already taken steps toward constitutional reform by the time it ruled on the matter in 2001. The Court did, however, express its approval of those reforms, while echoing the Commission's calls for reform of the law.[115] Thus *Olmedo Bustos*, which concerned a relatively minor rights violation, in comparison to many of the cases the Inter-American system had considered, saw the system take a momentous step forward in terms of its willingness to call for serious national-level legal reforms, implicitly suggesting the hierarchical superiority of the regional human rights order over every national constitutional order.[116]

113 Antkowiak, "Remedial Approaches to Human Rights Violations," 371–2. Antkowiak further notes that

> the new millennium … ushered in the era of multiple-victim cases before the Court. By way of comparison, in the 1996 decision el Amparo, the Tribunal granted reparations for sixteen victims, the largest case of the first decade in which it was considering contentious matters. In 2001, Baena-Ricardo v. Panama involved 270 state employees who had been arbitrarily dismissed from their jobs – setting the Court down a path to progressively larger cases that continues to the present day.

Idib., 372.

114 App. No. 11.803, Int.-Am. Comm. H.R. (September 29, 1998); App. No. 11.803, Int.-Am. Ct. H.R., Merits, Reparations and Costs (February 5, 2001).

115 Olmedo Bustos et al. v. Chile, App. No. 11.803, Int.-Am. Ct. H.R., Merits, Reparations and Costs (February 5, 2001), para. 89.

116 For more on the case, and the manner in which it has been interpreted as part of the system's "constitutionalization," see Eduardo Ferrer Mac-Gregor Poisot, "Conventionality

The second major decision in 2001 was in *Barrios Altos v. Peru,*[117] in which the Court staked out a clear, forceful position on amnesties. In 1991, a death squad linked to military intelligence attacked a neighborhood barbecue in the Barrios Altos neighborhood of Lima, Peru, killing fifteen people and injuring many others. An investigation was commenced, but halted shortly thereafter, when President Fujimori shuttered the legislature and judiciary and declared a state of emergency in the name of fighting terrorism. Attempts to resume investigations in 1995 were cut short by passage of an amnesty law. In late 2000 Fujimori was removed from office; shortly thereafter, the Inter-American Court issued its judgment. Emboldened by the supportive stance adopted by the new, rights-supportive representatives of the Peruvian government,[118] the Court not only found that Peru's amnesty laws were incompatible with the American Convention, but also went as far as to observe that due to that incompatibility those laws "lack[ed] legal effect."[119] In using such language the Court was not only suggesting, as it had before, that Peru should change its laws, but also implying that human rights law should be understood as having been consistently present and operative within the Peruvian domestic legal system all along, with the implication that the amnesty might be understood to have never had legal force to begin with.[120] Like *Olmedo Bustos,* therefore, albeit in a different fashion, the case advanced a view of human rights law as omnipresent and supreme within national legal orders.[121]

Control: The New Doctrine of the Inter-American Court of Human Rights," *American Journal of International Law Unbound* Symposium on the Constitutionalization of International Law in Latin America (November 11, 2015), citing Laurence Burgorgue-Larsen, "La Corte Interamericana de Derechos Humanos como tribunal constitucional," in Armin von Bogdandy et al. eds., *Ius constitutionale commune en America Latin* (Oxford University Press, 2014) and Eduardo Ferrer Mac-Gregor Poisot, "La Corte Interamericana de Derechos Humanos como interprete constitucional. Dimension transnacional del derecho procesal constitucional," in Deigo Valades and Rodrigo Rivas eds., *Memoria del IV Congreso Nacional de Derecho Constitucional* (Universidad Nacional Autónoma de México, 2001).

117 App. No. 11.528, Int.-Am. Ct. H.R., Merits (March 14, 2001).

118 For more on the human rights community in Peru in general, see Coletta Youngers, *Violencia politica y sociedad civil en el Perú: Historia de Coordinadora Nacional de Derechos Humanos* (Instituto de Estudios Peruanos, 2003).

119 Ibid., operative para. 4.

120 For emphasis on a similar point, see Poisot, "Conventionality Control."

121 The decision would be followed by several more decisions on amnesty laws in years to come, in particular Almonacid Arellano et al. v. Chile, App. No. 12.057, Int.-Am. Ct. H.R., Preliminary Objections, Merits, Reparations and Costs (September 26, 2006); Gomes Lund et al. v. Brazil, App. No. 11.552, Int.-Am. Ct. H.R., Preliminary Objections,

The third major 2001 decision came in *Mayagna Awas Tingni Community v. Nicaragua*,[122] in which the Court turned its attention to the rights of indigenous communities. The Awas Tingni were an indigenous community consisting of a few thousand people living in a densely forested area on the Atlantic coast of Nicaragua. The case was brought in large part as a challenge to a concession which would have allowed a significant portion of the rainforest area in which the Awas Tingni lived to be exploited by a logging company. In its judgment, the Court found that Nicaragua had violated the rights of the community, and called on Nicaragua to adopt "legislative, administrative, and any other measures required to create an effective mechanism for the delimitation, demarcation, and titling of the property of indigenous communities," and to carry out that demarcation within 15 months.[123] In addition, the case made clear that indigenous people have the right to participate in decisions affecting them. The case thus saw the system beginning to devote greater attention to the rights of indigenous communities, and represented a further development of its willingness to consider complex, collective claims on behalf of communities more broadly.[124]

These judgments were complemented by procedural developments. In the Court's decision in the Honduran cases, it set an important precedent relative to the role of individuals before it: while, as per the American Convention, the Commission was formally the party before the Court, from those early contentious hearings the Court allowed the Commission to consult with claimants' lawyers and to call them as

Merits, Reparations and Costs (November 24, 2010) (discussed further later); Gelman v. Uruguay, App. No. 12.607, Int.-Am. Ct. H.R., Merits and Reparations (February 24, 2011); and Massacres of El Mozote v. El Salvador, App. No. 10.720, Int.-Am. Ct. H.R., Merits, Reparations and Costs (October 25, 2012). *Almonacid* in particular has been hailed for further clarifying and emphasizing the domestic applicability of human rights law implied by *Barrios Altos*.

122 App. No. 11.577, Int.-Am. Ct. H.R., Merits (August 31, 2001).

123 Ibid., para. 164 and operative para. 3.

124 On the significance of the case, one pair of commentators have observed that while "the people of Awas Tingni did not set about to forge an international legal precedent with implications for indigenous peoples throughout the world … that is what they have done." Anaya and Grossman, "The Case of Awas Tingni v. Nicaragua," 1. See also Mario Melo, "Recent Advances in the Justiciability of Indigenous Rights in the Inter-American System of Human Rights," 4 *SUR International Journal of Human Rights* (2006), 31–50; S. James Anaya and Maia S. Campbell, "Gaining Legal Recognition of Indigenous Land Rights: The Story of the Awas Tingni Case in Nicaragua," in Deena R. Hurwitz and Margaret L. Satterthwaite eds., *Human Rights Advocacy Stories* (Foundation, 2009), 117–54.

witnesses freely.[125] By the beginning of the 2000s, claimants were granted the ability to directly represent themselves before the Court.[126] By the decade's end, information as to the Commission's findings was formally to be shared with claimants.[127] The decade saw the independence of the Commission and the Court enhanced as well, as the Executive Secretary of the Commission was given the power to appoint his own staff, including a newly created communication unit, while the Court took over the process of managing its Secretariat.

### *III.2 From Mass to Structural Violation*

The Inter-American system's trajectory in the new millennium has been more fraught. On the one hand, the system has continued to develop an expansive approach to its mandate, along the lines suggested by the developments considered earlier. This has been linked to several subsets of cases, including cases focused on repressive public order structures, as well as cases addressing indigenous peoples' rights, violence against women and marginalized groups' rights, areas of focus which are addressed in turn later. At the same time, the system has also faced numerous serious challenges to its legitimacy and ability to function, also addressed later.

125 Pressure toward reform of the system, and greater recognition for claimants and their representatives, began from the Court's first decisions as well, with Judge Piza in particular underscoring the importance of making claimants the parties before the Court. Velásquez Rodríguez v. Honduras, Case No. 7920, Int.-Am. Ct. H.R. (July 28, 1988), Separate Opinion of Judge Rodolgo E. Piza Escalante. In making this point, Judge Piza drew on his earlier emphasis on the importance of the participation of claimants in the Court's *Gallardo* decision, in his dissent to which he had noted that the limitation on such participation was:

> a "repugnant matter" (materia odiosa) and should thus be interpreted restrictively. Therefore, one cannot draw from that limitation the conclusion that the individual is also barred from his autonomous condition of "party" in the procedures once they have begun. On the other hand, it is possible, even imperative, to grant to the individual that role …

In the Matter of Viviana Gallardo et al., Int.-Am. Ct. H.R., Advisory Opinion No. G 101/81 (September 18, 1983), Dissenting Opinion of Judge Rodolgo E. Piza E., para. 40. In addition to the procedural developments pertaining to representation before the Court, the Honduras cases also saw the Court take the important procedural step of having the Honduran judge recuse himself.

126 In accordance with the Court's fourth rules of procedure, adopted in 2001. *See* Rules of Procedure, Int.-Am. Ct. H.R. (2001), Article 23.

127 See ibid., Article 43, stipulating that the Commission should share its initial reports with claimants.

One set of significant cases within the more recent history of the Inter-American system have focused on what might broadly be termed the reform of repressive public-order structures. While the jurisprudential content of such cases was not unusual in a human rights context, the cases in question were noteworthy because of the relatively holistic, broad-brush strokes they took toward such reform. Numerous cases falling upon such lines could be referenced; a small sample will, however, suffice. In *Hilaire,* which concerned the application of the death penalty in Trinidad and Tobago, the Court ordered Trinidad and Tobago to undertake legal reforms, to grant new trials and to reform its prison system.[128] In *Lori Berenson Mejia v. Peru,* the Court ordered Peru to amend its legal framework on terrorism and to reform its prison system.[129] In *Gutierrez-Soler*, the Court ordered Colombia to adopt a series of measures designed to dramatically reform the operations of its criminal justice and security systems.[130] In *Gomez-Palomino,* the Court ordered Peru to amend its law in order to firmly establish the criminality of enforced disappearance.[131] In *Palamara-Iribarne,* the Court

[128] See Hilaire et al. v. Trinidad & Tobago, App. Nos. 11.816 et al., Int.-Am. Ct. H.R., Merits, Reparations and Costs (June 21, 2002), operative paras. 8–9, 14. The system's advocacy on this issue was less than successful in practice, however, as, by the time of the Court's decision, Trinidad and Tobago had already withdrawn from the American Convention, in the face of the system's strong advocacy on the matter.

[129] See Lori Berenson Mejia v. Peru, App. No. 11.876, Int.-Am. Ct. H.R., Merits, Reparations and Costs (November 25, 2004).

[130] See Gutierrez-Soler v. Colombia, App. No. 12.291, Int.-Am. Ct. H.R., Merits, Reparations and Costs (September 12, 2005). Other similar cases include Caracazo v. Venezuela, Int.-Am. Ct. H.R., Reparations and Costs (August 29, 2002); Blanco-Romero et al. v. Venezuela, App. Nos. 12.256, 12.258, & 12.307, Int.-Am. Ct. H.R., Merits, Reparations and Costs (November 28, 2005); Ximenes-Lopes v. Brazil, App. No. 12.237, Int.-Am. Ct. H.R., Merits, Reparations and Costs (June 4, 2006); Montero-Aranguren v. Venezuela, App. No. 11.699, Int.-Am. Ct. H.R., Preliminary Objections, Merits, Reparations and Costs (July 5, 2006); Oscar Elias Biscet et al. v. Cuba, App. No. 12.476, Int.-Am. Comm. H.R. (October 21, 2006); and La Cantuta et al. v. Peru, App. No. 11.045, Int.-Am. Ct. H.R., Merits, Reparations and Costs (November 29, 2006).

[131] See Gomez-Palomino v. Peru, App. No. 11.062, Int.-Am. Ct. H.R., Merits, Reparations and Costs (November 22, 2005). Other, similar cases include Vargas-Areco v. Paraguay, App. No. 12.300, Int.-Am. Ct. H.R., Merits, Reparations and Costs (September 26, 2006), which also addressed the problem of child soldiers; and, relative to the necessity of adopting legal frameworks that effectively combat enforced disappearance, Goiburu et al. v. Paraguay, App. Nos. 11.560, 11.665, & 11.667, Int.-Am. Ct. H.R., Merits, Reparations and Costs (September 22, 2006); Heliodoro Portugal v. Panama, App. No. 12.408, Int.-Am. Ct. H.R., Preliminary Objections, Merits, Reparations and Costs (August 12, 2008); Radilla Pacheco v. Mexico, Int.-Am. Ct. H.R., Preliminary Objections, Merits, Reparations and Costs (November 23, 2009); Anzualdo Castro v. Peru, App. No. 11.385, Int.-Am. Ct.

ordered Chile to amend several components of its law to bring them into compliance with its obligation to uphold the right to freedom of expression, and to restrict and amend various components of its military justice system.[132] In *Apitz Barbera,* the Court called for reforms to Venezuela's domestic remedial system.[133] Above all, these cases were notable because of the manner in which they saw the Court approaching its case consideration mandate: rather than accepting that a case must be tightly focused on a narrow set of facts and legal claims, the Court adopted a broader approach, issuing remedial orders calling for extensive changes to major components of national legal and institutional systems.

Alongside its consideration of such cases, the Inter-American system continued to address amnesties. The significance of the system's amnesty cases was consistently recognized. Perhaps most widely known and commented on was the Court's 2006 judgment in *Almonacid Arellano,*[134] which concerned amnesty laws in Chile. *Almonacid* became well known for its enunciation of the doctrine of "conventionality control" – that is, the understanding that domestic judiciaries must ensure the compliance of their domestic legal orders with the obligations contained in the American Convention.[135] In clearly enunciating this obligation, the Court

H.R., Preliminary Objections, Merits, Reparations and Costs (September 22, 2009); and Gonzalez Medina and Family v. Dominican Republic, App. No. 11.324, Int.-Am. Ct. H.R., Preliminary Objections, Merits, Reparations and Costs (February 27, 2012)).

132 Palamara-Iribarne v. Chile, App. No. 11.571, Int.-Am. Ct. H.R., Merits, Reparations and Costs (November 22, 2005). In *Claude-Reyes v. Chile*, decided the following year, the Court went even further, at least in terms of requiring a positive legislative step rather than simply the amendment of negative components of existing laws, by ordering Chile to adopt a law on access to information. *See* Claude-Reyes v. Chile, App. No. 12.108, Int.-Am. Ct. H.R., Merits, Reparations and Costs (September 19, 2006).

133 See Apitz Barbera et al. v. Venezuela, App. No. 12.489, Int.-Am. Ct. H.R., Preliminary Objections, Merits, Reparations and Costs (August 5, 2008). Similar remedial orders came in Reveron-Trujillo v. Venezuela, App. No. 12.565, Int.-Am. Ct. H.R., Preliminary Objections, Merits, Reparations and Costs (June 30, 2009); Barreto Leiva v. Venezuela, App. No. 11.663, Int.-Am. Ct. H.R., Merits, Reparations and Costs (November 17, 2009); and Chocrón Chocrón v. Venezuela, App. No. 12.556, Int.-Am. Ct. H.R., Preliminary Objections, Merits, Reparations and Costs (July 1, 2011).

134 App. No. 12.057, Int.-Am. Ct. H.R., Preliminary Objections, Merits, Reparations and Costs (September 26, 2006).

135 To quote the Court at length:

> domestic judges and courts are bound to respect the rule of law, and therefore, they are bound to apply the provisions in force within the legal system. But when a State has ratified an international treaty such as the American Convention, its judges, as part of the State, are also bound by such Convention. This forces them to see that all the effects of the provisions embodied in the Convention are not adversely affected

made explicit an element of its approach to human rights law that was previously only implicit: the idea that regional human rights law should not be understood solely as part of international law, but rather as a field of law continuously operative, in one manner or another, within domestic legal systems as well.

Another amnesty decision four years later, this time concerning Brazil, was important not only because it concerned Latin America's largest and most powerful country, but also because the Court went further than it had done previously in stipulating the consequences that should flow from

> by the enforcement of laws which are contrary to its purpose and that have not had any legal effects since their inception. In other words, the Judiciary must exercise a sort of "conventionality control" between the domestic legal provisions which are applied to specific cases and the American Convention on Human Rights. To perform this task, the Judiciary has to take into account not only the treaty, but also the interpretation thereof made by the Inter-American Court, which is the ultimate interpreter of the American Convention.

Ibid., para. 124. For some later decisions further explicating and expanding the scope of the "doctrine," *see* Dismissed Congressional Employees v. Peru, App. Nos. 11.830 & 12.038, Int.-Am. Ct. H.R., Preliminary Objections, Merits, Reparations and Costs (November 24, 2006); Cabrera García and Montiel Flores v. Mexico, App. No. 12.449, Int.-Am. Ct. H.R., Preliminary Objections, Merits, Reparations and Costs (November 26, 2010); Atala Riffo and Daughters v. Chile, App. No. 12.502, Int.-Am. Ct. H.R., Merits, Reparations and Costs (February 24, 2012); Gelman v. Uruguay, App. No. 12.607, Int.-Am. Ct. H.R., Monitoring Compliance with Judgment (March 20, 2013). For academic commentary, see Ernesto Rey Cantor, "Controles de convencionalidad de las leyes," in Eduardo Ferrer Mac-Gregor Poisot and Arturo Zaldívar Lelo de Larrea eds., *La Ciencia Del Derecho Procesal Constitucional: Estudios en Homenaje a Héctor Fix-Zamudio en sus Cincuentas Años como Investigador del Derecho* (Juricentro, 2008); Oswaldo Ruiz-Chiriboga, "The Conventionality Control: Examples of (Un)Successful Experiences in Latin America," 3 *Inter-American and European Human Rights Journal* (2010), 200–19; Eduardo Ferrer Mac-Gregor Poisot, "Reflexiones sobre el control difuso de convencionalidad. A la luz del caso Cabrera García y Montiel Flores vs. México," 131 *Boletin Mexicano de Derecho Comparado* (2011), 917–67; Eduardo Ferrer Mac-Gregor Poisot, "Interpretación conforme y control difuso de convencionalidad. El Nuevo paradigma para el juez mexicano," 9 *Estudios Constitucionales* (2011), 531–622; Sergio García Ramírez, "El control judicial interno de convencionalidad," 5 *Revista IUS* (2011); Castan, *Transformation of the Inter-American System*; Claudio Nash Rojas, "Control de convencionalidad. Precisiones conceptuales y desafíos a la luz de la jurisprudencia de la Corte Interamericana de Derecho Humanos," in Christian Steiner ed., *Anuario de Derecho Constitucional Latinoamericano* (Konrad Adenauer Stiftung, 2013), 489–510; Dulitzky, "An Inter-American Constitutional Court?"; Poisot, "Conventionality Control." The development of the doctrine of conventionality control was helped by the willingness of several American states to incorporate the American Convention into domestic law in one way or another. On the inter-linked trend toward the "judicialization of politics" in Latin America, see Rachel Sieder, Line Schjolden, and Alan Angell eds., *The Judicialization of Politics in Latin America* (Palgrave, 2009); Sieder, Huneeus, and Couso eds., *Cultures of Legality*; Huneeus, "Constitutional Lawyers."

its declaration of the illegality, under human rights law, of a local amnesty law. Between 1972 and 1975, seventy members of the communist party and other poor rural workers were arbitrarily detained, tortured, and forcibly disappeared in the Araguaia region of Brazil. In 1979 an amnesty law was passed, preventing effective investigations into the disappearances, and blocking the release of information from state archives to victims' next of kin. In *Gomes Lund* the Inter-American Court found that the amnesty constituted a systematic violation of the Convention, and consequently found Brazil's amnesty law to "lack legal effect."[136] In addition to ordering Brazil to investigate the crimes in question and punish those responsible, the Court called on Brazil to unambiguously criminalize forced disappearance, to reform its justice and security systems,[137] and to develop initiatives aimed at the systematic collection and publication of information on all human rights violations that occurred during the military regime.[138] As a result the case was notable not only for its challenge to an amnesty law, but also for the holistic approach it took to the question of transitional justice, by highlighting the need for legal reform as well as the need to produce an honest accounting of the wrongs of the past, obligations advanced under the heading of the "right to truth."[139]

136 Gomes Lund et al. v. Brazil, App. No. 11.552, Int.-Am. Ct. H.R., Preliminary Objections, Merits, Reparations and Costs (November 24, 2010), operative para. 3.

137 See ibid., operative paras. 9, 14–15. In issuing such orders, the Court built on the strong judgment it had issued in *"Las Dos Erres" Massacre v. Guatemala* (App. No. 11.681, Int.-Am. Ct. H.R., Preliminary Objections, Merits, Reparations and Costs (November 24, 2009)), which, while it had not addressed amnesty laws as such, had addressed a major massacre committed in Guatemala on December 6, 1982, and the subsequent impunity of the perpetrators. In its judgment, the Court found that the massacre had formed part of a systematic pattern of human rights violations, and that the state's lack of action to address the violations constituted a systematic failure of justice. See ibid., paras. 152, 170–1, 182, 198–9, 233, 247, 253. The Court consequently ordered Guatemala to take a wide-ranging set of remedial measures, including concrete steps to combat impunity and to amend its law on legal protection. See ibid., paras. 231–42, operative paras. 8–10.

138 Gomes Lund et al. v. Brazil, App. No. 11.552, Int.-Am. Ct. H.R., Preliminary Objections, Merits, Reparations and Costs (November 24, 2010), operative para. 16. In addition, the Court ordered Brazil to:

> carry out a summons in, at least, one newspaper of broad national circulation and one in the region where the facts occurred in the present case, or by other appropriate means, in order for, in a period of 24 months as of the notification of the Judgment, the next of kin of the persons indicated in paragraph 199 of the present Judgment, provide irrefutable evidence that would allow the State to identify them, and where applicable, consider them victims …

Ibid., operative para. 18.

139 See ibid., paras. 200–2, operative para. 6.

Two decisions in the second decade of the new millennium helped further develop the system's approach to repressive public order structures. The Court's decision in *Mendoza* concerned life sentences imposed on Mr. Mendoza and others for actions they had taken while minors.[140] After their detention, the applicants were tortured and subjected to inhuman detention conditions, leading to the death of one prisoner and the blindness of another. Although the prisoners complained to the domestic remedial system, no effective action was taken. While the Court could have simply highlighted the violations against the five petitioners involved in the case, it chose to go further, addressing the issues before it as comprehensively as the case allowed by calling for an extensive and specific set of amendments to Argentina's law, policy, and practice relative to juvenile criminals, conditions of detention, and investigative procedures.[141] The Commission's decision in *Clarence Allen Lackey* provided another example along similar lines. The case concerned the application of the death penalty to foreign nationals in the United States, long a major concern of foreign governments and human rights advocates. In its holding the Commission called for a detailed set of measures to be taken, including extensive reforms to the laws and procedures in the United States pertaining to the detention, trial, and punishment of foreign nationals.[142]

Another area in and through which the Inter-American system expanded its jurisprudence and advanced its approach in the twenty-first century was relative to indigenous peoples' rights.[143] One early important case in this context in the new millennium was *YATAMA v. Nicaragua*,[144]

[140] Mendoza et al. v. Argentina, App. No. 12.651, Int.-Am. Ct. H.R., Preliminary Objections, Merits and Reparations (May 14, 2013).

[141] See ibid., operative paras. 20–3.

[142] See Clarence Allen Lackey et al. v. United States, App. Nos. 11.575, 12.333, & 12.341, Int.-Am. Comm. H.R. (July 15, 2013), paras. 251.2–251.9, 252.

[143] For more on indigenous peoples' struggle for rights in the Americas generally, see Alison Brysk, *From Tribal Village to Global Village: Indian Rights and International Relations in Latin America* (Stanford University Press, 2000); Florencia Mallon, *Courage Tastes of Blood: The Mapuche Community of Nicolás Ailío and the Chilean State, 1906–2001* (Duke University Press, 2005); Pasqualucci, "The Evolution of International Indigenous Rights"; Shannon Speed, *Rights in Rebellion: Indigenous Struggle and Human Rights in Chiapas* (Stanford University Press, 2007); Álvaro Bello and José Aylwin eds., *Globalización, Derechos Humanos y Pueblos Indígenas* (Dialog, 2008); Rachael Sieder ed., *Demanding Justice and Security: Indigenous Women and Legal Pluralities in Latin America* (Rutgers University Press, 2017).

[144] App. No. 12.388, Int.-Am. Ct. H.R., Preliminary Objections, Merits, Reparations and Costs (June 23, 2005).

unusual in the context of indigenous peoples' rights cases in that it did not concern land rights, but rather Nicaragua's electoral framework. Yapti Tasba Masraka Nanih Asla Takanka – YATAMA for short – was a regional political party representing indigenous peoples from Nicaragua's Atlantic coast. In 2000, candidates from the YATAMA party were barred from participating in elections, due to their failure to comply with certain technical components of the electoral law. In its judgment, the Court found that the manner in which this limitation on the right to political participation had been imposed had been unreasonable, noting along the way the need for greater leeway to be granted to vulnerable and marginalized communities. The Court ordered Nicaragua to enact a series of reforms to its electoral law in order to remedy the situation.[145]

Even more significant was the Court's 2005 judgment in *Moiwana Village v. Suriname*.[146] At first glance, *Moiwana* might not have appeared closely related to indigenous peoples' rights, insofar as, like the earlier *Aloeboetoe* case, *Moiwana* concerned the "Maroon" community in Suriname, a community made up not only of the original inhabitants of the Americas, but also and primarily of the descendants of escaped African slaves. The case concerned a 1986 attack on Moiwana village, in which some thirty-five of the village's inhabitants, mostly women and children, were killed, after which the survivors fled. Following stalled investigations, including the murder of the inspector assigned to lead the investigation, a case concerning the Moiwana attacks was brought to the Inter-American system. The Court's judgment was significant for several reasons. First, it reaffirmed the Court's emphasis on continuing violations, this time expanded from the context of enforced disappearance to the context of the manner in which the Moiwana massacre had left the community in a state of continual suffering and vulnerability – a broadening of the concept that suggested an expansive underlying understanding of the nature of human rights violations. *Moiwana* also further developed the Court's emphasis on strong remedial measures: the court ordered Suriname to create a large "community development fund," to be administered by a committee including both state and community representatives, and to construct a memorial.[147]

145 See ibid., operative paras. 9–11.

146 App. No. 11.821, Int.-Am. Ct. H.R., Preliminary Objections, Merits, Reparations and Costs (June 15, 2005).

147 See ibid., operative paras. 5, 7.

*Moiwana* was followed by two judgments regarding Paraguay, *Yakye Axa* and *Sawhoyamaxa*, both of which concerned the occupation of indigenous peoples' land and the impoverishment of their communities.[148] *Yakye Axa* saw the Court go even further than it had in *Awas Tingni*, by recognizing not only indigenous communities' rights to property, but also that such rights should, at least in some circumstances, prevail over individual property claims. In both cases, the Court continued its development of progressive and expansive jurisprudence, including by calling for measures to support landless community members, the establishment of an effective mechanism to handle indigenous peoples' land rights claims, the establishment of a fund the communities could use to purchase land, the implementation of community development funds and projects, the creation of a communications system to enable community members to access emergency health services, and the creation of a program that would issue identification documents to those without them.[149]

These judgments were followed, in the years to come, by judgments addressing the conflicts arising from the exploitation of indigenous peoples' land by major commercial ventures, in the cases of *Pueblo Saramaka v. Suriname*[150] and *Sarayaku v. Ecuador.*[151] *Pueblo Saramaka* concerned logging and mining concessions that had been granted within the traditional territory of the Saramaka people, a Maroon community living in the Upper Suriname River region. *Sarayaku* concerned grave harms committed against the Sarayaku people by Ecuadorian oil companies and CGC, an Argentinian subsidiary of the oil company Chevron, which were given a contract to exploit oil resources in the traditional area of Sarayaku habitation. With the help of armed forces, oil company employees entered Sarayaku lands and detonated 1.5 tons of explosives, destroying sacred sites and sparking confrontations, which led to the deployment of further violence against members of the Sarayaku community. Among other conclusions, in both judgments the Court underscored the importance

[148] Yakye Axa Indigenous Community v. Paraguay, App. No. 12.313, Int. Am. Ct. H.R., Merits, Reparations and Costs (June 17, 2005); Sawhoyamaxa Indigenous Community v. Paraguay, App. No. 12.419, Int. Am. Ct. H.R., Merits, Reparations and Costs (March 29, 2006).

[149] See Sawhoyamaxa Indigenous Community v. Paraguay, App. No. 12.419, Int. Am. Ct. H.R., Merits, Reparations and Costs (March 29, 2006), operative paras. 6–7, 9–12.

[150] App. No. 12.338, Int.-Am. Ct. H.R., Preliminary Objections, Merits, Reparations and Costs (November 28, 2007).

[151] App. No. 12.465, Int.-Am. Ct. H.R., Merits and Reparations (June 27, 2012).

of free, prior, and informed consent before any commercial venture on indigenous land.

Another area to which the Inter-America system devoted attention in the new millennium, developing its approach along the way, was relative to women's rights in general, and violence against women in particular. An important early instance was the Commission's 2001 decision in *Maria da Penha Fernandes v. Brazil*.[152] Maria da Penha Fernandes was shot in her sleep by her husband in 1983; although a case on her behalf was brought within the Brazilian legal system, no significant progress was made for almost two decades. The matter was then brought to the Inter-American system. While the case most immediately concerned Maria da Penha's situation, it was also explicitly framed as brought on behalf of all women in Brazil, directed at the inadequacy of Brazil's policies concerning domestic violence. In its holding, the Commission called for broad structural remedies, enumerating in some detail the steps Brazil should take in order to deal systematically with the problem of domestic violence.[153] While it took several years, Brazil ultimately responded by adopting a new law on domestic violence.[154]

At the end of the 2000s, the Court issued three major rulings concerning violence against women in Mexico. In the 1990s and early 2000s Ciudad Juárez became infamous as the site of extensive violence against women. In one incident characteristic of a much larger pattern three women's bodies were found in a cotton field on November 6, 2001. The identities of the perpetrators were never discovered. In 2009, the Court issued a ruling on the matter in the *Gonzalez* case.[155] The Court's ruling was notable for the emphasis it put on the systematic, structural nature of the violations in question.[156] The Court made it clear that it expected

152 App. No. 12.051, Int.-Am. Comm. H.R. (April 16, 2001).

153 See ibid., operative paras. 2, 4.

154 For more on women's movements in Brazil, see Sonia Alvarez, *Engendering Democracy in Brazil: Women's Movements in Transnational Politics* (Princeton University Press, 1990); Nathalie Lebon, "Brazil: Popular Feminism and Its Roots and Alliances," in Richard Stahler-Sholk, Harry Vanden, and Marc Becker eds., *Rethinking Latin American Social Movements: Radical Action from Below* (Rowman & Littlefield, 2014), 147–65.

155 Case of Gonzalez et al. ("Cotton Field") v. Mexico, App. Nos. 12,496, 12,497, & 12,498, Int.-Am. Ct. H.R., Preliminary Objections, Merits, Reparations and Costs (November 16, 2009). The issue had been considered by the Commission two years earlier in Gonzalez et al. (Campo Algodonero) v. Mexico, App. Nos. 12.496, 12.497, & 12.498, Int.-Am. Comm. H.R. (November 4, 2007).

156 In particular, the Court observed that "although there are different motives for the murders in Ciudad Juárez and different perpetrators, many cases relate to gender violence that occurs in a context of systematic discrimination against women" (Case of Gonzalez

Mexico to take strong, holistic measures to address the structural problem at issue, including reforming the practices of its police and remedial services.[157] The Court's subsequent rulings in *Fernandez Ortega et al. v. Mexico*[158] and *Rosendo Cantú et al. v. Mexico*[159] followed similar lines, while also calling for further reform measures in relation to Mexico's code of military justice and its legal standards on rape, as well as for the establishment of community and education programs and services for women and girls in the areas in which the violations took place.

A further significant case addressing violence against women concerned the region's most powerful state, and perhaps the state most reluctant to accept supranational oversight, the United States. In June 1999 Ms. Gonzales' three children were abducted by her estranged husband, and subsequently found dead in the trunk of his car. Ms. Gonzalez had taken out a restraining order against her husband, but Colorado police refused to enforce it. Following a later legal complaint by Ms. Gonzalez, the US Supreme Court stipulated that she had no constitutional right to such protection. In its holding in *Jessica Lenahan* the Commission found that "systemic failures" had taken place, observing that the harms in question

et al. ("Cotton Field") v. Mexico, App. Nos. 12,496, 12,497, & 12,498, Int.-Am. Ct. H.R., Preliminary Objections, Merits, Reparations and Costs, para. 133 (November 16, 2009)); cited the CEDAW Committee's recognition that "the murders, kidnappings, disappearances and the domestic violence 'are not isolated, sporadic or episodic cases of violence; rather they represent a structural situation'" (ibid.); observed that the pattern of violations in question was "generalized and systematic" and one of "structural discrimination" (ibid., paras. 373, 450); found a systematic deficiency in terms of the manner in which Mexico's remedial institutions dealt with the matter (see ibid., para. 344); and observed the necessity of responding to systematic patterns of violation with approaches that identify and attempt to combat those systematic patterns, while noting that "certain lines of inquiry, which fail to analyze the systematic patterns surrounding a specific type of violations of human rights, can render the investigations ineffective" (ibid., para. 366). In making this latter point, the Court relied on its decision in the earlier *Rochela Massacre* case, in which it found that the obligation to investigate had not been complied with due in part to the fact that the investigation had not taken a systematic enough view of the violations in question (which would have led, according to the logic of the judgment, to identification of higher-level responsible parties). See Rochela Massacre v. Colombia, App. No. 11.995, Int.-Am. Ct. H.R., Merits, Reparations and Costs (May 11, 2007).

157 Ibid., operative paras. 12–14, 18–23.

158 App. No. 12.580, Int.-Am. Ct. H.R., Preliminary Objections, Merits, Reparations and Costs (August 30, 2010).

159 App. No. 12.579, Int.-Am. Ct. H.R., Preliminary Objections, Merits, Reparations and Costs (August 31, 2010).

> took place in a context where there has been a historical problem with the enforcement of protection orders; a problem that has disproportionately affected women – especially those pertaining to ethnic and racial minorities and to low-income groups ... Even though the Commission recognizes the legislation and programmatic efforts of the United States to address the problem of domestic violence, these measures had not been sufficiently put into practice in the present case.[160]

In consequence of this finding, the Commission called upon the United States to adopt a range of structural reform measures.[161] In line with previous cases, the holding was notable for the level of detail the Commission put into the measures it called upon the United States to take, based in significant part on the broader "systemic" lens through which it contemplated the violations in question.

A final key set of group rights cases concerned the rights of discriminated against groups. An important judgment in this area came in 2005. *Yean and Bosico v. Dominican Republic*[162] concerned a systemic pattern of discrimination against girls of Haitian descent born in the Dominican Republic, who were denied Dominican nationality and opportunities for education, and constantly threatened with deportation. The case was noteworthy for the broad lens it adopted, contemplating not only the situation of the claimants before it, but also a wide range of evidence going to the situations of Haitians in the Dominican Republic more broadly. In its judgment, the Court ordered the Dominican Republic to take a range of measures to bring discrimination against persons of Haitian origin to an end.[163]

Another pair of important group rights cases came a few years thereafter, both of which involved Brazil. On September 13, 1998, Wallace de Almeida, a black Brazilian who was visiting family in the "Morro de Babilonia" favela of Rio de Janeiro, was shot and killed by police. In its holding in *Wallace de Almeida*,[164] the Commission again took a wide-angled perspective on the case, allowing the petitioners to provide evidence pertaining not only to the details of de Almeida's killing, but also to broader patterns of police violence and public discrimination against

160 Jessica Lenahan (Gonzales) et al. v. United States, App. No. 12.626, Int.-Am. Comm. H.R. (July 21, 2011), para. 161.

161 See ibid., operative paras. 4–7.

162 App. No. 12.189, Int.-Am. Ct. H.R., Preliminary Objections, Merits, Reparations and Costs (September 8, 2005).

163 See ibid., paras. 141, 240–41, operative para. 8.

164 Wallace de Almeida v. Brazil, App. No. 12.440, Int.-Am. Comm. H.R. (March 20, 2009).

Afro-Brazilians.[165] In its holding, the Commission called upon Brazil not only to provide reparations to de Almeida's family, but also to adopt a wide set of measures aimed at the elimination of racial discrimination in its police operations and criminal justice proceedings.[166]

In *Sebastião Camargo Filho*,[167] the Commission addressed the rights of Brazil's rural poor. In 1997 two hundred families belonging to the "Movement of Landless Rural Workers" occupied a pair of estates in the Marilena municipality. Following objections from the owners of those estates, an agreement was reached whereby the workers were to relocate to another pair of estates, which were to be declared social interest property. On February 7, 1998, a group of thirty masked and armed individuals came to the estates with the aim of violently evicting the families. In the course of their attempt to do so, one of the masked men shot and killed Sebastião Camargo Filho, from behind and at point-blank range. While official investigations followed the killing, they quickly stalled. In its holding, the Commission called on Brazil not only to thoroughly investigate the killing and hold those responsible to account, but also to take several measures aimed at addressing the underlying issues that had led to the confrontation, including adopting a comprehensive policy for eradicating rural violence, and dismantling the armed groups that were resisting land redistribution.[168]

165 In particular, the Commission observed "a pattern of extrajudicial executions by the police in Rio de Janeiro … that merits particular attention" (ibid., para. 53) and "a pattern of conduct outside the law on the part of the State's civil/military police" (ibid., para. 100) – findings which the Commission reached in part by drawing on its own earlier 1997 report on Brazil. In addition, the Commission observed that people of African descent in Brazil formed:

> a historically marginalized group in comparison with the white population that is politically and economically dominant … Differences still exist [in Brazil] that are far from a minimum acceptable level of equality and … discrimination is often reflected in patterns that violate human rights, particularly the rights to equality, non-discrimination, and dignity. The principal expression of these racial disparities is the uneven distribution of wealth and opportunities.

Ibid., para. 141.

166 See ibid., para. 168.4.

167 Sebastião Camargo Filho v. Brazil, App. No. 12.310, Int.-Am. Comm. H.R. (March 19, 2009).

168 In more detail, the Commission called on Brazil to:

> Adopt, on a priority basis, a global policy for eradicating rural violence, including preventive measures and measures to protect communities at risk, and stronger measures to protect leaders of movements working for the equitable distribution of rural land;

In 2012, the Court produced another similar ruling, *Nadege Dorzema*,[169] focused once again on the situation of Haitians and persons of Haitian descent in the Dominican Republic. On June 18, 2012, Dominican soldiers attacked a truck that was attempting to smuggle Haitians across the border, killing seven. The soldiers were acquitted of any wrongdoing in Dominican courts, while the survivors were summarily expelled. In their arguments to the Court, both the Commission and the representatives of the victims argued and took pains to highlight that the events were not an isolated occurrence, but rather that they had taken place in "a context of structural discrimination in [the] Dominican Republic against Haitians or those of Haitian origin."[170] While the Court refused to find whether there was discrimination specifically against persons of Haitian origin, it did find that there was discrimination against migrants in the Dominican Republic; on the question of racial discrimination, moreover, the Court held that it would consider the burden of proof to lie with the state to disprove discrimination, thereby essentially constructively finding that such discrimination did in fact exist.[171]

These four sets of cases – concerning the reform of repressive public order systems, indigenous peoples' rights, violence against women, and the rights of marginalized groups – were at the forefront of the system's ongoing development of a progressive and assertive approach to its work in the new millennium. That approach had multiple, interrelated characteristics, including the tendency on the part of both the Commission and the Court to adopt a wide-angled perspective, taking in broader structural

> Adopt effective measures to dismantle illegal armed groups involved in conflicts related to land distribution; [and]
>
> Adopt a public policy to tackle the impunity surrounding violations of the human rights of individuals involved in agrarian conflicts and seeking the equitable distribution of land.

Ibid., paras. 126.3–126.5.

169 Nadege Dorzema et al. v. Dominican Republic, App. No. 1351-05, Int.-Am. Ct. H.R., Merits, Reparations and Costs (October 24, 2012).

170 Ibid., para. 228; see also para. 40.

171 As the Court put it, given "the difficulty for those who are the object of discrimination to prove racial prejudice … in certain cases of human rights violations motivated by discrimination, the burden of proof falls on the State, which controls the means to clarify incidents that took place on its territory." Ibid., para. 229. The Court emphasized, moreover, that discrimination might be found based on impact alone, without any necessity of showing intent, ibid., paras. 234–5. The Court relied both on jurisprudence from the European Court and on its previous holding in *Gonzalez Medina* (para. 132), which had concerned forced disappearance.

issues; the assertion of the strength and hierarchical supremacy of human rights law, understood as having a degree of force on the national as well as on the international legal level; a willingness to prescribe sweeping, multifaceted, and forceful remedial measures; and a recognition of the interrelationship between rights and democracy, and of the need for rights work to be focused on rewriting the fundamental rules of society, with the aim both of addressing past wrongs, and of achieving more inclusive political cultures going forwards. In sum, the period saw the system continuing to evolve from its past focus on calling out widespread and serious violations, to a new emphasis on combatting structural forms of violence and inequality within societies.[172]

In short, the new millennium has seen the Inter-American system continue to chart its own approach to human rights, developing a forceful, structural approach that contrasts with the more cautious, individualized approach that was for long the norm within the European system. At the same time, the Inter-American system has been confronted by a diverse set of political challenges, which have grown in strength over time. The wave of challenges that have beset the systems in recent years began in the 1990s. In 1992 the Commission prepared an annual report criticizing the amnesty laws in Argentina and Uruguay. In response, those states, together with others resentful of the Commission's oversight, requested an advisory opinion from the Court as to the scope of the Commission's power. In 1993 they successfully secured a resolution by the General Assembly of the OAS, calling for a study of ways in which the system might be reformed. The end result of the process was not a diminishment of the Commission's powers, however: rather, both the study and the Court's judgment affirmed the Commission's ability to review national legal systems' conformity with regional human rights standards.[173]

A similar challenge came at a 1996 meeting of the General Assembly of the OAS.[174] At that meeting Mexico and Peru argued that the individual

[172] For a highly compelling summary of the nature of this evolution, see Abramovich, "From Massive Violations to Structural Patterns."

[173] See Certain Attributes of the Inter-American Commission on Human Rights, Int.-Am. Ct. H.R., Advisory Opinion No. OC-13/93 (July 16, 1993). For more on this confrontation, see Felipe Gonzales, *El Sistema Interamericano de Derechos Humanos: Transformaciones y Desafios* (Tirant lo Blanch, 2013), 63–7.

[174] The preceding year a fierce battle had been fought between the Commission and the OAS over the Commission's independence, resulting in the early resignation of Commissioner Reisman from his post in protest. The battle resulted in the removal of long-time Executive Secretary Edith Marquez and the appointment of Jorge Taiana, in the first relatively open

complaint system should be scrapped, now that authoritarian regimes in the region were on the decline. States' complaints resulted in the commencement of a "reform process." The process reached its conclusion with OAS General Assembly Resolution 1701, issued in 2000. The recommendations advanced by that resolution included that the Commission more clearly define its criteria for opening cases, declaring cases admissible, issuing provisional measures, and referring cases to the Court; that clear and prompt deadlines be instituted; and that friendly settlements continue to be pursued. In sum, while the "reform process" had been initiated due to states' desire to weaken the system, the ultimate result of the process was not the imposition of limitations, but rather an increase in procedural formality.[175]

Another more isolated challenge took place around the same time. In the late 1990s Trinidad and Tobago denounced the Convention, following a series of cases in which the Commission and the Court challenged the manner in which the death penalty was applied on the islands.[176] While Trinidad and Tobago's withdrawal had limited practical effect on the system overall, it set a worrying precedent insofar as it marked the first time a state had carried through on its threats to withdraw from the Convention.

While the first decade of the twenty-first century was marked by relative calm on the political front, the 2010s saw extensive turbulence. The first major pushback against the Inter-American human rights system began in 2011. The precipitating factor was the Commission's issuance of interim measures calling for a halt to ongoing work on the Belo Monte Dam in Brazil.[177] Brazil was incensed, and launched a sharp attack on the

Executive Secretary appointment procedure. See Richard Wilson, "The Inter-American Human Rights System: Principal Activities in 1996." By the end of the decade, Cesar Gaviria, Secretary-General of the OAS, was reportedly more supportive of the independence of the Commission, perhaps in part due to recognition that the independence of the Commission might prevent states coming to him with their complaints.

175 For more on this point, see Ariel Dulitzky and Ismene Zarifis, "Facing the Challenge: The Inter-American Commission on Human Rights' Adoption of New Rules of Procedure," 3 *Nordic Journal of Human Rights* (2003), 257–76.

176 For more, see Natasha Concepcion, "The Legal Implications of Trinidad & Tobago's Withdrawal from the American Convention on Human Rights," 16 *American University International Law Review* (2001), 847–90.

177 The Commission had developed a practice of ordering interim measures throughout the 2000s, including in cases involving state seizure of indigenous peoples' lands. The Commission had for instance granted interim measures relative to the Western Shoshone's claims to their land in the *Mary and Carrie Dann* case in 1993, as well as on behalf of the Sarayaku community in 2003, both of which measures were ignored by the states in

system, withdrawing its ambassador to the OAS and temporarily ceasing to pay its dues. While the Commission quickly backed down, withdrawing the interim measures in question, it took time to mend bridges with Brazil.[178] In the meantime, the governments of Venezuela, Ecuador, and Bolivia launched a concerted attack on the Commission at the 42nd General Assembly of the OAS in June 2012, motivated by what they saw as the system's persistent bias against the more left-leaning governments of the hemisphere. Venezuela became the second state to denounce the Convention shortly thereafter.[179]

Despite the concerted nature of these challenges, the ultimate result of the attacks was remarkably similar to the result of the earlier "reform process." In 2014 the Commission adopted yet another new set of procedural rules, once again deflecting pressure for retrenchment into a further formalization of the Commission's procedures. While a formal scaling back of the Commission's mandate was thereby avoided, the Commission continued to face challenges in the following years, in the form of increased efforts by states to fill the constituent bodies of the system with political appointments,[180] and in states' greater willingness to withhold funding. The latter challenge became particularly pressing in 2016, when, in the face of a budgetary shortfall, the Commission was faced with the prospect of having to lay off forty percent of its staff, though that outcome was ultimately averted.[181]

question. In 2010, the Commission issued interim measures calling on Guatemala to suspend extraction at the Marlin gold mine; while the attention resulted in some pressure on the Guatemalan government, the rights of the local community continued to be violated.

178 For more, see Douglas Cassel, "The Perfect Storm: Count and Balance," in DPLF, Reform of the Inter-American Commission.

179 For more, see Diego Mejía-Lemos, "Venezuela's Denunciation of the American Convention on Human Rights," 17 *American Journal of International Law Insights* (2013), www.asil.org/insights/volume/17/issue/1/venezuelas-denunciation-american-convention-human-rights.

180 In addition to political challenges, a crucial ongoing issue was ensuring personnel representative of the diversity of the Americas. The Inter-American system was historically underinclusive of women; even as late as 2015, only two (out of seven) commissioners were women, while all seven judges on the Court were men. For more, see Nienke Grossman and Anne H. Heindel, "Shattering the Glass Ceiling in International Adjudication," 56 *Virginia Journal of International Law* (2016), 339–406. In addition, serious accusations of sexual abuse have been made against Court staff. In 2018, following allegations of sexual assault by his wife and of sexual harassment by two nannies who worked at his home, Roberto Caldas, the President of the Court, resigned.

181 For more, see Raisa Cetra and Jefferson Nascimento, "Counting Coins: Funding the Inter-American Human Rights System," in DPLF, Changing Times, Ongoing Challenges; International Justice Resource Center, "Inter-American Commission: Funds Secured to Temporarily Mitigate Financial Crisis" (October 12, 2016).

The attacks on the system in 2011 and 2012 targeted the Commission, rather than the Court.[182] Subsequent resistance and attacks were directed against the Court as well. In 2014, perhaps influenced in part by domestic discontent with the stance the Court had adopted relative to racial discrimination in the Dominican Republic, the Constitutional Court of the Dominican Republic determined that the Dominican Republic's ratification of the jurisdiction of the Court had not complied with domestic constitutional requirements, leading to the conclusion that the Dominican Republic should not be understood as subject to the Court's jurisdiction. The judgment sparked an intercourt row, as the Inter-American Court refused to accept the Dominican Constitutional Court's view on the matter.[183]

In 2017 the Argentinian Supreme Court, a strong ally of the Inter-American system in the preceding decades, refused to comply with the Inter-American Court's decision in *Fontevecchia and D'Amico*,[184] in which the Court found the decision by Argentina's Supreme Court that journalists pay damages for having invaded the privacy of ex-President Menem in violation of the Convention, and ordered that the fine imposed by Argentina's Supreme Court not be enforced. In its response, the Argentinian Supreme Court took pains to assert its supremacy on the national level.[185]

[182] The Court, meanwhile, was busy attempting to amend the structural nature of its relationship with the Commission, as well as with rights claimants in the region as a whole. Pablo Saavedra-Alessandri, the Registrar of the Court from 2003 on, argued that states should allow public defenders to bring cases to the Inter-American system, and that some form of legal aid system should be created. See Pablo Saavedra-Alessandri, "The Inter-American Court of Human Rights, Present and Future Challenges," 24 *Netherlands Quarterly of Human Rights* (2006), 375–8. A step was taken in the latter direction through the creation of the new position of the "Inter-American Defender" in 2009. See 2009 Rules of Procedure, Int.-Am. Ct. H.R., Article 37. The aim of the creation of the new post was to ensure that "alleged victims will be guaranteed an attorney to represent their interests before the Court, and economic considerations will no longer impede access to legal consideration. Additionally, this reform prevents the Commission from having to take on a dual role before the Court, both as a representative of victims and an organ of the System." Int.-Am. Ct. H.R., Statement of Motives for the Reform of the Rules of Procedure.

[183] For more, see Dinah Shelton and Alexandra Huneeus, "In Re Direct Action of Unconstitutionality Initiated Against the Declaration of Acceptance of the Jurisdiction of the Inter-American Court of Human Rights," 109 *American Journal of International Law* (2015), 866–72.

[184] Fontevecchia and D'Amico v. Argentina, App. No. 12.524, Int.-Am. Ct. H.R., Merits, Reparations and Costs (November 29, 2011).

[185] See Ministerio de Relaciones Exteriores y Culto s/informe sentencie dictada en el caso "Fontevecchia y d'Amico v. Argentina" por law Corte Interamericana de Derechos Humanos; and Francisca Pou Giménez, "Quo vadis, Inter-American Court? Activism, Backlash and Latin American Constitutionalism," *ICON Blog* (April 11, 2018).

As of the end of the 2010s, therefore, the future of the Inter-American system was hard to predict.[186] On the one hand, the system had for decades been developing a body of progressive jurisprudence, carving out an increasingly assertive approach to its mandate along the way. From *Velásquez Rodríguez* on, the system developed an assertive approach to its case consideration role, premised on a willingness to adopt a wide-angled view of situations of violations, and to prescribe extensive and detailed remedial orders. This jurisprudence was defined, every step of the way, as much by the nature of the situations of violation the system confronted as by abstract considerations around the appropriate modalities through which to structure rights judgments. While the system's consistent development of and emphasis upon a progressive approach to jurisprudence suggested it would continue along similar lines in future, the second decade of the twenty-first century in particular saw the system increasingly running up against political pushback. How the system deals with that pushback in future, and whether it amends the assertive nature of its traditional approach, remains to be seen.

## IV Africa

### *IV.1 Early Challenges*

The African Charter was agreed in the early 1980s, after states' resistance to regional rights oversight decreased; the first Commission was composed in 1987. Among the first issues the newly formed Commission had to address was how to deal with the ambiguity bequeathed by Article 55 of the Charter, which explicitly referred to the fact that "communications other than those of State Parties" would be received. In adopting its first rules of procedure in 1988 the Commission stipulated that it read this rule as allowing individuals and organizations to submit information, though it did not make clear how it would treat such information after it had been

[186] As of the end of 2020, twenty-four of the thirty-five states in the Americas were party to the American Convention: Argentina, Barbados, Bolivia, Brazil, Chile, Colombia, Costa Rica, Dominica, Ecuador, El Salvador, Grenada, Guatemala, Haiti, Honduras, Jamaica, Mexico, Nicaragua, Panama, Paraguay, Peru, the Dominican Republic, Suriname, Uruguay, and Venezuela. The other eleven states of the region – Antigua and Barbuda, the Bahamas, Belize, Canada, Cuba, Guyana, St. Kitts and Nevis, St. Lucia, St. Vincent & Grenadines, Trinidad and Tobago, and the United States – were not. Of the twenty-four parties to the Convention, twenty-one had recognized the jurisdiction of the Court, the exceptions being Dominica, Grenada, and Jamaica.

submitted.[187] The Commission's rules of procedure also indicated that it aimed to adopt an inclusive approach to its work by allowing national liberation movements recognized by the OAU as well as NGOs, among others, to participate in its work and its sessions.[188]

While the Commission's approach to the issue of communications left open the door for more expansive interpretations of its mandate in time, other components of the rules limited the Commission's powers and independence. The rules affirmed the authority of the Secretary-General of the OAU over the Commission, by granting the Secretary-General a central position in the transmission of communications, and by giving the Secretary-General a key role in setting the Commission's agenda. The lack of independence of the Commission could also be seen in its composition in early years. The first set of Commissioners, appointed from 1987 to 1993, contained two members who were ministers in their countries (one minister of the interior, and one attorney-general), while several other members held lesser governmental positions.[189]

The Commission adopted an extremely cautious approach to publication of its work in its early years. The Commission decided to interpret the

[187] See 1988 Rules of Procedure, Af. Comm. H.P.R., Rule 114.

[188] See ibid., Rules 73–7.

[189] The composition of the Commission, its rules of procedure and its general lack of impartiality were all criticized by civil society. See, e.g., Intervention of Clement Nwankwo, Constitutional Rights Project of Nigeria, 10th Ordinary Session of the Af. Comm. H.P.R. (1991); Ankumah, *African Commission*, 18–19. As Murray has put it, these criticisms were concerned:

> Not just [with] the appearance of the lack of independence, with the inclusion of ambassadors amongst [the Commission's] members and senior government figures, but also evidence of an actual lack of impartiality. For example, missions taken to states were criticized for the one-sided manner in which they were conducted. Not all mission reports have been released and communications which prompted the missions in the first place have often only been published years after the visits. In the case of Nigeria, the communications were published after a change in government, suggesting that pressure from the previous regime may have had a role to play in the past.
>
> NGOs have consistently questioned the issue of Commissioner independence and at one stage it was a regular feature on the agenda of the Commission. One can only hope, therefore, for the position of Commissioner to gain a better profile and that NGOs and others can lobby at the national level for non-governmental nominations and thus influence subsequent appointments to the Commission.

Rachel Murray, "The African Charter on Human and Peoples' Rights 1987–2000: An Overview of its Progress and Problems," 1 *African Human Rights Law Journal* (2001), 7–8.

language of Article 59(1) of the Charter broadly,[190] to prevent any publication of information as to pending cases.[191] When the Commission did refer its final reports to the OAU, despite the Commission's fears that critical reports and commentary might be censored by the states concerned, the reports were generally adopted without comment.[192]

The end of the Cold War, which came shortly after the formation of the Commission, helped to remove fuel from several conflicts around Africa, and was followed by a number of transitions toward more democratic governance. In 1990 the OAU issued a declaration supporting the movement toward more democratic governance and greater popular participation.[193] Thanks to this new climate, the still young Commission was able to gradually adopt a more assertive stance. A first step came at the Commission's ninth ordinary session in 1991, at which the Commission adopted a more public approach to its proceedings, setting a new precedent for the years to come.

The question of how to handle individual communications remained challenging. Observers and commissioners were well aware of the Commission's weak mandate to receive such communications. As soon as the Commission was formed, however, communications had started to roll in,[194] leading Umozurike, one of the first chairs of the Commission, to

[190] That article reads "All measures taken within the provisions of the present Charter shall remain confidential until such a time as the Assembly of Heads of State and Government shall otherwise decide."

[191] On the problematic nature of the Commission's reading of this article, see Philip Amoah, "The African Charter on Human and Peoples Rights – An Effective Weapon for Human Rights?," 4 *African Journal of International and Comparative Law* (1992), 235–6; Mutua, "The African Human Rights Court," 347.

[192] The ready adoption of the Commission's reports in the early years was most likely due to a lack of attention; as Murray notes, the Commission's reports were typically "adopted without debate, usually late in the evening, after other, more high-profile, business was done." Murray, *Human Rights in Africa* 58, citing interview with Ben Kioko (2003). As Murray has further observed, this could be seen as indicative of the OAU's approach to human rights generally: having created the Commission, headquartered in distant Banjul, the OAU was free to largely ignore rights matters, ibid., 23. The initial reports of the Commission did not include holdings on cases; those were only included from the seventh activity report of the Commission on. For more on the Commission's early decisions – most of which did not find violations – see Frans Viljoen, *International Human Rights Law in Africa* (2nd edn., Oxford University Press, 2012), 335–6.

[193] See OAU, Declaration on the Political and Socio-Economic Situation in Africa and the Fundamental Changes Taking Place in the World, 26th session (July 11, 1990).

[194] Several of these communications concerned states not yet parties to the Charter. Despite the fact that the general rules of international law push strongly against the admissibility of such claims, there have often been those within the African system willing to mount a

observe that while under the Charter "it appears that a single breach is not enough, it must be massive and serious," the Commission was:

> likely to break out of this close confinement and make a report on every case that is reported to it provided it relates to a denial or violation of a right. Otherwise [the Charter] would not be talking of individual rights but the rights of the masses or peoples. The wrongful detention of citizen A cannot be regarded as massive and serious in the strict language of the Charter but [still] offends modern notions of human rights.[195]

Umozurike's prediction soon came to pass, as the Commission commenced accepting "individual" petitions shortly thereafter.[196] From the seventh activity report of the Commission on, moreover, the Commission's holdings were made public, though only after they had been adopted by the OAU.

Another important early procedural decision came at the Commission's fifteenth session, held in 1994. Having submitted a communication, Embga Mekongo Louis, a Cameroonian then living in exile in France, flew to the Commission session in order to advance his case, and asked for a hearing. While there was no applicable precedent in such cases, Louis's presence swayed the Commission, which decided to grant the hearing.[197] At the Commission's sixteenth ordinary session, held later that same year,

progressive, access to justice-based cases that such claims should be heard. For some later examples of such reasoning from the African Court, see Atabong Denis Atemnkeng v. African Union, App. No. 007/2011, Af. Ct. H.P.R. (September 2, 2011), dissenting opinion of Justices Akuffo, Ngoepe and Thompson; Femi Falana v. African Union, App. No. 001/2011, Af. Ct. H.P.R. (June 26, 2012), dissenting opinion of Justices Akuffo, Ngoepe and Thompson.

195 Oji Umozurike, "The African Commission on Human and Peoples' Rights: An Introduction," 1 *Review of the African Commission on Human and Peoples' Rights* (1991), 11.

196 For more on the debates that took place in the early years over whether and how the Commission might consider individual communications, see Edem Kodjo, "The African Charter on Human and Peoples' Rights," 11 *Human Rights Law Journal* (1990), 271–82; Wolfgang Benedek, "The African Charter and Commission on Human and Peoples' Rights: How to Make it More Effective," 11 *Netherlands Quarterly of Human Rights* (1993), 25–40; Rachel Murray, "Decisions by the African Commission on Individual Communications Under the African Charter on Human and Peoples' Rights," 46 *International and Comparative Law Quarterly* (1997), 412–34; Odinkalu, "Individual Complaints Procedures"; Odinkalu and Christensen, "The African Commission,", 239–44; Frans Viljoen, "Communications under the African Charter: Procedure and Admissibility," in Evans and Murray eds., *The African Charter*, 76–138.

197 The Commission ultimately found the Charter had been violated in Louis's case, moreover. See Embga Mekongo Louis v. Cameroon, Comm. No. 59/91, Af. Comm. H.P.R. (March 22, 1995).

the Commission took the further step of allowing lawyers to represent aggrieved parties within such hearings.

In 1995 the Commission adopted its second rules of procedure, which demonstrated the distance it had come on both the procedural and institutional fronts. The new rules formalized several of the developments that were already taking place, making public sessions the norm, making information about the cases before the Commission public, and allowing NGOs to participate more extensively in the Commission's work.[198] The new rules also asserted a far greater degree of independence for the Commission relative to the OAU. Communications were now to be submitted directly to the Commission, while the previous clause asserting that the Secretary-General of the OAU would have a role in setting the agenda of the Commission was removed.[199] In addition, the 1995 rules granted the Commission the power to make public statements on its own initiative, without requiring that such statements be vetted by the Secretary-General of the OAU.[200]

While the Commission's strength and independence may have increased, it was still well aware that its powers had limits. This recognition expressed itself in the Commission's keen desire to promote "friendly settlements" as a means of resolving communications.[201] While a case could be made for resolving disputes through friendly settlement with the parties' support, the Commission took its enthusiasm for friendly settlements further, including by dismissing a case after hearing from a government that the matter in question had been resolved, without consulting the applicants.[202]

198 See Rules of Procedure, Af. Comm. H.P.R. (1995), Rules 32, 72, 103.

199 See ibid., Rules 6–10, 102. It seems that the Secretary-General of the OAU at the time, Salim Ahmed Salim, was supportive of these changes.

200 See ibid., Rule 108. As one commentator has noted, the shift to greater transparency was made possible "by the simple device of reinterpreting Article 59(3) of the Charter to enable the Commission to publish its reports unless the OAU object[ed], instead of the previous interpretation which precluded the Commission from publishing the report unless the OAU authorizes its publication." Odinkalu, "Case and Complaints Procedures," 235.

201 In several cases, moreover, the Commission stressed "that the primary objective of the communication procedure is 'to initiate a positive dialogue, resulting in an amicable resolution between the complainant and the State concerned.'" See, e.g., Comité Culturel pour la Democratie au Benin et al. v. Benin, Comm. Nos. 16–18/88, Af. Comm. H.P.R. (April 27, 1994), para. 35; Free Legal Assistance Group et al. v. Zaire, Comm. Nos. 25/89, 47/90, 56/91, & 100/93, Af. Comm. H.P.R. (April 4, 1996), para. 39.

202 See Kalenga v. Zambia, Comm. No. 11/88, Af. Comm. H.P.R. (April 27, 1994). The Human Rights Committee, meanwhile, apprised of the same matter, ultimately found that Zambia's arrest and detention of Kalenga constituted violations of the International

From 1995 on the Commission began to demonstrate a greater willingness to reach decisions on individual case submissions. From the beginning, the Commission adopted a flexible approach, bringing together similar cases and considering recurrent patterns of wrongdoing in the course of reaching its holdings, as for instance in the case of *Krishna Achuthan (on behalf of Aleke Banda) and others v. Malawi*,[203] which concerned politically motivated detentions in Malawi. The Commission's holding in *Commission Nationale des Droits de l'Homme et des Libertés v. Tchad*,[204] which concerned several interconnected patterns of violation committed in the context of the Libya-backed Déby government in Chad, set a key precedent by finding that an exception to the rule of exhaustion would apply in instances of serious and massive violation – an exception that would pave the way for the Commission's prioritization of cases of serious and massive violation in the years to come.[205] The Commission continued to emphasize large-scale and serious violations in the following years. Thus the Commission's decision in *Free Legal Assistance Group and others v. D.R.C.*,[206] which concerned a range of deeply repressive

Covenant on Civil and Political Rights. *See* Kalenga v. Zambia, Comm. No. 326/1988, HRC (July 27, 1993). The Commission's approach was widely criticized, however (see, e.g., Odinkalu and Christensen, "The African Commission," 244–7), and, with time, the Commission's approach became more measured.

203 Comm. Nos. 64/92, 68/92, & 78/92, Af. Comm. H.P.R. (March 22, 1995).

204 Comm. No. 74/92, Af. Comm. H.P.R. (October 11, 1995).

205 As the Commission put it,

> S'agissant des communications d'où il ressort qu'aucun procès légal n'a été intenté par les victimes, étant donné le nombre important d'individus ayant souffert de violations de leurs droits, paraît-il, et le fait que les événements prétendus, s'ils sont vrais, constituaient "Un ensemble de violations graves et massives" il est clair que le gouvernement du Tchad a eu assez de notifications de la situation des droits de l'homme sur son territoire.
>
> La Commission doit interpréter l'Article 56.5 en se référant à sa mission de protection des droits de l'homme et des peuples telle que stipulée dans la Charte. La Commission ne peut pas absolument exiger que la demande d'épuisement des recours internes s'applique littéralement aux cas où le plaignant se trouve dans l'incapacité de saisir les tribunaux nationaux pour chaque plainte individuelle. En raison de la gravité de la situation des droits de l'homme et du grand nombre de personnes impliquées, les recours qui pourraient théoriquement exister devant les tribunaux nationaux sont dans la pratique inexistants ou, au terme de la Charte se prolongent d'une façon anormale.

Ibid., paras. 29–30. The passages in question in fact only appeared in the French judgment in the case, and not in its English translation.

206 Comm. Nos. 25/89, 47/90, 56/91, & 100/93, Af. Comm. H.P.R. (April 4, 1996).

and corrupt policies and practices employed by the government of the Democratic Republic of Congo, followed in the footsteps of the 1995 decisions by employing a liberal approach to joinder and underscoring the existence of an exception to the rule of exhaustion where there were "serious and massive" violations.[207]

In sum, while the prospects for the Commission might not have seemed promising when it was created, given the difficult context of its formation and the Commission's limited independence, by the mid to late 1990s the Commission had made huge strides. This was illustrated by the Commission's assertion of a greater degree of independence, its more forceful approach to publicity, its willingness to partner with civil society, and its willingness to consider "individual" communications – even if it still preferred that those communications concern widespread situations of violation.

The Commission continued to develop its approach in a series of decisions concerning Nigeria issued in the late 1990s. The decisions in these cases, and the implicit partnership with Nigerian civil society on which they were based, allowed the Commission to establish a clear and assertive position, supportive of and supported by civil society in the region.

For a clearer understanding of the Nigeria cases, a little context is necessary. In 1983, the civilian government in Nigeria was overthrown by a coup. The new leader, Muhammadu Buhari, was himself overthrown two years later by another general, Ibrahima Babangida. Babangida indicated that he would return the country to civilian rule; in 1989 a new constitution was prepared, and political activity permitted. In 1993 presidential elections were held, in which it appeared that Moshood Abiola would be the victor. Babangida annulled the election, leading to protests that eventually forced the handover of power to an interim government. The weakness of that government led to the assumption of power by the Defense Minister, Sani Abacha, who suspended plans for new elections and replaced elected governors with military officers. Abiola declared himself

[207] Other early cases involving widespread violations included *Organisation Mondiale Contre la Torture and others v. Rwanda* (Comm. Nos. 27/89, 46/91, 49/91, & 99/93, Af. Comm. H.P.R. (October 31, 1996)) (concerning the expulsion from Rwanda of large numbers of Burundian refugees, arbitrary arrests and detentions, and summary executions); *Rencontre Africaine pour la Défense des Droits de l'Homme v. Zambia* (Comm. No. 71/92, Af. Comm. H.P.R. (October 31, 1996)) (concerning the expulsion of hundreds of West Africans from Zambia); and *Union Interafricaine des Droits de l'Homme and others v. Angola* (Comm. No. 159/96, Af. Comm. H.P.R. (November 11, 1997)) (concerning mass expulsions of foreigners from Angola).

president, only to be promptly arrested, leading to strikes across the southwest of the country. The government refused to budge in the face of this resistance, however, instead deploying a range of repressive measures to deal with dissidents, including special tribunals empowered to issue the death penalty. Abacha's regime ended with his heart failure in 1998, after which he was replaced by Abdulsalami Abubakar, who organized elections. Olusegun Obasanjo won those elections and assumed power in 1999, ending a decade and a half of military rule.

Against this backdrop, numerous cases were submitted to the African Commission in the early 1990s. Once they were made aware of these communications, the Nigerian government showed up to the sixteenth session of the Commission in 1994 in force, perhaps hoping to intimidate the Commission into dismissing the cases. The Commission, however, held firm. At its seventeenth session, the Commission issued four decisions concerning Nigeria, two in cases brought by the Constitutional Rights Project, two in cases brought by the Civil Liberties Organisation.[208] The two *Constitutional Rights Project* cases concerned imposition of the death penalty, the first *Civil Liberties Organisation* case a government attempt to take control of the Nigerian Bar Association, and the second *Civil Liberties Organisation* case various decrees nullifying the jurisdiction of the courts.

In its decisions the Commission set several important precedents. The Commission accepted all the cases as admissible on the basis of exceptions to the rule of exhaustion, finding that there were no available and effective judicial remedies in Nigeria, in large part due to decree laws which had ousted the jurisdiction of the regular courts. In addition, the cases demonstrated the willingness of the Commission to begin to take an assertive stance on remedies: in the *Constitutional Rights Project* decisions the Commission called for the freeing of the complainants, while in the first *Civil Liberties Organisation* decision the Commission found that a law as such could be found to violate the Charter, and consequently called for the Decree Law in question "[to] be annulled."

A final, capstone ruling came three and a half years later, in *Media Rights Agenda and others v. Nigeria*.[209] The Commission's holding in the case was

208 Constitutional Rights Project v. Nigeria, Comm. No. 60/91, Af. Comm. H.P.R. (March 22, 1995); Constitutional Rights Project v. Nigeria, Comm. No. 87/93, Af. Comm. H.P.R. (March 22, 1995); Civil Liberties Organisation v. Nigeria, Comm. No. 101/93, Af. Comm. H.P.R. (March 22, 1995); Civil Liberties Organisation v. Nigeria, Comm. No. 129/94, Af. Comm. H.P.R. (March 22, 1995).

209 Comm. Nos. 105/93, 128/94, 130/94, & 152/96, Af. Comm. H.P.R. (October 31, 1998). The decisions the following year in *Constitutional Rights Project and others v. Nigeria* (Comm.

issued just as military rule in Nigeria was finally beginning to come to an end. *Media Rights Agenda* took a more comprehensive approach to the violations that had occurred in Nigeria in and following the annulment of the 1993 elections, including through an emphasis on various measures that had been taken to restrict freedom of expression and of the press in particular. The Commission's decision in the case was more detailed than those issued in previous years; in its holding, in addition to laying out the various ways in which Nigeria's laws had violated the Charter, the Commission called on Nigeria to "take the necessary steps to bring [those] laws into conformity with the Charter."[210]

### *IV.2 Coming to Grips with Violation as the Norm*

Following in the wake of its decisions concerning the military dictatorship in Nigeria the Commission issued a series of important judgments, before and after the turn of the millennium, that demonstrated both the Commission's newfound confidence and the basic shape that its vision of its human rights mandate would take. All four decisions concerned widespread patterns of violation, in Sudan, the Gambia, Mauritania and, once again, Nigeria.

The case against Sudan concerned violence that had occurred over the previous decade. On July 30, 1989, a weak coalition government, headed by Sadiq al-Mahdi, was overthrown by a military junta led by Omar al-Bashir. The period following the coup saw hundreds of arbitrary and unlawful detentions, instances of torture and other mistreatment, extrajudicial killings, and a variety of forms of discriminatory practice in the context of the new government's eager prosecution of war in the south of the country, and numerous instances of interference with the judiciary and of blatantly unfair trials. These events led to the submission of several applications, which the Commission consolidated into a single case, *Amnesty International and others v. Sudan*.[211] In its holding, the Commission called

Nos. 140/94, 141/94, & 145/95, Af. Comm. H.P.R. (November 5, 1999)) and *Constitutional Rights Project and Civil Liberties Organisation v. Nigeria* (Comm. Nos. 143/95 & 150/96, Af. Comm. H.P.R. (November 5, 1999)) were substantively very similar.

210 Ibid., holding.

211 Comm. Nos. 48/90, 50/91, 52/91, & 89/93, Af. Comm. H.P.R. (November 15, 1999). In explaining the approach it was adopting to joinder, the Commission observed that the:

> decision was based on the similarity of the allegations presented, on the one hand, and the human rights situation prevailing in Sudan during the period covered by

on Sudan to reform several of its laws, policies, and practices.[212] The decision was important both for the flexibility and initiative the Commission showed in confronting an extremely wide-scale problem, and for the assertive, if still broad and vague, remedial measures the Commission called upon Sudan to take.

The case concerning the Gambia also involved a coup. In July 1994, Dawda Jawara, the long-term president of the Gambia, was overthrown by a coup led by Yahya Jammeh. The aftermath of the coup saw abolition of the bill of rights, denial of the competence of the courts, the banning of political parties, arbitrary detentions, extrajudicial killings, and restrictions on numerous other rights. The Commission addressed this situation through its decision in *Jawara v. the Gambia*.[213] Once again, the case saw the Commission affirm and expand its jurisprudence on exceptions to the rule of exhaustion.[214] As in previous holdings, the Commission concluded its ruling by calling on the government to bring its laws into conformity with the Charter. *Jawara* was important for two further reasons as well. First, the Commission used the opportunity to definitively reassert its ability to consider individual communications, settling the matter once and for all.[215] In addition, the *Jawara* holding emphasized the binding force

> these allegations of violations, on the other. The communications were submitted by NGOs and allege many overlapping and inter-related details.

Ibid., para. 28. The holding also reinforced earlier judgments emphasizing the exception to the rule of exhaustion in cases of serious and massive violations, as well as where the jurisdiction of the courts had been denied. See ibid., paras. 33–39.

212 See ibid., para. 83.

213 Comm. Nos. 147/95 & 149/96, Af. Comm. H.P.R. (May 11, 2000).

214 In particular, admissibility was recognized on the basis of the denial of jurisdiction of the courts, the suspension of rights protections, the serious grounds for fear of harm should claimants attempt to bring domestic challenge, the government's disregard of the judiciary generally, and the lack of sufficient remedies. See ibid., paras. 33–40.

215 In particular, the Commission observed that:

> Article 55 of the Charter provides for the consideration of "communications other than those of States Parties." Further to this, Article 56 of the Charter stipulates the conditions for consideration of such communications (see also Chapter XVII [sic] of the Rules of Procedure entitled "Procedure for the Consideration of The Communications Received in Conformity with Article 55 of the Charter"). In any event, the practice of the Commission has been to consider communications even if they do not reveal a series of serious or massive violations. It is out of such useful exercise that the Commission has, over the years, been able to build up its case law and jurisprudence.

Ibid., para. 42.

of the obligations in the Charter, even in instances in which a domestic bill of rights was suspended. In so doing, the Commission went beyond the uncontroversial statement that domestic measures could not serve to limit international obligations, to suggest a broader view of the strength and force of international rights obligations, by referring to the "domestic effect of the Charter"[216] and by observing that "a violation of any provision of the Charter automatically means a violation of Article 1."[217] In short, the Commission gestured toward the applicability of the Charter within domestic legal orders.[218]

The case against Mauritania involved both a coup and a failed coup plot, against the background of a deeply troubling social context. Mauritania was the last country in the world to formally abolish slavery, only doing so in 1981. Slavery continued as a practice, however, as did extensive racial discrimination, especially with regard to various black ethnic groups in the south of the country.[219] In 1984 Maaouya Ould Sid'Ahmed Taya overthrew Mohamed Khouna Ould Haidallah in a coup. In 1987, following allegations of a coup plot by black army officers, suspects were arrested and tortured, while conflict broke out along the Senegalese border and repression of the black population of southern Mauritania intensified. The conflict resulted in the expulsion of tens of thousands of black Mauritanians to Senegal and Mali, while thousands of black soldiers and civil servants were tortured and arrested. In 1993, after the conflict had abated, the government issued an amnesty for any abuses that had been committed. In its holding in *Malawi African Association and others v. Mauritania,* the Commission found a wide range of interconnected violations. The Commission issued its most detailed remedial holdings to date, calling on the government to undertake a carefully specified set of reforms.[220] More than any other case, *Malawi*

[216] As the Commission put it, "the suspension of the Bill of Rights does not ipso facto mean the suspension of the domestic effect of the Charter." In Communication 129/94, the Commission held that "the obligation of ... a government remains unaffected by the purported revocation of the domestic effect of the Charter," Ibid., para. 49.

[217] Ibid., para. 46. This language was important insofar as it signaled a particularly broad understanding of Article 1, the article that requires domestic measures to give effect to the obligations imposed by the Charter, and therefore serves as a bridge of sorts between the national and international legal orders.

[218] That the Commission was willing to adopt such a firm position in *Jawara* was all the more striking given that the case concerned the home state of the Commission, in regards to which the Commission might have been expected to show extra deference.

[219] See Malawi African Association and others v. Mauritania, Comm. Nos. 54/91, 61/91, 96/93, 98/93, 164/97, 196/97, & 210/98, Af. Comm. H.P.R. (May 11, 2000), para. 1.

[220] See ibid., holding.

*African Association* saw the Commission move from a broad and vague approach to remedial measures, toward an approach based upon more detailed and extensive calls for reform.

The fourth key Commission case decided around the turn of the millennium concerned Nigeria. The case concerned extensive violations committed and permitted by Nigeria against the Ogoni people, a group living in an area in southeastern Nigeria cursed with extensive oil resources. Shell oil had been involved in extracting that oil since the 1950s, which, among other consequences, left the area severely polluted. In 1990, the Movement for the Survival of the Ogoni People, led by Ken Saro-Wiwa, organized protests aimed at asserting their rights. In 1993, following protests against a new pipeline, police raided the area, leading to thousands of deaths and the displacement of tens of thousands. In 1995 Ken Saro-Wiwa and several other leaders of the Ogoni people's movement were executed, following trial by special tribunal.

The Commission's decision in *Social and Economic Rights Action Center and Center for Economic and Social Rights v. Nigeria*[221] highlighted the environmental degradation and health problems caused by the oil extraction in the region, as well as the attacks by security forces on the Ogoni people.[222] The finding in the case was noteworthy for several reasons. First, the Commission explicitly recognized that the communication took the form of an *actio popularis,* not only affirming that it would consider cases brought in such a form, but also actively praising such a mode of case submission.[223] Even more significant was the nature of the violations in question. In the first place, the violations had to a significant extent been committed by private parties. Even so, the Commission found that they were violations that "the Nigerian government condoned and facilitated," or else had failed to prevent, implying that human rights obligations carried strong positive duties.[224] In addition, the case saw the Commission rule on articles of the Charter that had previously received little attention, including Article 21, on the right to free disposal of wealth

221 Comm. No. 155/96, Af. Comm. H.P.R. (October 27, 2001).

222 The plight of Ken Saro-Wiwa and his co-detainees was addressed in a separate complaint; see International PEN, Constitutional Rights Project, Civil Liberties Organisation and Interights (on behalf of Ken Saro-Wiwa Jnr.) v. Nigeria, Comm. Nos. 137/94, 139/94, 154/96, & 161/97, Af. Comm. H.P.R. (October 31, 1998).

223 See Social and Economic Rights Action Center and Center for Economic and Social Rights v. Nigeria, Comm. No. 155/96, Af. Comm. H.P.R. (October 27, 2001), para. 49.

224 See ibid., paras. 3, 57.

and natural resources, and Article 24, on the right to a satisfactory environment, two of the Charter's "peoples' rights." The Commission also read several articles of the Charter together to find that various rights not explicitly delimited in the Charter should also be understood as protected, including the rights to food and housing in particular.[225] Finally, the case concluded with a fairly specific list of steps for the Nigerian government to take, and by calling on the government of Nigeria to continue communicating with the Commission on measures taken to address the situation.

Taken together, these four cases helped to develop the contours of a broader vision of human rights work that would persist in the African system in the following years. All concerned wide-scale, complex violations, pertaining to factors such as the nature of political systems and accompanying policies, long-term structural violations, and violations linked to transnational resource extraction. In all four, the Commission indicated a willingness to set the exhaustion of domestic remedies requirement – not fit for purpose in the context of such violations – aside. In all four the Commission indicated its willingness to adopt an assertive, broad-ranging approach to remedies; in *Malawi African Association* in particular, it issued noticeably more detailed and extensive remedial orders.

In the following years the Commission continued along the lines initiated by these cases, while gradually refining the sophistication of its work and outputs.[226] Another high point in the Commission's work occurred in

[225] See ibid., paras. 60, 65.

[226] Among the important cases from the period were DRC v. Burundi, Rwanda and Uganda, Comm. No. 227/99, Af. Comm. H.P.R. (May 29, 2003) (pertaining to a series of wars centering on the Democratic Republic of Congo that began in 1996, ultimately involving nine African states and the deaths of over five million people); Institute for Human Rights and Development in Africa v. Guinea, Comm. No. 249/02, Af. Comm. H.P.R. (December 7, 2004) (concerning numerous violations committed against refugees from Liberia and Sierra Leone); Zimbabwe Human Rights NGO Forum v. Zimbabwe, Comm. No. 245/02, Af. Comm. H.P.R. (May 15, 2006) (concerning a constitutional referendum and elections held in Zimbabwe in 2000, both of which were accompanied by extensive political violence, initiated by the ruling ZANU-PF party, which subsequently absolved its agents through passage of an amnesty law); Article 19 v. Eritrea, Comm. No. 275/03, Af. Comm. H.P.R. (May 30, 2007) (concerning the incommunicado detention of journalists and former government officials, as well as a series of other limitations on freedom of expression); Sudan Human Rights Organisation and Centre on Housing Rights and Evictions (COHRE) v. Sudan, Comm. No. 279/03 and 296/05, Af. Comm. H.P.R. (May 27, 2009); (concerning massive and serious rights violations committed in Darfur from 2003 on); Kevin Mgwanga Gunme et al. v. Cameroon, Comm. No. 266/03, Af. Comm. H.P.R. (May 27, 2009) (concerning the desire of the English-speaking peoples of South-Western Cameroon for independence).

the late 2000s, when the Commission issued a string of sophisticated, compelling, and important judgments concerning issues such as the treatment of foreign workers in Angola, domestic political reform in Côte d'Ivoire, media laws in Zimbabwe, and indigenous peoples' rights in Kenya.

The case against Angola concerned the oil-rich state's mass deportation of foreign workers, some 100,000 of whom were detained and then forcibly deported around the beginning of 2004.[227] In its decision in *Institute for Human Rights and Development in Africa (IHRDA) v. Angola*[228] the African Commission challenged this action. The case was most notable for its remedial holding, which took a comprehensive approach, calling on Angola to implement structural reforms, to provide various forms of individual reparation, and to create a commission of inquiry.[229]

The Commission's two cases concerning Côte d'Ivoire in the period were similarly notable, this time for the energy with which they delved into sensitive domestic political matters. Côte d'Ivoire had a long history of labor immigration, as individuals and families, typically from neighboring countries such as Mali and Burkina Faso, had come to work on cocoa and coffee plantations, located in the north of the country. Such immigration produced tensions, however, leading the government to pass measures, beginning in the late 1990s, aimed at restricting the rights of individuals from the north, as part of a policy that came to be known as "*Ivoirité.*"

*Mouvement Ivoirien des Droits de l'Homme v. Côte d'Ivoire (1)*[230] challenged the *Ivoirité* laws on the grounds that they were discriminatory

[227] As one observer has noted,

> the 2004 [wave of deportations] coincide[d] with the MPLA's acquisition of control over the Lundas and recognition of the need to remove foreign UNITA supporters from the territory after an agreement was reached to work toward elections ... As a major oil-exporting country, Angola was partly insulated from international criticism ... even after news of the 2004 deportations had broken, the Bush administration still encouraged Dos Santos to stand for reelection and signed a deal for Chevron Texaco to extend its concessionary access to Angolan oil.

Alexander Betts, "Survival Migration: Failed Governance and the Crisis of Displacement" (2013); see also Médecins Sans Frontières, "Inhumane Treatment of Diamond Miners in Angola Continues" (April 29, 2004).

[228] Comm. No. 292/04, Af. Comm. H.P.R. (May 22, 2008). The case was brought specifically on behalf of fourteen Gambian deportees, but its ramifications extended to the wider deported population. See ibid., para. 3.

[229] See ibid., holding.

[230] Comm. No. 262/02, Af. Comm. H.P.R. (May 22, 2008).

against certain segments of the population. As with other significant cases, the Commission found the case admissible on the basis of an exception to the rule of exhaustion. Here, though, the Commission found such exception on a novel basis: the fact the laws in question could not be challenged at the national level, because no court empowered to hear rights-based claims was available.[231] Implicitly, therefore – if in a procedurally roundabout way – the Commission suggested that states have an obligation to establish remedial bodies with the ability to hear rights-based claims from individuals.[232] A second decision against Côte d'Ivoire, issued a month later, further advanced the assertive approach to human rights law seen in the first *Mouvement Ivoirien* case. In addition to challenging domestic law, *Mouvement Ivoirien des Droits de l'Homme v. Côte d'Ivoire (2)*[233] challenged discriminatory articles of the 2000 Ivorian Constitution. In finding that those articles violated the Charter, the Commission implied that Côte d'Ivoire would have to amend its constitution, emphasizing, as the Inter-American system had before it, the hierarchical supremacy of human rights law relative to national constitutional orders.

Another important case from the period was brought against Zimbabwe. *Scanlen and Holderness v. Zimbabwe*[234] concerned extensive violence deployed by the ZANU-PF party against opposition supporters in the context of Zimbabwe's 2002 elections, together with legislation clamping down on press freedoms passed in the aftermath of that election. The case was notable for the precision with which the Commission approached the problematic aspects of Zimbabwe's law as it related to the press, as the Commission's holding essentially provided a detailed roadmap of changes that would have to be made to the Zimbabwean law in order for it to be brought into compliance with the Charter, articulated to a level of specificity that was novel within a Commission judgment.

A fifth significant case from the period concerned indigenous peoples' rights in Kenya. The Endorois people lived for centuries in the Lake Bogoria region of Kenya. Beginning in 1973 a large game reserve was created around the lake, and from 1978 the Endorois people were

[231] See ibid., paras. 49–56.

[232] By the time the Commission reached its decision, the government had already amended the laws in question; the Commission went on however to call on the government "to ensure the effective application" of the new legal provisions, to ensure compensation for those wronged, and to ensure ongoing respect for the obligation of nondiscrimination in future. See ibid., Holding.

[233] Comm. No. 246/02, Af. Comm. H.P.R. (July 29, 2008).

[234] Comm. No. 297/05, Af. Comm. H.P.R. (April 3, 2009).

denied access to their traditional land. *Endorois v. Kenya*[235] challenged this exclusion. In its holding, the Commission found violations of both Article 21, on the right to free disposal of wealth and natural resources, and Article 22, on the right to economic, social, and cultural development, of the Charter; recognized rights to shelter and to one's traditional place of dwelling, deriving from numerous articles of the Charter read together; and recognized the obligation of consultation, drawing upon international and Inter-American human rights jurisprudence. The case was hence notable both for turning the African Commission's attention to the rights of indigenous peoples, and for continuing the progressive approach to interpretation of the Charter laid out by *Social and Economic Rights Action Center.*

In sum, the decisions of the late 2000s demonstrated the Commission's continued allegiance to the sort of approach it had begun pursuing so forcefully at the beginning of the new millennium, as well as the distance it had advanced down that path. Once again, the Commission demonstrated its willingness to adopt a broad perspective, focusing on the rights of migrants as well as indigenous communities, while also delving into sensitive questions pertaining to domestic political issues. The cases were also marked by a more detailed approach to remedies, including in terms of specifying measures designed to ensure remedies reached a broad claimant base, as in *IHRDA*, and in terms of a focus on detailed changes to law and policy, as in *Scanlen and Holderness.* In the decisions concerning Côte d'Ivoire, meanwhile, the Commission advanced the expansive understanding of rights it had hinted at in *Jawara*, underlining the necessity for compliance of domestic constitutions with the Charter, and implicitly suggesting that rights-based judicial review should be available within national judicial systems.

In 2010 the Commission adopted new rules of procedure, which were generally seen as a positive step toward addressing some limitations of previous rules.[236] Despite that positive step, however, as the first decade of the third millennium came to an end, the Commission's assertiveness

[235] Centre for Minority Rights Development (Kenya) and Minority Rights Group (on behalf of Endorois Welfare Council) v. Kenya, Comm. No. 276/03, Af. Comm. H.P.R. (November 25, 2009).

[236] See 2010 Rules of Procedure, Af. Comm. H.P.R. *Inter alia,* the 2010 rules addressed the Commission's relationship with the Court, and included strict timelines, intended to speed up the system's case processing times, See, ibid., Rules 83–123. The timelines were little complied with in practice over the following decade.

cooled off. While the 2010s saw some key decisions being issued,[237] together with guidelines, model laws, and general comments addressing numerous key areas,[238] political and institutional challenges meant that the Commission's commitment to promptly address the caseload before it waned, with no sign of improvement as of the end of 2020.[239] At the end of the decade just as at its beginning, the Commission adopted new

[237] Notable judgments included Abdel Hadi & others v. Sudan, Comm. No. 68/09, Af. Comm. H.P.R. (November 5, 2013) (concerning several individuals who fled Southern Sudan for an IDP camp in Khartoum, where they were arbitrarily detained); and Dabalorivhuwa Patriotic Front v. South Africa, Comm. No. 335/06, Af. Comm. H.P.R. (April 23, 2013) and Front for the Liberation of the State of Cabinda v. Angola, Comm. No. 328/06, Af. Comm. H.P.R. (November 5, 2013) (both of which were notable, despite no violations being found, for demonstrating the Commission's willingness to consider complex, large-scale cases on behalf of extended groups of claimants).

[238] Including the Model Law for African States on Access to Information and the Guidelines and Principles on Economic, Social and Cultural Rights (both issued in 2011), the General Comments on Article 14(1)(d and e) of the Protocol to the African Charter on the Rights of Women in Africa (issued in 2012), General Comment No. 2 on Article 14(1)(a, b, c, and f) and Article 14(2)(a and c) of the Protocol to the African Charter on the Rights of Women in Africa (issued in 2014), the Guidelines on the Conditions of Arrest, Police Custody, and Pre-Trial Detention in Africa and General Comment No. 3 on the Right to Life (issued in 2015), the Principles and Guidelines on Human and Peoples' Rights while Countering Terrorism in Africa (issued in 2016), and the Guidelines on Policing Assemblies, General Comment No. 4 on the Right to Redress for Victims of Torture and Other Cruel, Inhuman or Degrading Punishment or Treatment, the Guidelines on Freedom of Association and Assembly in Africa and the Guidelines on Combatting Sexual Violence and its Consequences in Africa (issued in 2017).

[239] As one commentator has observed, the Commission's disappointing output of communication decisions was due both to the fact that "as the special mechanisms of the Commission increased, it gradually started to neglect its core protective function by finalizing fewer and fewer communications at its sessions" and to "continuous fluctuation in the … staff of [the Commission's] Secretariat [limiting] the building of institutional memory and capacity." Viljoen, *International Human Rights Law in Africa*, 296, 299. Particularly significant in this context was the issuance of Decision 1015 (Decision on the Report on the Joint Retreat of the Permanent Representatives' Committee (PRC) and the African Commission on Human and Peoples' Rights (ACHPR), Doc.EX.CL/Dec.1015(XXXIII)) by the Executive Council of the African Union in June 2018, which came in large part in response to the African Commission's granting of observer status to the Coalition of African Lesbians, and sought both to have that observer status rescinded – a "request" with which the Commission complied – and more generally to reign in the independence of the Commission. For more on the political tensions generated around that issue, see Global Campus Africa, "Diffusing Tension, Building Support: Proposals on Guiding Principles Applicable during Consideration of the Activity Reports of the African Commission on Human and Peoples' Rights," Policy Briefs (2018); Independence of the ACHPR Campaign, "Tracking Decision 1015," available at: https://achprindependence.org/decision-1015/

rules of procedure; how efficacious these new rules will prove in practice remains to be seen.[240]

The decline in the Commission's case-based output in the 2010s was initially balanced out by the emergence of the Court as a new locus for the consideration of complaints. The Court's ability to assume such a role was enabled by several states' acceptance of the Court's jurisdiction over directly submitted individual complaints.[241] The Court's first major decision concerned Tanzania. In the early 1990s Tanzania adopted constitutional amendments limiting participation in various political races to members of official political parties or candidates supported by those parties. These amendments were challenged in the Tanzanian judicial system, and while the High Court struck the amendments down, the Court of Appeal, Tanzania's highest judicial body, overturned one of the High Court rulings, stipulating that the matter was a political one and hence that judicial review was inappropriate. The issue was then brought to the African Court, which, in *Tanganyika Law Society et al. v. Tanzania*,[242] found Tanzania's electoral structure in violation of the Charter, and ordered Tanzania to "take constitutional, legislative and all other measures within a reasonable time to remedy the violations."[243] In its very first merits decision, therefore, the Court demonstrated its willingness to wade into the potentially contentious area of electoral law as well as to call for changes both to legislation and to domestic constitutional law.

Two of the Court's next significant decisions concerned freedom of expression and of the press in Burkina Faso. The first concerned Norbert Zongo, a prominent journalist who was assassinated along with several companions in December 1998. At the time, Zongo was investigating corruption in the highest circles of power in the country. Following Zongo and his colleagues' deaths, investigations stalled. In *In the Matter of Beneficiaries of Late Norbert Zongo et al. v. Burkina Faso*[244] the Court found Burkina Faso had violated the Charter through its failure to adequately investigate the assassinations and to hold those responsible to account, and on the basis of the chilling effect that failure had on freedom

240 2020 Rules of Procedure, Af. Comm. H.P.R.

241 By the end of 2020 ten states had accepted the ability of individuals to submit cases directly – Benin, Burkina Faso, Côte d'Ivoire, Gambia, Ghana, Malawi, Mali, Rwanda, Tanzania, and Tunisia. Four of these states withdrew their acceptance by the decade's end, however, as detailed later.

242 App. Nos. 009/2011 & 011/2011, Af. Ct. H.P.R. (June 14, 2013).

243 Ibid., holding para. 3.

244 App. No. 013/2011, Af. Ct. H.P.R. (March 28, 2014).

of expression. In its ruling the Court also gave notice that it would be playing close attention to the question of remedies, by requiring separate briefs on remedial measures.

The Court's second decision concerning Burkina Faso concerned another journalist investigating state wrongdoing, Lohé Konaté, who wrote two articles accusing a state prosecutor of corruption in 2012. Mr. Konaté and one of his colleagues were subsequently found criminally liable for defamation, public insult, and contempt of court. In *Konaté v. Burkina Faso*[245] the Court found that the state had thereby violated the right to freedom of expression, and adopted a holding laying out in detail a variety of measures Burkina Faso must take in order to bring its law into conformity with its obligations in regard to freedom of expression, while once again ordering the parties to submit further briefs concerning personal reparations.

A couple of years later, the Court turned its attention once more to the design of electoral systems, with its ruling in *Actions Pour la Protection des Droits de l'Homme (APDH) v. Côte d'Ivoire.*[246] The complaint accused the Ivoirian electoral commission of lacking independence. The Court found that the manner in which Côte d'Ivoire had established its electoral commission was indeed in violation of the principles including in the African Charter on Democracy and the ECOWAS Democracy Protocol, as well as of the rights to equality before the law and political participation protected by the African Charter, and ordered Côte d'Ivoire to revise the law establishing the electoral commission. While the standards advanced by the Court in the case may not have been radical in themselves, the decision was notable both for the manner in which the Court drew upon the broader frameworks for the establishment of democratic systems in Africa, and for the Court's willingness to once again move into the contentious area of political system design, reinforcing the approach to such issues developed by the Commission's Côte d'Ivoire decisions and the Court's decision in *Tanganyika Law Society.*

As had been true of the other regional systems, the Commission was initially reluctant to refer cases to the Court. The Commission conquered its reluctance in 2011 by referring a case concerning violations committed during the fighting in Libya,[247] and followed up in 2012 by referring the

[245] App. No. 004/2013, Af. Ct. H.P.R. (December 5, 2014).

[246] App. No. 001/2014, Af. Ct. H.P.R. (November 18, 2016).

[247] The Commission referred this case directly, prior to reaching its own decision on the matter, on the basis that it concerned serious and massive violations. See African Commission on Human and Peoples' Rights v. Great Socialist People's Libyan Arab Jamahiriya, App.

*Ogiek* case, concerning the rights of the Ogiek people, another indigenous community in Kenya.[248] In 2017, the Court issued its ruling in the latter case, finding that Kenya had violated the rights of the Ogiek people by expelling them from their land against their will and without prior consultation or compensation.

The Court was not the only body that began to take up the slack left by the Commission's retreat from its caseload mandate in the 2010s. The African Committee of Experts on the Rights and Welfare of the Child made its first decision in 2011.[249] The ECOWAS Court's acquisition of a mandate to consider rights issues in 2005 saw it too start to develop a strong body of rights-based jurisprudence,[250] and the East African Court of Justice commenced issuing rights-based decisions around the same time as well.[251]

No. 004/2011, Af. Ct. H.P.R., Order for Provisional Measures (March 25, 2011); African Commission on Human and Peoples' Rights v. Great Socialist People's Libyan Arab Jamahiriya, App. No. 004/2011, Af. Ct. H.P.R., Order Striking Out the Case (March 15, 2013).

248 African Commission on Human and Peoples' Rights v. Kenya, App. No. 006/2012, Af. Ct. H.P.R. (May 26, 2017). In this instance, the Commission referred the case following Kenya's failure to comply with interim measures it had suggested. The case took its name before the Court from the fact that the African Commission had referred the case, though it was already apparent to many at the time that such a naming convention could not persist for long, given the sheer number of cases that would otherwise be distinguishable only on the basis of their case numbers.

249 The Committee was the body tasked with overseeing the African Charter on the Rights and Welfare of the Child (ACRWC), which had come into force in 1999. The Committee's first decision was IHRDA and OSJI (on behalf of children of Nubian descent in Kenya) v. Kenya, Comm. No. 002/09, ACRWC Committee (March 22, 2011). This was followed by other important decisions, including Michelo Husungule and others (on behalf of children in Northern Uganda) v. Uganda, Comm. No. 1/2005, ACRWC Committee (April 19, 2013) and Centre for Human Rights and Rencontre Africaine pour la Défense des Droits de l'Homme v. Senegal, Comm. No. 003/12, ACRWC Committee (April 15, 2014).

250 See, e.g., Essien v. The Gambia, Judgment ECW/CCJ/APP/05/05, ECOWAS Ct. (March 17, 2007); Manneh v. The Gambia, Judgment ECW/CCJ/JJD/03/08, ECOWAS Ct. (June 5, 2008); Karaou v. Niger, Judgment ECW/CCJ/JJD/06/08, ECOWAS Ct. (October 27, 2008); Registered Trustees of SERAP v. Nigeria, Judgment ECW/CCJ/JUD/07/10, ECOWAS Ct. (November 30, 2010).

251 See, e.g., Anyang' Nyong'o and others v. Attorney General of Kenya and others, Reference 1 of 2006, EAC Ct. (November 27, 2006); Katabazi and others v. Secretary General of the EAC and another, Reference 1 of 2007, EAC Ct. (November 1, 2007). The East African Court has also encountered some resistance to its human rights jurisprudence, however, in particular due to its decision in the *Anyang' Nyong'o* case, which touched on sensitive issues of Kenyan politics. The Kenyan government responded by suggesting a restructuring of the Court, ultimately leading to amendments that created an appellate division and provided that judges might be removed for "misconduct," after an independent tribunal

The Commission's gradual relinquishment of its work deciding individual cases was hence counterbalanced in the early 2010s by other institutions' development, and acceptance of increasing numbers of case submissions, in the same period. As the decade progressed, however, worrying signs developed elsewhere as well. Several of the states that had previously accepted the ability of the Court to hear individual complaints directly withdrew that acceptance. Rwanda withdrew its assent in 2016, following a complaint by an opposition politician arrested and imprisoned in 2010. Aware of state resistance, the Court took some steps to mollify states. A 2017 decision of the Court barred civil society organizations recognized by the African Commission, but not the African Union, from requesting advisory opinions.[252] While an unfortunate limitation, this decision was limited insofar as civil society organizations recognized by the African Union might still request advisory opinions, and have taken use of this power to produce several important decisions in recent years.[253] In the later 2010s the Court began to reduce the types of remedies it was willing to award and to focus its energy on more individualized, localized cases. The Court's willingness to soften its approach had limits, however: in those cases the Court did hear, it often issued strong judgments, in accordance with rights standards. This led to ongoing backlash, however, as Tanzania withdrew its assent to the Court's ability to hear cases directly in November 2019, and Benin and Côte d'Ivoire shortly thereafter, in April 2020.

had looked into the charge. See Joint Communique of the eighth Summit of the EAC Community Heads of State (November 30, 2006). As with other reform processes, the result was an increase in the formality of the system, rather than an out and out weakening of it. The process that led to the amendments was itself challenged in *East Africa Law Society and others v. Attorney General of Kenya and others* (Ref 3 of 2007, EAC Ct. (September 1, 2008)), in which the Court found that the process that had been followed had not allowed for adequate consultation, and that in particular further amendments should only be adopted following a more consultative process.

252 See African Court on Human and Peoples' Rights, Request for Advisory Opinion by the Centre for Human Rights at the University of Pretoria and the Coalition of African Lesbians, Request No. 002/2015, Af. Ct. H.P.R. (September 28, 2017).

253 See, e.g., Request for Advisory Opinion by The Pan African Lawyers Union (PALU) on The Compatibility of Vagrancy Laws with the African Charter on Human and Peoples' Rights and Other Human Rights Instruments Applicable in Africa, Advisory Opinion Request No. 001/2018, Af. Ct. H.P.R. (December 4, 2020); Request for Advisory Opinion by The Pan African Lawyers Union (PALU) on The Right to Participate in the Government of One's Country in the Context of an Election Held During a Public Health Emergency or a Pandemic, such as the COVID-19 Crisis, Advisory Opinion Request No. 001/2020, Af. Ct. H.P.R. (July 16, 2021).

## V Conclusion

The systems' distinct foundational moments helped set them off on different paths. While those moments played a significant role in the formation of each of the systems, the systems' subsequent evolutionary paths cannot be understood on the basis of those moments alone. From the moment each rights treaty and set of institutional mechanism was initially agreed upon and established, that system set off on a course of gradualist evolution. Many factors have been influential in such regards, including the character of individuals who have assumed key roles within the systems, and the ongoing input of state parties. More than any other factor, however, the systems' respective evolutions have been shaped by the nature of the rights violations they have encountered, and the extensive work done by individuals and organizations to bring those violations before them. As the preceding discussion has recounted, the types of violations most frequently and impactfully faced have neither been the same across the various systems nor within each system over time, pushing each system in different directions as time has gone on. What impacts have these different processes of struggle had within the different rights systems?

### *V.1 Europe*

From early in its existence the European Commission was confronted with cases that involved widespread and serious violations. The Commission did not distinguish itself in its first encounters with such violations, however, adopting an understandable but nonetheless weak approach to the violations brought to its attention.[254] At least as significant, though less widely recognized, was the manner in which the Commission decided to structure its broader approach in response to such cases: separating off its case consideration into two tracks, one track available on the inter-state level, focused on the contemplation of general situations of violation, and another available to individuals, focused on narrower issues and complaints.[255]

254 See Greece v. United Kingdom, Eur Comm. H.R., 2 Eur. Ybk. Hum. Rts. 182 (1958–1959).

255 In this context both were applied to complaints brought by Greece; the first Greek case (Greece v. United Kingdom, App. No. 176/56, Eur. Comm. H.R., Admissibility (June 2, 1956)) was declared admissible on the basis that "the provision of Article 26 concerning the exhaustion of domestic remedies according to the generally recognized rules of international law does not apply to the present application, the scope of which is to determine the compatibility with the Convention of legislative measures and administrative

The result was that the majority of the system's early work came to concern relatively discrete matters: much of the system's early casework, for instance, related to procedural issues pertaining to detention and the conditions in which detained individuals were held.[256] With time, the system's relatively cautious initial decisions were replaced by a more forceful set of holdings, issued in the 1970s. Key cases from this period concerned corporal punishment, freedom of the press, inheritance laws, and access to council.[257] In and through decisions concerning these matters, the Court developed the ideas of progressive interpretation and European consensus and the margin of appreciation and subsidiarity doctrines, all of which have become widely recognized cornerstones of the European system's approach to human rights.

As time went on, the European system continued to evolve along the lines set out in its initial decades, developing increasingly detailed standards relative to the rights guarantees provided by the Convention, while the doctrinal devices enumerated previously became more sophisticated and entrenched. The result was a system that could think of itself as playing a constitutional role, insofar as its work was targeted at developing legal standards as such. At the same time, in part because of its emphasis on judicial procedures, in part because of its emphasis on more individualized cases, and in part because of the greater sophistication of national-level judicial actors in Europe, the system's relationship with rights advocacy communities, while strong, was at a greater remove than that which developed in the other systems.

The European system had a moment of triumph in the 1990s, as the dual commission/court structure was replaced by a unified court. At the same time, the system expanded its jurisdiction to the east, encompassing

practices in Cyprus"; the second Greek case (Greece v. United Kingdom, App. No. 299/57, Eur. Comm. H.R., Admissibility (October 12, 1957)) concerned a bundled collection of applications on behalf of individuals, some of which the Commission found admissible, others of which it did not.

256 See, e.g., Neumeister v. Austria, App. No. 1936/63, Eur. Ct. H.R. (June 27, 1968); Wemhoff v. Germany, App. No. 2122/64, Eur. Ct. H.R. (June 27, 1968); Stögmüller v. Austria, App. No. 1602/62, Eur. Ct. H.R. (November 10, 1969); Matznetter v. Austria, App. No. 2178/64, Eur. Ct. H.R. (November 10, 1969); Ringeisen v Austria, App. No. 2614/65, Eur. Ct. H.R. (July 16, 1971).

257 See Golder v. United Kingdom, App. No. 4451/70, Eur. Ct. H.R. (February 21, 1975); Tyrer v. United Kingdom, App. No. 5856/72, Eur. Ct. H.R. (April 25, 1978); Sunday Times v. United Kingdom, App. No. 6538/74, Eur. Ct. H.R. (April 26, 1979); Marckx v. Belgium, App. No. 6833/74, Eur. Ct. H.R. (June 13, 1979); Airey v. Ireland, App. No. 6289/73, Eur. Ct. H.R. (October 9, 1979).

several countries that were transitioning away from Soviet rule. The combination of the system's reputation as an effective mechanism, the thickening of its jurisprudence over time, its transition into a purely juridical system and the expansion of its coverage to several more jurisdictions, however, all contributed to the system's growing "caseload crisis," driven both by the number of cases submitted, and by the fact that in several cases, national situations of widespread, structural violation continued regardless of the Court's rulings condemning them.

In a number of cases faced in this period the European system was called upon to address situations of serious and widespread violations, similar to those that arose early and often before the Inter-American and African regional human rights systems. While the immediacy with which such cases confronted the Inter-American and African systems meant they played a major role shaping those systems' approaches, however, in the European system they arrived after a particular approach had become entrenched, and hence had far less effect on the nature of the system as a whole. The European system refused to deal with cases concerning violations against the Kurds in Turkey and against the Chechen population in Russia in a more collective fashion, deeming an individualized approach more suitable.[258] While the system has supported transitions toward more democratic governance, it has tended to do so through individual case determinations advancing particular standards, rather than through more holistic judgments.[259] Similarly, while the European system has considered cases alleging discrimination against members of particular groups, it has preferred to address such issues from a more individualized perspective, leading, for instance, to a refusal to consider indigenous peoples' rights claims altogether.[260]

[258] See Reidy, Hampson, and Boyle, "Gross Violations"; Leach, "The Chechen Conflict"; Koroteev, "Legal Remedies"; Leach et al., *Responding to Systemic Human Rights Violations*, 163–4. For a general criticism of the system's approach to entrenched situations of widespread violation, see Gross, "'Once More unto the Breach.'"

[259] On this theme, see James Sweeney, *The European Court of Human Rights in the Post-Cold War Era: Universality in Transition* (Routledge, 2013). In addition, the system also relied on the efforts of other organizations, such as the Venice Commission, which did much valuable work supporting transitions, itself built upon the standards developed by the European Court. See Drzemczewski, "The Council of Europe's Cooperation and Assistance Programmes"; Jowell, "The Venice Commission."

[260] See Giovanna Gismondi, "Denial of Justice: The Latest Indigenous Land Disputes Before the European Court of Human Rights and the Need for an Expansive Interpretation of Protocol 1," 18 *Yale Human Rights and Development Journal* (2017), 1–58. That said, the European Court has at least adopted a somewhat more flexible approach to evidence in

In sum, the European system has developed an approach that tends to focus more narrowly on individual situations, that pursues the gradual development of jurisprudence, and that deploys a range of tools in order to lessen or avoid the tension that might otherwise be produced by judgments against states. This approach has been challenged in recent decades, leading to significant reforms, including for instance adoption of the pilot judgment procedure. The European system as a whole remains tightly bound to a jurisprudential, constitutionalist vision of rights work, however, within which framework the struggles of the 2010s over caseload, enforcement, and appropriate levels of subsidiarity are likely to continue.

### *V.2 The Americas*

The Inter-American system encountered instances of widespread and serious violations from its earliest days. The system's encounters with the military dictatorships in countries such as Brazil, Uruguay, Chile, and Argentina from the 1960s through the 1970s were particularly formative.[261] It was also called upon to engage with similarly serious, entrenched and widespread violations in Central America, in which context the Court's dramatic first full decision in a contentious case, in *Velásquez Rodríguez v. Honduras*, helped to cement the system's willingness to directly confront serious violations within popular imaginations of the system's work.[262] Cases involving widespread, serious, and systematic violations, including several instances of mass killing, have continued to form a central part of the system's work ever since.[263]

cases of discrimination, as demonstrated by its decision in *Nachova and others v. Bulgaria* and *D.H. and others v. The Czech Republic. See* Nachova and others v. Bulgaria, App. Nos. 43577/98 & 43579/98, Eur. Ct. H.R. (2005), paras. 147, 157; D.H. and others v. The Czech Republic, App. No. 57325/00, Eur. Ct. H.R. (November 13, 2007), paras. 176–80.

261 The Commission's reports on Chile and Argentina were particularly important; see Report on the Status of Human Rights in Chile, Findings of "on the spot" Observations in the Republic of Chile (July 22–August 2, 1974), OEA/Ser. L/V/II.34, Doc. 21 (October 25, 1974); Report on the Status of Human Rights in Argentina, OEA/Ser. L/V/II.49, Doc. 19 corr.1 (April 1, 1980).

262 Velásquez Rodríguez v. Honduras, App. No. 7920, Int.-Am. Ct. H.R. (July 29, 1988); see also Saul Godinez Cruz v. Honduras, App. No. 8097, Int.-Am. Ct. H.R. (January 20, 1989), and Francisco Fairen-Grabi and Yolanda Solis-Corrales v. Honduras, App. No. 7951, Int.-Am. Ct. H.R. (March 15, 1989).

263 See, e.g., Garrido v. Argentina, App. No. 11.009, Int.-Am. Ct. H.R., Reparations and Costs (August 27, 1998); Plan de Sanchez Massacre v. Guatemala, App. No. 11.763, Int.-Am. Ct. H.R. (April 29, 2004); Mapiripan Massacre v. Colombia, App. No. 12.250, Int.-Am. Ct. H.R. (March 7, 2005); Gomez-Palomino v. Peru, App. No. 11.062, Int.-Am. Ct. H.R.

The repeated early engagement by the Inter-American system with widespread and serious violations had numerous effects. Most broadly, the encounter with such violations led the system to adopt a more structural understanding of rights violations, focused on examining situations of violation from a holistic, rather than an individuated, viewpoint. This applied temporally as well, as the system came to understand violations as ongoing states of affairs, rather than as isolated events – a shift in viewpoint that carried procedural implications.[264] More practically, where widespread and serious violations took place, national political opposition was often rendered impossible, driving many of those who might otherwise have fought for gradual domestic reforms into exile. In such instances, the energy those individuals might otherwise have devoted to more overtly political work was often channeled into appeals to international human rights mechanisms, which were often strongly supported by one or another exiled community.[265]

Over time, the Inter-American system began to encounter other sets of violations as well. From the 1990s on, the system began to encounter an increasing number of cases from states transitioning to more democratic modes of governance, including Argentina, Brazil, Uruguay, Chile and Peru. The more rights-hospitable context provided by such transitions helped to encourage the system to move beyond calling out violations, and to devote greater attention to measures that might aid states with the

(November 22, 2005) (in which the Court noted that "the forced disappearance of persons became a systematic and generalized practice implemented by the State" between "1989 and 1993" (para. 54.1)); Ituango Massacres v. Colombia, App. Nos. 12.050 & 12.266, Int.-Am. Ct. H.R. (July 1, 2006); Las Dos Erres v Guatemala, App. No. 11.681, Int.-Am. Ct. H.R. (November 24, 2009); Gomes Lund et al. v. Brazil, App. No. 11.552, Int.-Am. Ct. H.R. (November 24, 2010).

264 In this context, the Inter-American system's contemplations of the notion of continuing violations, and its interrelated contemplation of the notion of whether unenforced laws might be considered to violate rights, are particularly notable; see Blake v. Guatemala, App No. 11.219, Int.-Am. Ct. H.R., Preliminary Objections (July 2, 1996); El Amparo v. Venezuela, App. No. 10.602, Int.-Am. Ct. H.R., Reparations, Trindade dissent, paras. 2–3, 5, 7, 10 (September 14, 1996); ibid., Interpretation of Reparations, Trindade dissent, paras. 22–3 (April 16, 1997); Genie Lacoyo v. Nicaragua, App. No. 10.792, Int.-Am. Ct. H.R., Application for Review, Trindade dissent, paras. 9, 27 (September 13, 1997); Suarez Rosero v. Ecuador, App. No. 11.273, Int.-Am. Ct. H.R., para. 98 (November 12, 1997); Moiwana v. Suriname, App. No. 11.821, Int.-Am. Ct. H.R., Preliminary Objections, Merits, Reparations and Costs (June 15, 2005). See also Trindade, "The Inter-American Court of Human Rights at a crossroads," 182.

265 For more, see Sikkink, "Emergence, Evolution, and Effectiveness"; Keck and Sikkink, *Activists Beyond Borders*; Markarian, *Left in Transformation*; Kelly, *Sovereign Emergencies*.

process of democratic, rights-based transition. While the Inter-American system was not alone in playing this function, it was the most heavily shaped by it, developing a body of jurisprudence specifically aligned to such a context.[266] Among other features, this could be seen in the system's strong opposition to amnesty laws, and in its development of the concept of "the right to truth."

The system's amnesty decisions were important in their own right.[267] In addition, they played a key role within the system's development of a more forceful position on the strength of regional human rights law within national legal systems. This was due in significant part to the peculiar nature of amnesty laws, which act as purported "absolutions," legal acts claiming the power to de-link individuals from responsibility for their past acts – rather than, like most laws, serving the role of establishing rules governing all in society impartially and in an ongoing way. Relative to most laws, the separation of the national and international legal orders presents less of a problem for international rights bodies. If a human rights body declares a national law in violation of a state's international human rights obligations, the state may bring its violation to an end simply by bringing its law into compliance with the terms laid out by the rights body's judgment, and there is accordingly no need for the human rights body in question to insist on the direct applicability of their judgment, or

[266] The Inter-American system's development of a progressive, "transformative" approach in this context was fueled in substantial part by a dynamic interplay between regional and national level developments. For more, see Armin von Bogdandy, Eduardo F. Mac-Gregor, Mariela M. Antoniazzi, and Flávia Piovesan eds., *Transformative Constitutionalism in Latin America: The Emergence of a New Ius Commune* (Oxford University Press, 2017).

[267] For some of the Inter-American Court's key amnesty decisions, see Barrios Altos v. Peru, App. No. 11.528, Int.-Am. Ct. H.R., Merits (March 14, 2001); Almonacid Arellano et al. v. Chile, App. No. 12.057, Int.-Am. Ct. H.R. (September 26, 2006); Gomes Lund et al. v. Brazil, App. No. 11.552, Int.-Am. Ct. H.R. (November 24, 2010); Gelman v. Uruguay, App. No. 12.607, Int.-Am. Ct. H.R. (February 24, 2011); Massacres of El Mozote v. El Salvador App. No. 10.720, Int.-Am. Ct. H.R. (October 25, 2012). For more, see Douglass Cassel, "La Corte Interamericana de Derechos Humanos," in *Víctimas sin mordaza. El impacto del sistema interamericano en la justicia transicional en Latinoamérica: los casos de Argentina, Guatemala, El Salvador y Perú* (Due Process of Law Foundation, 2007), https://dplf.org/sites/default/files/1202485080.pdf; Lisa Laplante, 'Outlawing Amnesty: The Return of Criminal Justice in Transitional Justice Schemes', 49 *Virginia Journal of International Law* (2009), 915–84. A number of African cases have also challenged amnesties, including Malawi African Association and others v. Mauritania, App. Nos. 54/91, 61/91, 96/93, 98/93, 164/97, 196/97, & 210/98, Af. Comm. H.P.R. (May 11, 2000) and Mouvement Ivoirien de Droits de l'Homme v. Cote d'Ivoire (2), App. No. 246/02, Af. Comm. H.P.R. (May 22, 2008).

of human rights law in general, on the national legal level. With amnesty laws, however, to pursue such an approach poses more challenges. While, following a judgment finding an amnesty law in violation of its international human rights obligations, a state might remove that amnesty law from its books, the effect of such a removal is less than clear. Should that removal be understood to annul the previously granted amnesty, or should that amnesty be understood to have taken effect upon the issuance of the initial law, such that while the law might be repealed, it is too late to relink the individuals in question to the responsibility for their acts the amnesty severed? While accountability advocates might prefer the former approach, thorny due process questions would be raised. One way around such challenges, however, is to insist that the amnesty law in question was never effective in the first place, and that the responsibility of individuals for serious rights violations was thereby never severed. In order to do so, it is necessary to suggest in one way or another that the rights violation committed by such an amnesty law in essence meant that it could never really take effect. In the human rights context, the clearest way of advancing such an understanding is to suggest that human rights law does not only have effect on the international but also on the national level. This, in essence, is what the Inter-American Court came to suggest, albeit in a somewhat indirect and ambiguous manner.[268]

In addition to being driven to adopt a more assertive vision of the force of human rights law by its amnesty cases, the Inter-American system's encounter with situations of transitional justice also led it to develop the concept of the "right to truth," with further implications for the system's broader rights vision. The seeds of the concept developed in relation to cases of enforced disappearance, a composite form of rights violation in which the most severe violations – torture and extrajudicial killings – were combined with the active propagation of a veil of secrecy, aimed both at shielding perpetrators from accountability, and at generating a wider

[268] For an extensive, compelling account of both the nature of the Inter-American system's amnesty caselaw, and its effect on the approach of the system as a whole, see Castan, *Transformation of the Inter-American System*. The Court's ability to advance a more assertive vision of human rights law in the context of amnesties was aided both by the gravity of the harms in question, which justified the adoption of a particularly forceful response, and by contemporaneous developments in international criminal law, which even more clearly broke down the distinction between the international and national legal orders, and similarly tended to find amnesties, at least those that purported to forgive the most serious rights violations, in violation of higher-order legal obligations and as such lacking in legal consequence.

aura of terror. Enforced disappearances were perhaps the most emblematic form of violation committed by the authoritarian regimes of Latin America in the 1960s, 1970s, and 1980s, embodying both their brutality and their desire to insulate government decisions from public view, oversight, and control. Consequently, the experience of addressing them was central to the Inter-American system's formation.

The complex nature of enforced disappearances pushed the Inter-American system to develop more experimental and expansive approaches. The nature of the violations was such that they required both a liberal approach to standing and evidence, and a recognition not only of the concrete violations in question but also of the underlying policies that gave rise to them. As the Inter-American Court put it in *Velásquez*,

> Disappearances are not new in the history of human rights violations. However, their systematic and repeated nature and their use not only for causing certain individuals to disappear, either briefly or permanently, but also as a means of creating a general state of anguish, insecurity and fear, is a recent phenomenon ... The phenomenon of disappearances is a complex form of human rights violation that must be understood and confronted in an integral fashion.[269]

While its encounter with enforced disappearances imbued the Inter-American system with an enhanced awareness of the importance of establishing accurate accounts, to the extent possible, of past violations, it was only when it encountered transitional contexts that the system came to articulate the concept of the right to truth as such. As the Commission has put it, its recognition of the right to truth arose out of its confrontation with "multiple and repeated breaks with the democratic and institutional order" in which "mass and systemic violations of human rights [were] frequent."[270] Over time, the idea of the right to truth gradually broadened, coming to encompass an understanding that "society as a whole ... has the inalienable right to know the truth about past events, as well as the motives and circumstances in which aberrant crimes came to be committed, in order to prevent recurrence of such acts in the future."[271] The aim

[269] Velásquez Rodríguez v. Honduras, App. No. 7920, Int.-Am. Ct. H.R., paras. 149–50 (July 29, 1988).

[270] See Int.-Am. Comm. H.R., The Right to Truth in the Americas (2014), paras. 2, 4.

[271] Ibid., para 15; see also paras. 55–60, 71, 81. As the Commission would further put it,

> satisfaction of the collective dimension of the right to truth requires a procedural examination of the most complete historical record possible, and a judicial

was not only to provide victims and relatives with an accurate account of past rights violations due to the personal benefits they might derive from that knowledge; rather, it was also to establish an account society as a whole might rely upon, in order to enable a process of collective healing and reconciliation, and to make the recurrence of such violations less likely in future.[272]

The development of the idea of the right to truth by the Inter-American system further developed the approach employed by that system. First, while the right to truth might be understood as possessed by every individual, it is also and overarchingly a right possessed by society as a whole – in short, a quintessential "group" right. Second, the idea of the right to truth helps to push rights bodies toward more encompassive visions of their work, because that work can no longer be geared simply to providing justice in individual cases, but rather must involve the production of wide-ranging and detailed accounts of the historical record, with the implicit purpose of reorienting societies toward more rights-respecting futures.

Another set of cases that contributed to the vision and approach that developed within the Inter-American system over the course of the first two decades of the twenty-first century were cases concerning group-based rights violations. Important group rights cases included most prominently indigenous peoples' rights case,[273] but also cases concerning

> determination as to the patterns of joint action and the identity of all those who, in one way or another, participated in the violations and their respective responsibility. Fulfillment of these obligations is necessary to guarantee a full reconstruction of the truth and a thorough investigation of the structures in which the human rights violations took place.

Ibid., para. 20; see also para. 82.

272 As the Commission has further put it, the right to truth serves to "enable society to rebuild the past, recognize the mistakes made, make reparations to victims and form the vigorous public opinion that is instrumental in rebuilding democracy and restoring the rule of law"; to "preserve memory" in order to avoid "a recurrence of violations in the future"; to help dismantle "the authoritarian structures that seek to survive the transition to democracy"; to help promote "accountability and transparency in government"; and to prevent "corruption and authoritarianism," ibid., para. 109; see also paras. 81–6.

273 See, e.g., Aloeboetoe v. Suriname, App. No. 10.150, Int.-Am. Ct. H.R., Reparations and Costs (September 10, 1993); Mayagna Awas Tingni Community v. Nicaragua, App. No. 11.577, Int.-Am. Ct. H.R., Merits (August 31, 2001); Mary and Carrie Dann v. United States, App. No. 11.140, Int.-Am. Comm. H.R. (December 27, 2002); Moiwana Community v. Suriname, App. No. 11.821, Int.-Am. Ct. H.R. (June 15, 2005); Yakye Axa Indigenous Community v. Paraguay, App. No. 12.313, Int.-Am. Ct. H.R. (June 17, 2005); Yatama v. Nicaragua, App. No. 12.388, Int.-Am. Ct. H.R. (June 23, 2005); Sawhoyamaxa Indigenous

rights violations committed against groups defined by race or ethnicity,[274] gender,[275] and age.[276] The system's ability to consider such cases was not pre-given – rather, the way was paved by the system's early encounters with widespread and serious violations, which accustomed it to adopting wide-angled, comprehensive approaches.[277] The development of a group rights paradigm in the United States, earlier in the twentieth century, perhaps provided an inspirational model as well.[278] Once recognized, group-based rights violation claims further encouraged the system's adoption of a more holistic, structural approach, insofar as they compelled the system not only to confront specific instances of harm inflicted on particular communities, but also to consider the longer-term, underlying structural forces that enabled such harms to take place. Moreover, the system's encounter with such violations tended to place emphasis on the need for specific, as opposed to universalized, responses[279] – emphasizing, in other words, the importance of the remedial as opposed to the jurisprudential function of case consideration.[280]

Community v. Paraguay, App. No. 322/2001, Int.-Am. Ct. H.R. (March 29, 2006); Pueblo Saramaka v. Suriname, App. No. 12.338, Int.-Am. Ct. H.R. (November 28, 2007); Sarayaku v. Ecuador, App. No. 12.465, Int.-Am. Ct. H.R. (June 27, 2012).

274 See, e.g., Yean and Bosico v. Dominican Republic, App. No. 12.189, Int.-Am. Ct. H.R. (September 8, 2005); Simone Andre Diniz v. Brazil, App. No. 12.001, Int.-Am. Comm. H.R. (October 21, 2006); Wallace de Almeida v. Brazil, App. No. 12.440, Int.-Am. Comm. H.R. (March 20, 2009); Nadege Dorzema et al. v. Dominican Republic, App. No. 1351–05, Int.-Am. Ct. H.R. (October 24, 2012).

275 See, e.g., Maria da Penha Fernandes v. Brazil, App. No. 12.051, Int.-Am. Comm. H.R. (April 16, 2001); Gonzalez et al. v. Mexico, App. Nos. 12.496, 12.497, & 12.498, Int.-Am. Ct. H.R. (November 16, 2009); Fernandez Ortega et al. v. Mexico, 12,580 (August 30, 2010); Rosendo Cantú et al. v. Mexico, App. No. 12.579, Int.-Am. Ct. H.R. (August 31, 2010); Jessica Lenahan (Gonzales) et al v. United States, App. No. 12.626, Int.-Am. Comm. H.R. (July 21, 2011).

276 See, e.g., Villagran Morales et al. v. Guatemala, App. No. 11.383, Int.-Am. Ct. H.R., Merits (November 19, 1999); Juvenile Reeducation Institute v. Paraguay, App. No. 11.666, Int.-Am. Ct. H.R. (September 2, 2004).

277 On this point, see Abramovich, "From Massive Violations to Structural Patterns."

278 For more on the "minority rights revolution" in the United States, see John Skrentny, *The Minority Rights Revolution* (Harvard University Press, 2002).

279 This position, which flows organically from the confrontation with group-based rights violations, has been emphasized on the theoretical level by critical race theorists, who have observed that "Critical race theory cannot be understood as an abstract set of ideas or principles. Among its basic theoretical themes is that of privileging contextual and historical descriptions over transhistorical or purely abstract ones." Mari Matsuda, Charles R. Lawrence III, Richard Delgado, and Kimberlè Williams Crenshaw, *Words That Wound: Critical Race Theory, Assaultive Speech, and the First Amendment* (Westview, 1993), 3.

280 On the evolution of remedial approaches in the Inter-American system, see Antkowiak, "Remedial Approaches to Human Rights Violations."

### V.3 Africa

In Africa just as in the Americas, widespread and serious violations were at the forefront of the system's attention from its founding in the shadow of events in Uganda and the Central African Republic, leading to explicit reference to "serious or massive violations" in Article 58(1) of the African Charter. Since the Commission's creation it has been repeatedly called upon to address situations involving widespread and serious violations in several countries.[281] This repeated engagement with egregious violations, set against a backdrop of poorly functioning national remedial systems, had a significant effect on the approach adopted in the system. From the beginning, separating out individuals' stories from wider background political contexts was challenging and made little functional sense. The system was thus conditioned from its first moments not to focus on individuals and individual instances of violation, a form of attention sometimes mistakenly understood to be inherent to human rights as such, but rather to focus on big picture situations, taking the prevalence of rights violations as given and attempting to provide wide-ranging and cross-cutting responses thereto. To put it another way, as several astute commentators on the African system have put it, encounters with mass violations helped to render the "exception" the norm.[282]

As in the Americas, the African system's approach was further shaped by encounters with situations of democratic transition, which took place

[281] See, e.g., Commission Nationale des Droits de l'Homme et des Libertés v. Tchad, App. No. 74/92, Af. Comm. H.P.R. (October 11, 1995); Free Legal Assistance Group and others v. DRC, App. Nos. 25/89, 47/90, 56/91, & 100/93, Af. Comm. H.P.R. (April 4, 1996); Organisation Mondial Contre la Torture and others v. Rwanda, App. Nos. 27/89, 46/91, 49/91, & 99/93, Af. Comm. H.P.R. (October 31, 1996); Amnesty International and others v. Sudan, App. Nos. 48/90, 50/91, 52/91, & 89/93, Af. Comm. H.P.R. (November 15, 1999); DRC v. Burundi, Rwanda, and Uganda, App. No. 227/99, Af. Comm. H.P.R. (29 May 2003); Sudan Human Rights Organisation and COHRE v. Sudan, App. Nos. 279/03 & 296/05, Af. Comm. H.P.R. (May 27, 2009). In addition, a number of other cases have addressed the institution of authoritarian systems (see, e.g., Civil Liberties Organisation v. Nigeria, App. No. 129/94, Af. Comm. H.P.R. (March 22, 1995); Jawara v. the Gambia, App. Nos. 147/95 & 149/96, Af. Comm. H.P.R. (May 11, 2000)) and violence against opposition parties (see, e.g., Zimbabwe Human Rights NGO Forum v. Zimbabwe, App. No. 245/02, Af. Comm. H.P.R. (May 15, 2006); Association of Victims of Post Electoral Violence and INTERIGHTS v. Cameroon, App. No. 273/03, Af. Comm. H.P.R. (Nov. 25, 2009)).

[282] See An Na'im, "The Legal Protection of Human Rights in Africa"; Odinkalu, "Back to the Future," 4; Takele Bulto, "Exception as Norm: The Local Remedies Rule in the Context of Socio-economic Rights in the African Human Rights System," 16 *International Journal of Human Rights* (2012), 555–76.

in several Southern African countries as well as Benin, Mali, and Tanzania over the course of the 1990s. The Commission's encounters with various violations committed by Nigeria's military dictatorship were particularly important, thanks in part to the significance of Nigeria as such and the sophistication of the rights advocacy organizations who brought the cases, but most overarchingly to the fact that Nigeria underwent a transition toward more democratic governance while several key cases concerning the repressive governance put in place under the military government were still before the system, allowing the system to deliver more assertive judgments than it might otherwise have deemed possible.[283] While not as much of a leader in terms of transitional justice jurisprudence as the Inter-American system, the African system proved itself willing to support many similar steps, including endorsing the right to truth.[284] In its decisions concerning Gambia and Côte d'Ivoire the system adopted a strong vision of the effect of international human rights law on the national level, while in numerous other holdings issued over the course of the 2000s, including cases concerning various group rights in particular[285] – facilitated, in the African system, not only by the system's previous encounters with widespread and systemic violations, but also by its explicit mandate to protect "group rights" – the system dramatically increased the detail of its remedial orders. Beginning in the early 2010s, the Court picked up on this progressive trend, issuing forceful and detailed holdings in several major cases.

The African system's gradual development of a wide-angled and assertive approach to its rights mandate ran into serious obstacles in the 2010s.

283 See Media Rights Agenda and others v. Nigeria, Comm. Nos. 105/93, 128/94, 130/94, & 152/96, Af. Comm. H.P.R. (October 31, 1998); Constitutional Rights Project and others v. Nigeria, Comm. Nos. 140/94, 141/94, & 145/95, Af. Comm. H.P.R. (November 5, 1999); Constitutional Rights Project and Civil Liberties Organisation v. Nigeria, Comm. Nos. 143/95 & 150/96, Af. Comm. H.P.R. (November 5, 1999).

284 See African Commission on Human and Peoples' Rights, General Comment No. 4 on the African Charter on Human and Peoples' Rights: The Right to Redress for Victims of Torture and Other Cruel, Inhuman or Degrading Punishment or Treatment (Article 5) (March 4, 2017), para. 44.

285 See, e.g., Malawi African Association and others v. Mauritania, App. Nos. 54/91, 61/91, 96/93, 98/93, 164/97, 196/97, & 210/98, Af. Comm. H.P.R. (May 11, 2000); Institute for Human Rights and Development in Africa v. Guinea, App. No. 249/02, Af. Comm. H.P.R. (December 7, 2004); Institute for Human Rights and Development in Africa v. Angola, App. No. 292/04, Af. Comm. H.P.R. (May 22, 2008); Centre for Minority Rights Development (Kenya) and Minority Rights Group (on behalf of Enderois Welfare Council) v. Kenya, App. No. 276/03, Af. Comm. H.P.R. (November 25, 2009).

First, the Commission retreated from its case consideration mandate. While the Court began to pick up the slack, its assertive jurisprudence led to several states withdrawing their previous acceptances of its direct jurisdiction. As of the end of the 2010s, the African system looks set to continue to face serious challenges in the years ahead.

# 4

# Comparisons

## I Introduction

The previous chapters have considered the two major factors that have shaped the regional systems, as they have evolved over time: their foundational moments, plural and extended as they inevitably were; and the various gradual developments that have taken place in between such moments of major institutional reconstruction, as the systems have struggled to engage with and address the rights violations they have encountered. Implicit in the account is the suggestion that complex institutions like the regional human rights systems cannot be understood based on either the circumstances of their foundation(s) or the manner in which they have gradually evolved over the course of their existence alone – rather, the character of any such system is shaped by both sets of factors.

Assessing the evolution of the European, Inter-American, and African regional human rights systems along these vectors leads to two types of insights. First, it becomes apparent that in certain ways, all three systems have evolved in similar manners over time. Presumably, these similarities have been due to certain shared structural factors common to all three systems, features that might hence be expected to shape the evolution of every such similar system. Multiple elements that have been common to the evolution of each system are identified in the Section II. The first element is *political opportunity*: each system's development has been significantly influenced by the occurrence, from time to time, of background moments in which the regional space for advancing human rights work has opened up. The second element is *legitimacy management*: members of all three systems have worked hard to maintain and, where possible, advance the legitimacy of the system over time. Third, all three systems have been characterized by the development of *symbiotic relationships* between the systems and the human rights advocacy communities in each region. Finally, all three systems have been characterized by processes of *juridification*, becoming more formal, legalistic, and judicialized over time.

Recognizing similar dynamics that have shaped the evolution of all three systems is interesting and important, insofar as it helps us understand the broader structural context in which such systems can be expected to continue to operate in future. Even more interesting and important, however – and also significantly less-studied – are the differences between the systems the previous chapters have helped to bring out. Some important differences are on the level of jurisprudence. Perhaps even more significant, however, are differences in the institutional form each system has assumed – differences that are closely linked to the systems' different approaches to and understandings of human rights work. Recognizing these differences is important both insofar as such recognition serves to broaden understandings of human rights work, and because a broader picture of substantive, institutional, and procedural possibilities will help scholars and rights' advocates better understand the range of institutional design choices available, and the implications those choices may have.

## II Similar Dynamics

Four general dynamics that have shaped system evolution stand out. First, the evolution of the regional human rights systems has been significantly shaped by moments of *political opportunity*.[1] Such critical junctures have

[1] The term "political opportunity" originated and has primarily been used in the social movement context; see Doug McAdam, "Clarifying the Concept of Political Opportunity," in Doug McAdam, John McCarthy, and Mayer Zald eds., *Comparative Perspectives on Social Movements: Political Opportunities, Mobilizing Structures, and Cultural Framings* (Cambridge University Press, 1996). Scholars such as Martha Finnemore and Michael Barnett, Karen Alter, Mikael Madsen and Suzanne Katzenstein have similarly recognized and emphasized the importance of major crises and global political shifts to the evolution of international affairs and international institutions. See Martha Finnemore and Michael Barnett, "The Politics, Power, and Pathologies of International Organizations," 53 *International Organization* (1999), 699–732; Martha Finnemore and Michael Barnett, *Rules for the World: International Organizations in Global Politics* (Cornell University Press, 2004); Karen Alter, "The Evolving International Judiciary," 7 *Annual Review of Law and Social Science* (2011), 387–415; Madsen, "Explaining the Power of International Courts," 24; Karen Alter, *The New Terrain of International Law: Courts, Politics, Rights* (Princeton University Press, 2014); Suzanne Katzenstein, "In the Shadow of Crisis: The Creation of International Courts in the Twentieth Century," 55 *Harvard International Law Journal* (2014), 151–209. Katzenstein helpfully cites a number of different labels under which scholars have recognized the importance of such moments to broader change, highlighting Reiter's invocation of "formative events" (see Dan Reiter, *Crucible of Beliefs: Learning, Alliances, and World Wars* (NCROL, 1996), 184–89), Widmaier et al.'s use of the term "exogenous shocks" (see Wesley Widmaier, Mark Blyth, and Leonard Seabrooke,

arisen in the wake of major global political shifts, as in the post–World War II period and following the end of the Cold War; in the context of more gradually political shifts in which greater emphasis has come to be placed on human rights, as occurred in the 1970s; and following more localized crises, such as those that took place in the context of the Dominican Republic and Cuba in the Americas, and the Central African Republic and Uganda in Africa. As Haas has emphasized, "Decision makers do not always recognize that their understanding of complex issues and linkages is limited, and it often takes a crisis or shock to overcome institutional inertia and habit."[2] Moments of political opportunity, in other words, which are also moments of crisis, uncertainty, or changing normative alignments of one sort or another, shake up the status quo and existing power arrangements, allowing new voices and ideas to arise, that at least on occasion are able to rewrite the existing order and to alter previously dominant approaches.

Second, the evolution of the regional systems has been characterized by ongoing, careful attempts at *legitimacy management* by the various commissions and courts that have been established. A core challenge for such institutions concerns the different communities they must answer to: they must attempt to satisfy a human rights community eager for strong statements and judgments, while simultaneously avoiding giving such offense to states that those states withdraw from their jurisdiction or strip them of their powers. Careful attention to legitimacy management is not a feature of regional rights institutions alone, of course – rather, judicial and quasi-judicial bodies on all levels constantly work to preserve their legitimacy, and have developed a range of techniques through which to do so. Classic strategies of judicial self-protection include declaring matters outside a particular body's jurisdiction; declaring a matter inadmissible for one reason or another; narrowing a ruling; or following up forceful rulings with weak remedial orders.

"Exogenous Shocks or Endogenous Constructions? The Meanings of Wars and Crises," 51 *International Studies Quarterly* (2007), 747–59), Abbott's reference to "turning points" (see Andrew Abbott, "On the Concept of Turning Point," 16 *Comparative Social Research* (1997), 85–105), and Capoccia, Kelemen, Hoan, and Doyle's discussion of "critical junctures" (see Giovanni Capoccia and R. Daniel Kelemen, "The Study of Critical Junctures Theory, Narrative and Counterfactuals in Historical Institutionalism," 59 *World Politics* (2007), 341–69); John Hogan and David Doyle, "A Comparative Framework: How Broadly Applicable is a 'Rigorous' Critical Junctures Framework?," 44 *Acta Politica* (2009), 211–40).

2 Peter Haas, "Introduction: Epistemic Communities and International Policy Coordination," 46 *International Organization* (1992), 14.

While all of the regional rights systems have worked to manage their legitimacies, the extent to which they have had to do so has varied a great deal from institution to institution and over time. In this respect the early European system enjoyed a uniquely advantageous position, both because it was comparatively free to choose the pace of development of its jurisprudence, thanks to the fact that international human rights standards were not yet extensively developed, and because it was able to operate in the context of a set of states which were comparatively rights-respecting. Against this background, the European system was able to develop some of the most sophisticated and effective mechanisms of legitimacy management, including the European consensus approach[3] as well as the margin of appreciation doctrine. The Court's recent "procedural turn" may be understood as playing such a role as well.[4]

The Inter-American and African systems, in contrast, have faced more challenging contexts, both because they have generally had to make decisions against the backdrop of an international legal system in which human rights law has been comparatively thick, limiting their room to develop their standards gradually, and because they were faced from their initial moments with clear and serious rights violations, in the face of which equivocation would have been an evasion of duty. At the same time, in the early years the legitimacy of both of those systems benefited, ironically, from the fact that their suggestions were relatively easy to ignore, especially before the coming into operation of the courts in each system.[5]

3 On the idea of European consensus, see Alec Stone-Sweet and Thomas Brunell, "Trustee Courts and the Judicialization of International Regimes," 1 *Journal of Law and Courts* (2013), 61–88; Luzius Wildhaber, Arnaldur Hjartarson, and Stephen Donnelly, "No Consensus on Consensus? The Practice of the European Court of Human Rights," 33 *Human Rights Law Journal* (2013), 248–63; Paul Mahoney and Rachael Kondak, "Common Ground: A Starting Point or Destination for Comparative-Law Analysis by the European Court of Human Rights?," in Mads Andenas and Duncan Fairgrieve eds., *Courts and Comparative Law* (Oxford University Press, 2015), 119–40; Kanstantsin Dzehtsiarou, *European Consensus and the Legitimacy of the European Court of Human Rights* (Cambridge University Press, 2015); Panos Kapotas and Vassilis Tzevelekos eds., *Building Consensus on European Consensus: Judicial Interpretation of Human Rights in Europe and Beyond* (Cambridge University Press, 2019).

4 On the "procedural turn" see Arnardóttir, "The 'procedural turn'"; Gerards and Brems eds., *Procedural Review*.

5 For a variety of texts exploring the manner in which legitimacy challenges become more serious as the strength of the demands made by a particular body increase, see Daryl Levinson, "Rights Essentialism and Remedial Equilibration," 99 *Columbia Law Review* (1999), 857–940; Sonja Starr, "Rethinking 'Effective Remedies': Remedial Deterrence in International Courts," 83 *New York University Law Review* (2008), 693–768; and in

Thus, their weakness protected them from challenges to their legitimacy. More recently, both systems' courts have encountered pushback from domestic forces, leading to state withdrawal from their jurisdiction and calls for the adoption of the more cautious margin of appreciation approach of the European system.[6]

In all three contexts, legitimacy management is not only a matter of acquiring the right procedural tools – institutions must also have access to information concerning which issues are most sensitive for states and other interested parties. Where they lack such knowledge, confrontations that might otherwise be avoided may occur.[7] At other times, state opposition may be driven by internal political forces, in which case there is likely little a regional rights system can do to avoid it – though it may still attempt to minimize it, for instance by weakening the force of its orders and recommendations.[8]

The history explored has shown that, from time to time, state parties are likely to attempt to undermine the work of regional rights systems, even when they may have previously supported them. Measures states may adopt toward such an end include appointing new, less independent commissioners, judges, or members of registries or secretariats; imposing budgetary restrictions; or pressuring the system into moderating its approach through covert or overt political pressure.[9] In some instances, as

a different way, Mark Tushnet, *Weak Courts, Strong Rights: Judicial Review and Social Welfare Rights in Comparative Constitutional Law* (Princeton University Press, 2008); Daniel Bodansky, "Legitimacy in International Law and International Relations," in Jeffrey Dunoff and Mark Pollack eds., *Interdisciplinary Perspectives on International Law and International Relations* (Cambridge Unversity Presss, 2012), 325.

6 See Sergio Vergudo and José Francisco García, "Radiografía al Sistema Interamericano de Derechos Humanos," 25 *Actualidad Jurídica* (2012), 175–216; Contesse, "Contestation and Deference"; Follesdal, "Exporting the Margin of Appreciation." On the Inter-American system's resistance to such calls, see Contreras, "National Discretion and International Deference."

7 This was arguably relative to the Inter-American Commission's issuance of interim measures concerning the Belo Monte Dam in Brazil. For more on the importance of information in such a context, see Madsen, "Explaining the Power of International Courts"; Yonatan Lupu, "International Judicial Legitimacy: Lessons from National Courts," 14 *Theoretical Inquiries in Law* (2013), 437–54.

8 On this issue, see Laurence Helfer and Karen Alter, "Legitimacy and Lawmaking: A Tale of Three International Courts," 14 *Theoretical Inquiries in Law* (2013), 479–502. The UK's opposition to the European Court's ruling that prisoners should be able to vote illustrates this dynamic. For more, see Ed Bates, "Analysing the Prisoner Voting Saga and the British Challenge to Strasbourg," 14 *Human Rights Law Review* (2014), 503–40.

9 For more on such issues generally, see Laurence Helfer and Anne-Marie Slaughter, "Why States Create International Tribunals: A Response to Professors Posner and Yoo," 93

in the cases of Trinidad and Tobago and Venezuela relative to the Inter-American Court, and of Rwanda, Tanzania, Benin, and Côte d'Ivoire relative to the African Court, states may withdraw their assent to a particular supranational body's jurisdiction.

States are not the only entities with which the regional rights institutions have come into conflict. From time to time, tensions have also simmered up between those bodies and national courts.[10] Such clashes are often short-lived and marked by a tendency toward resolution and compromise, however, likely due to a recognition by courts on both levels of the risks such clashes pose for their own legitimacy.[11]

Third, the evolution of the systems has been characterized by the formation of *symbiotic relationships* between the systems and human rights advocates. Human rights advocates rely on the systems to magnify the effects of their advocacy, while the systems rely on rights advocates to acquire information, develop their outputs, and enhance their authority. The development of symbiotic relationships has been undergirded both by the mandates of the systems to advance human rights, as well as by the fact that the systems' mandates and broader sociocultural contexts have

*California Law Review* (2005), 942–54; Thordis Ingadottir, "The Financing of International Adjudication" and Tom Ginsburg, "Political Constraints on International Courts," both in Cesare Romano, Karen Alter, and Yuval Shany eds., *The Oxford Handbook of International Adjudication* (Oxford University Press, 2014). The recent financial challenges of the Inter-American system constitute one example of financial pressure in action.

10 For further exploration of such tensions *see* Nico Krisch, "The Open Architecture of European Human Rights Law," 71 *Modern Law Review* (2008), 183–216; Lord Hoffmann, "The Universality of Human Rights," 125 *Law Quarterly Review* (2009), 416–32; Huneeus, "Rejecting the Inter-American Court."

11 On the ability of national and supranational courts to benefit from collaborative approaches, see Eyal Benvenisti, "Reclaiming Democracy: The Strategic Uses of Foreign and International Law by National Courts," 102 *American Journal of International Law* (2008), 241–73; Eyal Benvenisti and George Downs, "National Courts, Domestic Democracy and the Evolution of International Law," 20 *European Journal of International Law* (2009), 59–72; André Nollkaemper, *National Courts and the International Rule of Law* (Oxford University Press, 2011); Shai Dothan, "How International Courts Enhance Their Legitimacy," 14 *Theoretical Inquires in Law* (2013), 455–78; Erik Voeten, "Public Opinion and the Legitimacy of International Courts," 14 *Theoretical Inquires in Law* (2013), 411–36. For more on the importance of finding ways through which to enhance the quality of the relationship between the European Court of Human Rights and national judicial systems, see Helfer, "Redesigning the European Court." For an argument that the Inter-American system should adopt a more "integrated" relationship with national courts, see Dulitzky, "An Inter-American Constitutional Court?" On some of the positive functions such clashes may serve, see Krisch, "Open Architecture"; Nico Krisch, *Beyond Constitutionalism: The Pluralist Structure of Postnational Law* (Oxford University Press, 2010).

geared them to be sympathetic to human rights claims. While they may not have the resources of state parties, rights claimants often have greater expertise in the field of human rights law than the state advocates who oppose them, at least when repeat institutional players are involved.

The symbiotic relationships between the systems and regional rights advocates has often taken institutional form as well. As the regional systems have developed their jurisprudence and procedure, they have come to need increasingly technically proficient staff. The strong correlation between technical expertise in human rights law and support for rights, however, means that as secretariats and registries become increasingly professionalized, they tend to fill up with strong rights advocates, the occasional state-planted oppositional figure notwithstanding. As the workload and formalization of the systems have advanced, their secretariats and registries have not only become more independent and professionalized, but also larger and more powerful, to the point that in many instances their power may be understood as commensurate with or perhaps even greater than that of the systems' formal representatives (judges and commissioners). This is especially true where, as is usually the case, secretariat staff serve unlimited terms, during which they are employed full-time, whereas formal representatives serve for set periods of time and on a part-time basis.[12]

The symbiotic relationships that have formed between rights advocates and the regional systems have also had an external component: the more cases that have been decided, the more the knowledge of each system has expanded, leading to the submission of ever greater numbers of cases.[13]

[12] The greater the number of official representatives of a system, moreover, and the greater the cultural and linguistic diversity among them – as with the European Court and its 47 judges from 47 different states – the weaker they are likely to be as a collective force in relationship to the secretariat.

[13] Often, each system has ended up having extensive interactions with one country or another at an early point in its existence, resulting both in models of productive work being set, and in cadres of human rights lawyers within those countries being developed, who have then been able to push forward the work of the systems as a whole. In Africa, Nigeria has been such a key country. In the European system, early interactions with the United Kingdom were particularly important. As Villiger has put it,

> The dynamics of the Convention changed … when British lawyers at the end of the 1960s and in the 1970s discovered the Convention. They realized that the Commission's report and the Court's judgment could be a valuable tool in implementing their clients' rights in the domestic sphere. With their polished, at times brilliant presentations in often spectacular cases, they drew the attention of other lawyers to the Strasbourg complaints system.

The strength of these feedback loops has been such, in fact, that they have come to generate problems for the systems, leading to growing caseloads.

Fourth, the evolution of all three systems has been characterized by *juridification* – that is, a constant and ongoing movement in the direction of increasing legalization and judicialization.[14] Numerous factors have been responsible for this development. First, most simply, the tendency toward juridification has been encouraged by the fact that many rights advocates, across time, have viewed courts as an optimal mechanism through which to obtain more vigorous and effective rights protection. Second, the movement toward juridification has been driven by the professional interests of the international juridical community.[15] Third, structural forces have played a role as well. As Shapiro and Stone Sweet have observed, iterated processes of claim-making and dispute resolution tend to produce increasingly judicialized bodies over time.[16] When created, dispute resolution bodies are likely to operate on the basis of fairly loose and informal frameworks – something that was true relative to all three regional rights systems. Once they begin resolving disputes, however, such bodies must be careful, if they hope to continue to exist and to be relied upon, to preserve their good reputations. In order to promote their legitimacy in this context, dispute resolution bodies tend to develop

Villiger, "Comment," in Wolfrum and Deutsch eds., *European Court of Human Rights*, 22. In addition, all three systems have benefited from the support of human rights law faculties within their respective regions. In Europe such support has arrived from an extensive set of institutions, spread across numerous countries. In the Americas support from faculty at law schools in the United States has always been important, despite the United States' unwillingness to submit itself to the oversight of the system. In Africa, the Centre for Human Rights at the University of Pretoria has been particularly influential.

14 From a broader perspective, the regional human rights systems form only one small part of a broader trend toward juridification. For more on that broader trend, see Benedict Kingsbury, "International Courts: Uneven Judicialization in Global Order," in James Crawford and Martti Koskenniemi eds., *The Cambridge Companion to International Law* (Cambridge University Press, 2012), 203–27; Karen Alter, "The Multiplication of International Courts and Tribunals after the End of the Cold War," in Romano, Alter, and Shany eds., *International Adjudication*, 63–89.

15 See Mikael Madsen, "Beyond Prescription: Towards a Reflexive Sociology of Human Rights," in Mikael Madsen and Gert Verschraegen eds., *Making Human Rights Intelligible: Towards a Sociology of Human Rights* (Hart, 2013), 94–5. See also John Hagan and Ron Levi, "Justiciability as Field Effect: When Sociology Meets Human Rights," 22 *Sociological Forum* (2007), 372–80; Judith Blau and Alberto Moncada, "Sociologizing Human Rights: Reply to John Hagan and Ron Levi," 22 *Sociological Forum* (2007), 381–4.

16 See Martin Shapiro, *Courts: A Comparative and Political Analysis* (University of Chicago Press, 1981); Alec Stone Sweet, "Judicialization and the Construction of Governance," 31 *Comparative Political Studies* (1999), 147–84.

clear procedural rules and to issue increasingly detailed judgments over time, in order to satisfy parties that their positions have been heard, fairly weighed, and taken into account. Such a general process, as described by Shapiro and Stone Sweet, has certainly operated in the regional human rights context, as the formality of the procedural rules and the level of detail provided by judgments has continuously increased in each system over time. In fact, procedural developments have often come about as the direct result of challenges to the legitimacy of the systems, as those legitimacy challenges have been defused through agreement on more tightly defined sets of rules.

## III Alternative Approaches

Foregrounding the similar dynamics that have helped to shape all three systems is helpful, insofar as it makes apparent the sorts of challenges and patterns of developments that may be taken as typical in the human rights context. In addition to the similarities, it is also important to recognize the differences between different human rights systems. Among other things, recognizing those differences may be valuable both to those interested in strengthening the existing systems as well as to those interested in supporting the creation of new ones, insofar as it can help broaden understandings of the ends to which human rights work can be oriented, as well as of the different substantive, institutional, and procedural design choices that may be made in pursuit of those ends.

In what have the differences between the systems consisted? The first area where one might investigate differences is relative to substantive jurisprudence. In some areas, the systems have followed clearly differentiated paths: thus, for instance, the European system has refused to consider indigenous peoples' rights claims,[17] whereas the Inter-American and African systems have been more willing to recognize the rights and struggles of such populations. The European system has also been reluctant to challenge the vagrancy law legacy, a subject on which the African Court in contrast has adopted a bold, progressive stance.[18] The Inter-American

[17] See Giovanna Gismondi, "Denial of Justice: The Latest Indigenous Land Disputes Before the European Court of Human Rights and the Need for an Expansive Interpretation of Protocol 1," 18 *Yale Human Rights and Development Journal* (2017), 1–58.

[18] See Request for Advisory Opinion by The Pan African Lawyers Union (PALU) on The Compatibility of Vagrancy Laws with the African Charter on Human and Peoples' Rights and Other Human Rights Instruments Applicable in Africa, Advisory Opinion Request No. 001/2018, Af. Ct. H.P.R. (December 4, 2020); Lăcătuş v. Switzerland, App. No. 14065/15,

system has also been more receptive to litigation pertaining to the relationship between rights and the environment,[19] as in theory is the African system, thanks to Article 24 of the African Charter guaranteeing to "all peoples … the right to a general satisfactory environment favourable to their development," though the African system has yet to produce the same volume of jurisprudence as the Inter-American on the subject. In general, however, the substantive differences between the systems are not overly extensive – unsurprisingly, given that epistemic and communal pressures push supranational human rights systems toward harmonious standards, such that there is significant pressure for the diminishment of differences over time.[20]

To focus on jurisprudential differences alone is already to adopt a limited view, however – to imagine, as participants in the European system have often done, that the solitary or at least the main function of a human rights system should be to advance substantive human rights jurisprudence. In addition to their jurisprudential differences, the systems are marked by notable institutional and procedural differences, differences which have shaped the manner in which the systems have interacted with human rights communities in their respective regions, defined the relative distributions of their energy and attention, and, in and through such processes, served to provide the different systems with their respective visions of and approaches to human rights work.

The following sections consider the different institutional and procedural approaches that have evolved in the European, Inter-American, and African regional human rights systems over time. These approaches cannot be understood in isolation from the broader historical backgrounds of each of the systems – rather, the choices that have been made, and the manner in which each system has evolved, have been heavily conditioned

Eur. Ct. H.R. (January 19, 2021); Corina Heri, "Beg Your Pardon!: Criminalisation of Poverty and the Human Right to Beg in Lăcătuş v. Switzerland," Strasbourg Observers Blog (February 10, 2021); Christopher Roberts, "The Beginning of the End for Vagrancy Laws?," ICON Blog (July 9, 2021).

19 See Riccardo Pavoni, "Environmental Jurisprudence of the European and Inter-American Courts of Human Rights: Comparative Insights," in Ben Boer ed. *The Environmental Dimension of Human Rights* (Oxford University Press, 2015), 69–106.

20 Nonetheless, certain systems may remain permanently on the more conservative side of the spectrum, others on the more progressive side. On the European system's conservatism as of the mid-1990s, in relationship to situations of emergency in particular, for example, see Fionnuala Ni Aolain, "The Emergency of Diversity: Differences in Human Rights Jurisprudence," 19 *Fordham International Law Journal* (1995), 101–42.

by the understandings of rights work possessed by each system's participants, background political conditions, and the situations of violation the system has encountered over time. This relationship has, moreover, been co-constitutive, as the manner in which each system's institutions have been designed, and the procedural rules they have adopted, have helped to shape the sorts of rights violation it has been possible to render visible in each system at particular points in time. Broader background conditions, personal understandings of rights work, concrete rights struggles, and institutional and procedural design choices have hence all influenced each other, in an ongoing process of co-constitution. As such, the approach of each system is not presented in a temporal vacuum, but rather with reference to the circumstances of its gradual development over time. Nonetheless, the differences between the systems have been such that three broad models can be identified: the judicial model, most extensively developed in the European system; the strongly integrated dualist model, which developed in the Inter-American system; and the weakly integrated dualist model, which developed in the African system.

### *III.1 The Judicial Model*

Several key decisions were made at the time of the European system's founding that have continued to shape the system to the present day. First, social and economic rights were excluded from the European Convention.[21] Second, the right of individual petition and the jurisdiction of the court were made optional features of the system – orienting the attention of regional rights advocates from the beginning to establishing both features as mandatory ones. Third, the system was framed as geared to protecting the rights of Europeans in particular, to the potential – and often real – exclusion of the rights of outsiders. Finally, the system's application to European colonial possessions was also rendered optional, further entrenching the exclusionary and limited vision of rights established. While the European system was given an early chance to address colonial rights violations via the *Cyprus* case, the Commission shied away from an assertive holding. Along the way, the Commission created a two-track system of cases: one track for inter-state cases, which could address big picture, structural and systemic violations, and another track for individual cases, in which the system's lens would be more tightly focused.

21 While they were later included in the "European Social Charter," that Charter has never achieved a level of utilization or influence similar to that of the European Convention.

As time went on, three progressive developments came to define the system. First, the place of individuals within the system increased over time. Initially, the ability of individuals to bring complaints was an opt-in feature, and the Court was shielded from hearing individual complainants directly, in part due to the suggestion that to allow individuals to directly confront states before the Court would constitute an unacceptable challenge to sovereign power. Over time, the barriers to individuals' participation were stripped away, until ultimately the ability of individuals to bring their cases to the Court was made a nonnegotiable feature of the European system's operation. Second, over the course of the 1970s the European system gradually developed the fundamental principles that would define its approach in the decades to come. The doctrine of progressive interpretation and the idea of European consensus helped to define the system's belief in incremental progress, to be achieved through the gradual leveling-up of standards across European states. The doctrines of the margin of appreciation and subsidiarity meanwhile served as valuable tools of calibration and legitimacy balancing. Taken together, these ideas helped develop and cement an incrementalist approach in which central emphasis was placed on the system's jurisprudential function. This incrementalist jurisprudential role was one at which the European system excelled, as over time it produced increasingly thick, detailed standards relative to the rights covered by the Convention, leading the global development of rights-based standards in numerous areas. Third, while acceptance of the Court's jurisdiction was initially optional, and the Commission the more active body, as time went on the European Court became an increasingly central part of the system. The end result was the phasing out of the Commission in favor of a unified court system in the 1990s.

These developments represented the outcome both of the understandings of system participants as to optimal human rights system design, and external forces exerting pressure on the organs of the systems. In particular, the European system's existence in the context of state parties where the rule of law was strongly established helped exert pressure on the system to temper its rulings, while adopting a more judicial posture. In comparison to the Inter-American and African systems, moreover, the European Commission on Human Rights did not function for long on its own: within less than a decade of its creation, it was complemented by a Court, that was soon issuing important judgments. In contrast to the other two systems, therefore, there was little opportunity for the European Commission to develop in a forceful, independent manner. When it was functioning, the European Commission tended to act more as a court of first instance without binding power of judgment than as an alternative form of rights body, in contrast to the more expansive, experimental approach adopted by the commissions in the other two regional systems. These factors helped contribute to a broader understanding in the European context that the existence of a Commission was suboptimal and that it had only been created because a fully judicialized system had not initially been possible. In light of this background, it is unsurprising the Commission was abolished by Protocol 11, and similarly unsurprising that development was celebrated at the time.

Functionally, since the end of the 1990s the European system has been close to fully judicialized, excepting the persisting role for the Committee of Ministers. This judicialization is closely linked to limitations in the sorts of claims the system will and will not allow. The European system's nonrecognition of group rights is something many of the system's participants would likely consider as natural, the ideological content of which only becomes apparent in comparative perspective. While the European system does recognize a certain degree of extension of the concept of victim, and grounds for exceptions to a rigid rule around representation, it does not recognize *actio popularis* claims.[22] Formally, the European system has a fairly broad rule on joinder;[23] in practice, it has been less willing than the other systems to liberally join cases, doubtless in significant part because joinder in the other systems has mostly been undertaken by those systems' more flexible commissions. Like the other systems, the European system recognizes an extensive regime of exceptions to the rule of exhaustion. While a more extensive study would be necessary to identify the percentage of cases admitted under exceptions to the rule of exhaustion in each system, a much higher proportion appear to be accepted in the Inter-American and African systems, suggesting, albeit in a far from conclusive way,[24] a greater flexibility on the part of those systems in such regards.

[22] See *Practical Guide on Admissibility Criteria* (Updated December 31, 2018), para. 15–52.

[23] See Rule 49, 2018 Rules of Court.

[24] There are several complications to bear in mind here. Generally speaking, one might expect far greater numbers of cases to be submitted together with arguments that an exception to the rule of exhaustion should apply when the states from which those cases arise have less developed and rights-respecting judicial systems. As such, it is natural that more such case submissions would take place in the Americas and Africa, in comparison to Europe, and even if Europe admits less cases on the basis of exceptions to the rule of exhaustion proportionally, that does not necessarily mean Europe applies a higher standard in such regards.

While Protocol 11 was initially widely celebrated, the subsequent years have put the new system under pressure. This has led to several procedural developments designed to increase efficiency, including for instance Protocol 14, which allowed for the quick filtering out of cases in which no "significant disadvantage" had been demonstrated and for admissibility decisions to be made by single judges, and which provided for a summary procedure through which repeat applications could be resolved.[25] The development of the pilot judgment procedure, meanwhile, suggested that even for a system as structurally and culturally adverse to group judgments as the European human rights system, broader systemic pressures pushing in such a direction could not be ignored.

From a schematic, simplified, and comparative viewpoint, the approach that has developed within the European system may be described through reference to five key features. First, the European approach tends to prioritize and valorize the individual and an individualized approach to rights case resolution. As noted, the fight for individuals to be able to bring their claims directly to the European Court of Human Rights was a long and protracted one, the success of which was celebrated as a victory for human rights in general, and relative to the dignity of the individual person in particular. Maintaining a focus on individuals is easier where rights violations are less extensive, as well as where claims tend to be brought after domestic remedies have been exhausted, because cases that have satisfied the rule of exhaustion will already have passed through the domestic legal system, which tends to shape cases along more individualized lines. In addition, the more carefully individualized a case is, the less "political" it will seem – both because the broader impacts may more readily be left as matters of implication rather than direct prescription, and because it is rhetorically possible to shift the focus of attention to the rights of the individual in question, and away from broader policy implications.

Second, the European approach is deeply committed to the superiority of courts as a means of rights protection and advancement. This can be seen both from the manner in which the European Commission functioned when it did exist, as well as through the decision that was taken to abolish the Commission in favor of a unified court system through Protocol 11. As with the struggle for the full recognition of the individual, the struggle to achieve a more fully judicialized system helped to cement

[25] For more, see Beernaert, "Protocol 14"; Greer, "Protocol 14"; Caflisch, "Reform of the European Court"; Greer, *The European Convention on Human Rights*, 136; Gattini, "Mass Claims", 288. Protocol 15 went further along similar lines.

the idea in the minds of many participants in the European system that such a system was the optimal one. In addition to constituting a practical, organizational matter, the system's reliance on a more fully judicialized approach tends to structure the sorts of outcomes produced. In the first place, it complements the system's tendency to focus on individuals. In addition, it tends to exert a conservative influence, deriving both from judicial culture as such, as well as from the fact that the greater weight of a court's decisions exerts pressure on the system to limit the progressivity built into any particular decision.[26] As highlighted elsewhere, the system's frequent use of and close association with a number of legitimacy balancing tools – including the margin of appreciation and subsidiarity doctrines, as well as the recent "procedural turn" – is closely related to its reliance on a more judicialized approach as well.

Third, closely related to its orientation toward a more judicialized approach, the European system has tended to adopt a "constitutional" vision of its role. To speak of a "constitutional" vision can mean many things; as deployed here and in the context of the European Court of Human Rights, the term speaks to the manner in which the court sees its primary role as the production of standard-setting jurisprudence relative to the various states over which it has jurisdiction.[27] Both the idea of progressive interpretation and that of European consensus are closely connected to this function, the former as a doctrine providing the space for creative interpretation, the latter as a methodology and a form of justification.

Fourth, whereas the Inter-American and African systems quickly came to adopt an extensive and assertive approach to remedies, the European system has been far more cautious in such regards. For much of its existence the European system preferred to employ a declaratory approach, perhaps complemented with largely symbolic monetary remedies.[28] This

[26] On this dynamic, see Levinson, "Rights Essentialism"; Starr, "Rethinking 'Effective Remedies'"; Tushnet, *Weak Courts, Strong Rights*; Bodansky, "Legitimacy in International Law."

[27] To note that the European system sees its constitutional role as primary is not to say that it sees that as its only function, rather that it sees it as its most important, fundamental, and ennobling function. In practice, the European system has also always played a substantial role as an individual complaint resolver, a fact that has contributed to its caseload crisis, leading to reflections on manners in which the system's constitutional role can be enhanced. See, e.g., Wildhaber, "Constitutional Future"; Greer and Wildhaber, "Revisiting the Debate."

[28] On which see Huneeus, "Reforming the State from Afar."

lack of emphasis on the remedial side of the equation has both derived from, and has helped to reinforce, the emphasis on the production of jurisprudence stressed erlier. In addition, it accords closely with the system's emphasis on subsidiarity.[29] The European system's resistance to issuing extensive and tightly prescriptive remedial orders has also helped to shape the vision of the force of human rights law it has put forward, emphasizing, as the system often puts it, that its role is to lay out the obligations prescribed by international law, while leaving it to state parties to determine how to ensure compliance with those obligations on the national level. While the Court has recently gone further, this development has come late, in response to extensive pressure from multiple sources, and has been limited, in comparison to the other two systems.

Fifth and finally, in comparison to the Inter-American and African systems the European system has managed to present its work as less overtly confrontational, doing its best both to foreground its role as the provider of technical expertise and to adopt a gradualist, as opposed to confrontational, position wherever possible. As with the other features detailed above, this characteristic has rested on the system's historical experience fine-tuning jurisprudence through interactions with states in which the rule of law has been relatively well-respected, interactions which have pushed it toward the adoption of a more conciliatory stance. In addition, the fact that the European system never had a multifunction commission, and now has no commission at all, has tended to keep the regional community of rights advocates one step further removed than they might otherwise be, reducing the pressure on the system to adopt more forceful, confrontational positions.[30]

In sum, the judicial model of supranational human rights oversight that has developed within the European system has been closely

[29] Itself initially formulated relative to the question of concrete remedial orders – see "Belgian Linguistics" case, App. Nos. 1474/62, 1677/62, 1691/62, 1769/63, 1994/63, & 2126/64, Eur. Ct. H.R., Merits (July 23, 1968), para. 10.

[30] This is by no means meant to suggest that that community has not been important to the development of the European system – as highlighted above, relationships with civil society have been key to the development of all of the systems. For more on the relationship between civil society and the European regional human rights system in particular, see Rachel Cichowski, "Civil Society and the European Court of Human Rights," in Christoffersen and Madsen eds., *The European Court*, 77–97. In comparison to the Inter-American and African systems, however, the more fully judicialized approach in Europe has provided civil society with fewer avenues through which to interact with and influence the European regional human rights system.

related to various other features of the system, including an emphasis on the importance of the individual, and adoption of an individualized approach to rights issues; a constitutional vision of rights work; a more limited approach to remedies, that preserves the distinction between the national and international legal orders; and a more conciliatory posture relative to state parties, tied to a patient, gradualist approach to rights advancement.

### *III.2 The Strongly Integrated Dualist Model*

As with the European system, the model that has evolved in the Inter-American system cannot be understood in isolation from the system's history. Agreement on the American Declaration on the Rights and Duties of Man was not accompanied by agreement to create oversight institutions. A decade later, however, tensions in and around the Caribbean prompted the states of the Americas into action, leading to the creation of the Commission. For the next several decades the Commission was the sole rights institution in the region, and it handled itself with aplomb, managing to prove its value to the region's most powerful states, assertively developed its mandate, and confront some of the region's worst rights abusers, all the while consistently avoiding overly forceful blowback.

As the 1960s gave way to the 1970s, the Commission benefited from and contributed to the ongoing expansion of the global human rights project, directing its attention to some of the worst forms of authoritarian rule and rights violations in the region, including through widely noticed and influential fact-finding trips to Chile and Argentina in particular. Over the decades that followed the Commission continued to direct attention to the region's worst violations, though it was often unable to bring those violations to a halt or bring those responsible to justice. When the Court received its first referrals in the late 1980s, it picked up on the dynamism imparted by the Commission, adopting an assertive and expansive approach toward some of the most serious and widespread rights violations committed in the region in its first contentious decisions.

Over the course of the 1980s and 1990s numerous authoritarian regimes collapsed across the Americas, providing the organs of the Inter-American system enhanced political space in which to advance their work. Over the following period, both the Commission and the Court developed newfound confidence, expressed and advanced through procedural and institutional reforms as well as through the development of a new, more expansive approach to their casework, while on the national level state authorities and members of the legal community began to take increasing notice of the regional system's recommendations and judgments.

As the region changed, the system's focus gradually shifted from the widespread and systematic violations of the past to the challenges involved in supporting transitions toward democracy, and to the need to challenge the deeper, ongoing structural violations found across the Americans. This last focus expressed itself in the system's extensive development of its jurisprudence pertaining to the rights of particular communities, including its focus on indigenous peoples' rights, women's rights, and the rights of other marginalized and discriminated-against communities. Along the way, the main characteristics of the system's new approach became increasingly clear: a willingness to adopt a wide-angled view of cases brought before it; a liberal approach to procedure; an assertive approach to remedies; an insistence on the applicability of regional human rights law on the national level; and an emphasis on using the cases that came before it to address broader, underlying, structural violations, rather than carefully tailoring its judgments in the interests of limiting the pushback they might provoke.

The system that has developed in the Americas, over the course of this long history, is one in which both Commission and Court have been preserved. In particular, the Inter-American system can be understood as employing a "strongly integrated dualist" model, dualist insofar as two institutions exist, and strongly integrated in that there is no possibility of approaching the Court without first having recourse to the Commission. In contrast to the European system, many in the Americas seem to appreciate the work the Commission has done, not least the Commission's extensive non-case-oriented activities, an area in which the Inter-American Commission has far outstripped its European counterpart. That said, the possibility of abolishing the Commission has never been seriously on the cards in the Americas, for the simple reason that not every state in the region has accepted the Court's jurisdiction.

Just as the place of the Commission in the current Inter-American system is due to the history of the system, so too has the Commission influenced that history. The Inter-American Commission was created and set about its work in 1960. The Court was only created in 1979, and issued its first judgment in a contentious case in 1989. For three decades, therefore, the Inter-American Commission was the premier organ within the Inter-American human rights system. The frontline role played by the Inter-American commission not only allowed it to entrench itself, but also allowed it to set the tone for rights work in the region. In particular, the Commission's broad lens, together with the nonbinding nature of its judgments, helped develop a bigger picture, holistic approach to rights questions across the system as a whole.

Over the course of its existence, the Inter-American Commission has engaged in a wide variety of tasks beyond the consideration of cases. These have included developing soft law instruments, conducting fact-finding missions and promotional visits, and issuing reports, including both country-specific and issue-based reports, as well as annual reports highlighting the overall state of respect for rights across the region.[31] The commission has also made it a practice to hold regular sessions, at which civil society groups are able to come together, to form coalitions, and to conduct advocacy campaigns. In addition to the value for civil society of the Commission's sessions, the holding of those sessions allows the Commission to more deeply appreciate civil society organizations' concerns, and to develop closer relationships with regional rights advocates.

In addition to its non-case-oriented activities, the Inter-American Commission's quasi-judicial nature has allowed it to adopt a more flexible approach to case consideration. While it was initially ambiguous whether the Inter-American Commission could receive communications, the Commission wasted no time in interpreting its mandate as allowing it to do so. Over time, the Commission has continued to develop its flexible approach to that mandate. While the Declaration on the Rights and Duties of Man and the American Convention on Human Rights do not include group rights, the Inter-American system has in practice come to recognize such rights, in the context of indigenous peoples in particular. In addition, the Inter-American system has been flexible relative to questions of standing, including by adopting a more liberal approach to questions of representation, that is, to the circumstances in which one may bring a claim on behalf of another, and a more expansive understanding of victimhood, that is, when an individual may claim to be a victim of a particular rights

[31] In this context, Chapter IV.B of the Inter-American Commission's Annual Reports, in which the Commission outlines the worst ongoing rights violation in the Americas, is particularly significant. Chapter IV.B is addressed by Rule 59(6) of the Commission's 2013 Rules of Procedure, which states that the chapter should cover instances in which a state "has committed or is committing massive, serious and widespread violations of human rights," where there are instances of serious democratic breakdown, where states of emergency have been declared, and where "other structural situations that seriously affect the use and enjoyment of fundamental rights" persist. States have consistently fought hard against their inclusion in the chapter, testifying to the seriousness with which they take that component of the Commission's work.

violation. The adoption of a more liberal approach to representation has been driven by the system's encounters with incommunicado detentions and forced disappearances, in which context communication with victims has been impossible, as well as by its encounters with large-scale atrocity, in which context individuation of victims has been impossible. Expansions in notions of victimhood meanwhile have been enabled by the adoption of broader, more victim-sympathetic approaches toward violations and their consequences.[32] The Inter-American system has also adopted a more flexible approach to joinder.[33] The system has also been flexible relative to the exhaustion of domestic remedies rule, in recognition of the limitations human rights advocates often encounter when attempting to have their rights vindicated through domestic systems in less than fully rights-respecting states.

Like the European system, the Inter-American system's overall approach can be reasonably approximated through reference to five factors. Once again, these descriptions are simplified for the sake of analytical purchase, and must be understood comparatively, rather than in absolute terms. First, in contrast to the more individuated lens of the European system, the Inter-American system has employed a wider-angled view of violations. This has been closely linked to the adoption of procedures through which it has been possible to view situations in their entirety, instead of examining violations or the circumstances of individual claimants piecemeal. The Inter-American Commission's more holistic tools, such as its state-based and annual reports, have required the adoption of such a lens; that lens has seeped into the Commission's casework as well, influencing the Court in turn as cases have been referred on.

Second, in contrast to the European system's more judicialized approach, the Inter-American system has utilized a more informal, less judicialized approach. While less binding judgments have thereby been issued, the comparative lack of formality has enabled the Inter-American

32 Thus for instance the Court has found that the children of the disappeared may appropriately be classified as victims, observing that "The fact of living in an environment of suffering and uncertainty owing to the failure to determine the whereabouts of the disappeared victims, despite the ceaseless efforts of their parents, harmed the mental and moral integrity of the children who were born and lived in that environment." Contreras and others v. El Salvador, App. Nos. 12,494, 12,517, & 12,518, Int.-Am. Ct. H.R., para. 122 (August 31, 2011).

33 The Inter-American Commission's joinder rule provides: "If two or more petitions address similar facts, involve the same persons, or reveal the same pattern of conduct, the Commission may join them and process them together in the same file." Int.-Am. Comm. H.R., 2013 Rules of Procedure, Rule 29(5).

system to pursue more flexible and experimental approaches, as well as to more readily develop progressive jurisprudence. In addition, the system has been able to build a much closer relationship with regional rights advocates. Both factors are closely linked to a different understanding of the efficacy of rights work: rather than imagining change as coming from above, through formal decisions, as a judicial model tends to do, the more informal approach and proximity to civil society of the Inter-American system suggests change is more likely to come "from below," linked to the recognition and magnification of the voices of rights advocates.

Third, whereas the European approach to human rights valorizes a constitutional vision focused on the production of novel jurisprudential standards, the Inter-American approach has tended toward what might be termed a responsive vision, focused more centrally on mobilizing energy to push back against ongoing violations, including wide-scale, systematic and structural violations in particular. This distinction has, of course, been produced in large part by the different situations faced by the different systems. Whereas the European system was able to achieve great success from an early stage through a focus on the development of its jurisprudence, the Inter-American system has frequently been called upon to respond to situations in which no novel jurisprudence was necessary, yet nonetheless violations persisted, underscoring the extent to which rights-attainment requires political will, more than and in addition to legal wisdom.

Fourth, the Inter-American system has been at the forefront of the development of novel, extensive and forceful remedial measures. On the most direct level, this has involved a concrete, observable feature of the system's holdings and judgments. More broadly, this emphasis may be understood as linked to a different understanding of how the focus of rights work should be distributed, in which greater weight is placed on dealing with specific, historically generated situations of structural violation by means of clearly laid out steps that aim to alter societal relationships, including potentially through a significant redistribution of resources.[34] Adopting a more forceful approach to remedies also suggests and has been closely linked to an understanding of human rights obligations as operative on

[34] As the Inter-American Court put it in *Gonzalez et al. v. Mexico*, "bearing in mind the context of structural discrimination in which the facts of this case occurred … the reparations must be designed to change this situation, so that their effect is not only of restitution, but also of rectification. In this regard, reestablishment of the same structural context of violence and discrimination is not acceptable." App. Nos. 12.496–8, Int.-Am. Ct. H.R. (November 16, 2009), para. 450.

the national level, as may be discerned from the Inter-American system's adoption of such a viewpoint.[35]

Fifth and finally, whereas the European system has preferred to deploy a more cautious, step-by-step, deferential approach, the Inter-American system has tended to be more directly confrontational. This more confrontational posture initially arose because the system was frequently confronted by widespread and serious violations, in which context it had little choice, given its mandate, but to directly and forcefully call out those violations. As time has gone on, this characteristic has become somewhat entrenched, linked among other things to the system's comparatively closer relationship with rights advocates observed earlier, which has tended to push it toward the adoption of more forceful rights-supportive positions, as well as its stronger approach to remedies, which has limited its ability to deploy a more deferential, subsidiarity-based approach.

In sum, the Inter-American system's dualist, less-judicialized approach can be understood as closely linked to several other elements that have characterized the system's overall approach: it has tended to view violations from a broad, holistic viewpoint; it has been able to adopt more flexible and experimental approaches to case determination and rights work broadly, and to forge closer relationships with right advocates; it has tended to focus more on addressing ongoing situations of violation, and less on the development of jurisprudence as such; it has foregrounded the importance of remedies, and frequently produced extensive and detailed remedial measures; and it has tended to adopt a more direct, confrontational posture in support of rights claims. Just as with the European system, these elements are not merely contingently related, but rather form part of a consistent whole, a vision of human rights which, while historically determined, has a high degree of internal coherence.

### *III.3 The Weakly Integrated Dualist Model*

In the years following World War II, the Inter-American, United Nations, and European human rights systems all took their first steps. It was not possible for an African regional human rights system to be formed in the same moment, however, for the simple reason that the people of Africa

[35] See Almonacid Arellano v. Chile, App. No. 12.057, Int.-Am. Ct. H.R., Preliminary Objections, Merits, Reparations and Costs (September 26, 2006); Ramírez, "El control judicial interno"; Dulitzky, "An Inter-American Constitutional Court?"; Poisot, "Conventionality Control."

were still subject to European colonization. The hypocrisy of Western European states simultaneously proclaiming their allegiance to rights while at the same time violating those rights through the dramatic escalation of their attempts to crush resistance movements went anything but unnoticed by independence leaders, who repeatedly called for rights standards to be respected in regards to their polities as well.

Global rights standards gained an importance place in the constitutions of numerous African states as decolonization gathered momentum, and regional leaders continued to deploy the language of rights to decry ongoing apartheid governance and Portuguese colonialism into the late 1960s, 1970s and beyond. At the same time, those new leaders were wary of accepting the call by rights advocates for the creation of a regional rights system, afraid of the limitation on their sovereignty the creation of such an institution might entail. Their resistance weakened, however, following foreign intervention in the Central African Republic and cross-border adventurism by Idi Amin in the late 1970s, which prompted key regional leaders to adopt a more favorable view relative to the creation of regional rights institutions. Though advocates were in favor of the creation of a court, as elsewhere this proved a step too far for state representatives initially. A regional Charter was, nonetheless, adopted, and a Commission established. Notably, the new Charter did not merely aim to protect human rights but also "peoples' rights," encouraging the adoption of a broad lens relative to rights issues.

In the decades that followed, the distinctive nature of the African Charter was reflected in the approach to human rights adopted by the region's new human rights institutions. It took the Commission several years to get up to speed; once it did, however, it set about its task with vigor, tackling big picture, politically contentious questions, prescribing broad remedies, calling, at least at times, for detailed reforms to national legal orders, and advancing an assertive and incisive view of the nature of African human rights law. Meanwhile, the window of political opportunity that opened in the 1990s allowed for the formation of the African Court, which set about its task in the early 2010s with the same vigor the Commission had brought to its role.

The approach to human rights that has developed in the African system has been similar to that which developed in the Inter-American system. As in the Inter-American system, the African system relies on both a Commission and a Court, the former charged with a range of tasks, the later primarily with case resolution. While the African system is therefore dualist, it employs a more weakly integrated form of dualism than the Inter-American system, in that while the Commission may refer cases to the Court, it is also possible for individuals to bring cases to the Court directly, where a state party has accepted that jurisdictional possibility. The vast majority of the Court's cases have been received through this latter avenue. While on the one hand this testifies to the virtues of that approach – since it allows for case processing without need for the involvement of an over-stretched Commission – it is a procedural possibility with drawbacks as well, as most clearly observable in the fact the four of the ten states that had signed up to allow complaints to go directly to the Court had withdrawn that assent by the end of 2020.[36]

The approach that has developed in the African system clearly owes something both to the broader background circumstances of the region, as well as to the circumstances of the system's development. The inclusion of group rights in the Charter, together with Article 58(1), requiring special attention to situations involving "a series of serious or massive violations," oriented the system from the beginning toward the adoption of big-picture approaches – an orientation reinforced by the widespread and serious violations the system has repeatedly encountered. As in the Inter-American system, moreover, the African system functioned for a substantial period of time with a commission alone: the African Commission was created in 1987, the African Court in 2006, and the African Court's first full judgment on the merits issued in 2013. Even granted that the Commission got off to a slow start, it was issuing important holdings and engaging in other activities by the early to mid-1990s, and was hence for two decades or so the leading regional rights body in Africa. As in the Americas, the African Commission has pursued a diverse range of tasks, including promulgating regional standards, holding sessions, conducting country visits, and undertaking state party reviews.

In its case consideration function, the African Commission has adopted an expansive approach. That the Commission would adopt an expansive approach to questions of representation was essentially established from the beginning, with the system's recognition of people's rights. The African system doubled down in this area, by recognizing that claimants may advance cases on the basis of the principle of "*actio popularis,*"

[36] The ten states that had accepted the ability of individuals to submit cases directly by the end of 2020 were Benin, Burkina Faso, Côte d'Ivoire, Gambia, Ghana, Malawi, Mali, Rwanda, Tanzania, and Tunisia. Rwanda, Tanzania, Benin, and Côte d'Ivoire subsequently withdrew their acceptances.

meaning that any applicant may raise a claim pertaining to an issue of public concern.[37] The African Commission has also adopted a flexible approach to joinder, joining together multiple complaints to reach its holdings, including relative to some of the most serious situations of violation it has considered. In addition, the African system has addressed the challenges that would be faced by claimants should it require rigorous adherence to admissibility rules by working to expand the existing regime of exceptions to the rule of exhaustion where local remedies are "unavailable, ineffective or insufficient,"[38] including by entrenching and expanding the existence of an exception to the rule relative to cases of widespread and serious violations in particular.[39]

From a broad, schematic angle, the approach of the African system in such regards is similar to that of the Inter-American system. Overarchingly, it has deployed a dualist approach. This has been linked to a tendency to adopt a wide-angled view relative to violations; reliance on an assortment of methods of rights advocacy; a greater proximity to the work of civil society; a more responsive vision of human rights work; an expansive approach to remedies; a willingness to suggest the need for domestic legal orders to be reformed;[40] and a tendency to be more directly confrontational.

That the African system's approach has been similar to that of the Inter-American system so far, with the exception of the potential it offers for individuals to bring their cases directly to the regional court, does not mean it will permanently remain so tightly aligned to its sister regional system. In particular, it would be hard to argue that the promise contained within the Charter's inclusion of "peoples' rights" has yet been fulfilled,

[37] See Social and Economic Rights Action Center and Center for Economic and Social Rights v. Nigeria, App. No. 155/96, Af. Comm. H.P.R., para. 49 (October 27, 2001); Article 19 v. Eritrea, App. No. 275/03, Af. Comm. H.P.R., para. 65 (May 20, 2007). The African system's approach contrasts with the vast majority of international rights bodies, which have refused to recognize *actio popularis* claims. For more, see William Aceves, "Actio Popularis – The Class Action in International Law," 1 *University of Chicago Legal Forum* (2003), 353–402.

[38] See, e.g., Jawara v. the Gambia, App. Nos. 147/95 & 149/96, Af. Comm. H.P.R. (May 11, 2000), paras. 31–7.

[39] See, e.g., Free Legal Assistance Group and Others v. Zaire, App. Nos. 25/89, 47/90, 56/91, & 100/93, Af. Comm. H.P.R. (April 4, 1996); Organisation Mondiale Contre la Torture and others v. Rwanda, App. Nos. 27/89, 46/91, 49/91, & 99/93, Af. Comm. H.P.R. (October 31, 1996); Amnesty and others v. Sudan, App. Nos. 48/90, 50/91, 52/91, & 89/93, Af. Comm. H.P.R. (November 15, 1999); Article 19 v. Eritrea, App. No. 275/2003, Af. Comm. H.P.R. (May 30, 2007); Haregewoin Gabre-Selassie and IHRDA v. Ethiopia, App. No. 301/05, Af. Comm. H.P.R. (October 12, 2013).

[40] See, e.g., Mouvement Ivoirien des Droits de l'Homme v. Côte d'Ivoire, Comm. No. 246/02, Af. Comm. H.P.R. (July 29, 2008).

including insofar as the African regional system has yet to turn its attention to big picture questions of national and international socioeconomic justice, despite the mandate it has to do so.

### *III.4 Optimal System Design?*

As the preceding outline of the different positions that have been reached by the different systems suggests, their varying approaches have not been the result of choices made by omniscient system designers, but rather products of the complex dynamics that have unfolded in each system over time. There is no doubt, moreover, that the idea of a one-size-fits-all approach to rights work has serious limitations, and that suggestions relative to ideal system design offered on the most general, abstract level may not always be optimal in practice.

That said, the survey conducted here makes it hard to avoid the conclusion that the dualist model is superior to the judicial model. The dualist model preserves a role for a court; it does not rely solely upon a court, however, but rather complements the court with a commission, which is able to undertake a number of additional rights tasks. Such a model is valuable because it has the ability to engage in a wider range of methods of work. Different approaches are necessary within the broader field of rights work at different times: at times, it may be necessary to reach novel decisions on important points of jurisprudence; at other times, the primary task may be finding the most effective modes of responding to and attempting to mitigate and bring to an end entrenched, structural situations of rights violation. At times, in other words, courts will be called for; at other times, commissions will be able to make more effective interventions. Far from distracting from the work of a court, moreover, a commission can enhance its work, by freeing up the court to pursue the function to which it is best suited and to which members of a rights-based judiciary generally seek to devote their attention: advancing rights-based jurisprudence. In addition, dualist models draw strength from the simple fact they utilize more than one institution, increasing their capacity for progressive experimentation, allowing one institution to take up the burdens of advancing rights where the other becomes a target of state attacks, and making state capture more difficult, by increasing the number of institutions states would have to capture in order to render the system as a whole ineffective.[41]

[41] Challenges arise from the multiplication of institutions as well, of course, including challenges relative to ensuring harmonious interactions and efficient divisions of work among

Including a commission within a human rights system tends to produce a number of additional effects as well. In particular, commissions tend to develop much closer relationships with civil society, thanks both to the fact one function of commissions is typically the holding of regular sessions, as well to the fact their quasi-judicial status removes some barriers to socialization. This in turn tends to lead to a different model of human rights work, focused less on change from above, through court orders, and more on change from below, through civil society advocacy supported and enabled by the voice-magnifying opportunities provided by a regional rights system. If at the end of the day progress on rights issues depends first and foremost on the efforts and achievements of such communities – as all evidence suggests – then the importance of enabling bottom-up approaches is hard to over-emphasize.[42]

More of an open question persists around the question of whether or not to favor a strongly or a weakly integrated dualist approach. The weakly integrated approach offers the ability for a regional court to function even where the regional commission is unable to handle the task of referring cases – as was the case in the African system in the late 2010s, where the Commission's case output slowed to a trickle, with referrals to the Court few and far between. As observed earlier, the weakly integrated dualist approach comes with challenges as well, however, as faced in the form of the numerous withdrawals from the Court's system that

those institutions. For some compelling recommendations pertaining to inter-institution complementarity in the context of the Inter-American system's interactions with other regional mechanisms, see Gabriela Kletzel and Camila Baretto Maia, "The Challenge of Complementarity in Latin America's New Institutional Architecture for Human Rights," in Kelly A. Reynolds, ed., *Changing Times, Ongoing Challenges* (Due Process Law Foundation, 2016), 17–52.

42 For emphasis on the virtues of such an approach in the regional rights context, see Cavallaro and Schaffer, "Less as More"; Cavallaro and Brewer, "The Virtue of Following"; Cavallaro and Brewer, "Reevaluating Regional Human Rights Litigation." For wider emphasis on the virtues of such an approach, see William Eskridge, "Public Law from the Bottom Up," 97 *West Virginia Law Review* (1994), 142–80; Rajagopal, *International Law*; Boaventura de Sousa Santos and Cesar A. Rodriguez-Garavito eds., *Law and Globalization from Below* (Cambridge University Press, 2005); Jonathan Berger, "Litigating for Social Justice in Post-Apartheid South Africa: A Focus on Health and Education," in Varun Gauri & Daniel Brinks eds., *Courting Social Justice: Judicial Enforcement of Social and Economic Rights in the Developing World* (Cambridge University Press, 2008), 38–99; Obiora Okafor, "National Human Rights Institutions in Anglophone Africa: Legalism, Popular Agency, and the Voices of Suffering'", in Ryan Goodman and Thomas Pegram eds., *Human Rights, State Compliance, and Social Change: Assessing National Human Rights Institutions* (Cambridge University Press, 2011), 124–49.

took place following Court rulings against states on politically sensitive issues. The weakly integrated dualist model may also give rise to caseload-related problems, especially where, as in Africa, a flexible approach to exhaustion has developed. The strongly integrated dualist system, in contrast, offers the commission as a case filtering and processing system, granting such powers to a body better suited, thanks to its more flexible procedures, to handle them, avoiding the potential of the court becoming bogged down by its caseload, as occurred in Europe, and allowing for the referral of cases involving novel or contentious jurisprudential standards. Of course, the success of the strongly integrated model requires that the commission be sufficiently resourced, independent, and strongly rights-oriented – not characteristics that can be taken for granted. Where a commission does possess such characteristics, the strongly integrated dualist system presents the most compelling case, from among the approaches considered, to represent the most broadly optimal model of rights system design.

## IV Structural Context, Path Dependence, and Choice in Rights System Design

In addition to the similarities and differences between the regional human rights systems that have developed in Europe, the Americas, and Africa considered in this chapter, it is possible in light of the comparative investigation of those three systems to reflect on one further set of closely related questions: to the extent each system has embarked down its own course, what factors drove that system in such a direction, to what extent might that course have been different, and to what extent is it possible for each system to change course today, after many decades of existence and experience?

Core components of the shape and trajectory of each system were put in place during that system's initial foundational moment. At the same time, subsequent decisions made by each of the systems, after they began functioning, played a key role. In the European system, as observed, the Commission had several major decisions to make when confronted with the case of *Greece v. the United Kingdom*.[43] In addition to adopting a cautious approach, the Commission decided to establish two separate case paths, a systemic path that might be followed in inter-state cases, and a

[43] Eur Comm. H.R., 2 European Yearbook on Human Rights (1958–1959).

more individuated path to be followed in cases brought by individual claimants. The Inter-American and African systems' commissions also had early decisions to make, that were remarkably similar to those faced by their sister institutions. Neither commission's mandate clearly provided the power to hear case submissions from nonstate parties; as such, both commissions had to decide whether to hear such submissions at all. In both instances, rather than adopting a cautious position, the Inter-American and African commissions decided to consider the cases being submitted to them, thereby launching each system down the path toward more extensive interaction with civil society.

Clearly, the systems possessed a degree of institutional flexibility in their early moments. How much flexibility they truly had during those periods is a difficult question to answer, however. The European system's tendency toward a more cautious, formal, judicialized approach was not an accident, but rather a product of several interrelated aspects of its structural position: the fact that the rule of law was comparatively sophisticated and respected within the majority of its member states; the system's strong need in its early years to shore up political support, especially in light of the fact states only signed up for its jurisdiction for limited periods; its frequent encounters with relatively technical jurisprudential issues; and the fact that the early years of the European system's evolution took place while the field of international human rights law was still relatively nascent. The Inter-American and African systems' evolution in the direction of more multifaceted, systemic approaches was similarly determined by the contexts in which they found themselves in their early years, including in particular their frequent encounters with situations of serious and massive violation, as well as the fact that they frequently interacted with domestic legal systems in which remedies were far from available, effective, and sufficient.

Even if one considers that the systems' respective paths of travel were not predetermined, it is hard to avoid the conclusion that such flexibility as they enjoyed in their early years has diminished over time. As time has passed, each system has developed its formal institutional shape and its procedural rules; has laid down an increasingly thick web of substantive jurisprudence; and has helped to set expectations and understandings of rights work within the wider regional community. These factors, combined with the structural factors laid out previously, suggest that the space each regional system has to maneuver today may be somewhat limited. Each system's commitment to a particular approach has been reinforced by the extent to which that system has experienced major moments of triumph in the past, allowing the system to expand along certain lines and for a broader narrative as to the nature of successful rights work to develop. In the European system, both the Court's discovery of its voice in the 1970s and the optimism, expansion, and reform of the 1990s were key moments in terms of entrenching an optimistic, jurisprudence- and judicialization-oriented approach. In the Inter-American system, the period of transitions toward democratic governance, coinciding with the coming online of the Court in the late 1980s, marked the system's most triumphant period, in which the system's self-image as a strong ally of civil society and supporter of transitional justice and legal reform were similarly entrenched.[44]

Of course, even where a particular approach and narrative has become historically entrenched, change is not impossible. As observed earlier, to the extent change has come historically, it has typically been premised on moments of political opportunity, themselves opened up by moments of crisis or structural change of one form or another. The shape such change takes, however, is determined not only by the nature of the crisis or structural change in question, but also by the ideas as to system redesign held by individuals in key positions in and around each system. As such, further major change may be expected, as and when each region encounters a period of crisis, or when key elements within its broader background structural context change.

Significant structural change can be observed to have taken place in both the European and Inter-American systems over the past several decades, as both regions have come, in terms of the structural factors that impact on regional system functioning, to more closely resemble one another. The European Court, long used to dealing with state parties in which the rule of law has been relatively well-respected, has for the last several decades been called upon to deal more frequently with situations of widespread and serious violations as well, occurring in countries such as Russia, Turkey, and Ukraine. The Inter-American system, meanwhile, long used to confronting situations of serious and widespread violation, has increasingly had to interact with national legal systems in which the rule of law is more entrenched and developed, placing a growing pressure on the system to adopt a more cautious, incremental approach.[45]

44 The African system, in contrast, has yet to experience as formative a period as those experienced in the European and Inter-American systems, such that its approach remains relatively fluid.

45 This has been expressed through calls for the Inter-American Court to adopt the European system's margin of appreciation approach. See Vergudo and García, "Radiografía"; Contesse,

While the structural context of both the European and the Inter-American systems has been changing, neither has yet adopted changes as extensive as their new situations seem to require. The systems' reluctance to adjust their approaches may be explained through reference to the dynamic of path dependence.[46] In the Inter-American system, the force of path dependence may be observed in the system's resistance to the increasing calls for it to adopt the European system's margin of appreciation approach, a resistance rooted in the system's long history of adopting a more confrontational approach to violations.[47] In the European system, the force of path dependence can be seen in the dynamics around reform in the face of the system's caseload crisis. On the one hand, several steps have been taken to attempt to address that crisis.[48] When viewed in light of comparative approaches, the steps taken in the European system appear half measures, however. Relative to case processing, for instance, the European Court adopted the pilot judgment approach, rather than the more liberal approach to joinder employed in the other systems;[49] relative

"Contestation and Deference"; Follesdal, "Exporting the Margin of Appreciation." On the Inter-American system's resistance to such calls, see Contreras, "National Discretion and International Deference."

[46] On path dependence and the related concept of "imprinting," see James Mahoney, "Path Dependence in Historical Sociology," 29 *Theory and Society* (2000), 507–48; Scott Page, "Path Dependence," 1 *Quarterly Journal of Political Science* (2006), 87–115; Christopher Marquis and András Tilcsik, "Imprinting: Toward a Multilevel Theory," 7 *Academy Management Annals* (2013), 193–243. Page identifies four subcategories of path dependence: increasing returns; self-reinforcement; positive feedbacks; and lock-in. The second of these factors – self-reinforcement, meaning that a past choice has "pu[t] in place a set of forces or complementary institutions that encourage that choice to be sustained" – is most relevant to the regional rights institutions. In addition, the psychological element of path dependence is also significant in the context of the regional rights institutions – that is, the belief of system participants in the appropriateness and value of certain approaches, and/or their failure to recognize the potential for things to be done differently. On the significance of psychological factors to the manner in which international organizations approach their work, see Finnemore and Barnett, "Politics, Power, and Pathologies"; Finnemore and Barnett, *Rules for the World.*

[47] On the debates in this area, see Contreras, "National Discretion and International Deference." As Contreras notes, the Inter-American Court has mentioned the margin of appreciation approach on occasion (see ibid., 57–60), but has not given it as regular or central a place as it occupies within the European Court's work.

[48] For more, see Sadurski, "Partnering with Strasbourg"; Huneeus, "Reforming the State from Afar."

[49] For more on the calls for a more expansive, perhaps even "class action" approach within the European system, see Gattini, "Mass Claims," 291; Greer and Wildhaber, "Revisiting the Debate."

to remedies, the European Court has expanded its approach, but has still refused to issue anything close to the remedial orders the Inter-American and African systems have been willing to call for.[50]

[50] On the European system's development of a more assertive approach to remedies, see Alastair Mowbray, "An Examination of the European Court of Human Rights' Indication of Remedial Measures," 17 *Human Rights Law Review* (2017), 451–78; Alice Donald and Anne-Katrin Speck, "The European Court of Human Rights' Remedial Practice and its Impact on the Execution of Judgments," 19 *Human Rights Law Review* (2019), 83–117.

# 5

# Conclusion

There are two broad lessons that may be drawn from examination of the comparative historical evolution of the world's three most institutionally developed regional human rights systems. In the first place, that exploration helps to reveal the many ways in which the systems have been propelled forward and shaped by similar dynamics and forces. As observed, they have all been significantly impacted by the possibilities opened up by major moments of political opportunity, including in particular the post–World War II period, the 1970s, and the end of the Cold War, all of which provided fertile milieus for human rights advancements across regional contexts. In addition, all three systems have shown themselves to be driven by similar underlying dynamics, of which their commitment to legitimacy balancing has been most obvious and widely recognized. While the importance of the relationship between rights advocates and rights institutions is plainly apparent, the manner in which the systems have tended to become increasingly close to rights experts over time, as their jurisprudence and procedures have become more complex and sophisticated, has been less widely recognized, though it is no less significant a structural feature. Finally, all three systems' evolution have participated in a process of juridification over time. This has involved both the gradually increasing sophistication of each system's formal procedures and jurisprudential output, as well as, most dramatically, the establishment of human rights courts in all three regions studied, despite strong initial resistance to such institutions. As in other areas, the history of the regional human rights systems testifies to the strength the idea of supranational judicial oversight has had over the course of the three-quarters of a century following World War II.

At least equally as important to recognize as these similarities are the systems' differences. In the first place, it is illuminating to recognize that diversity as such. The reality of contemporary rights discourse is that many – including both friends and critics of "human rights" – tend to speak of "human rights" as if were a simple, unitary concept, and of "*the* human rights movement" as if a homogenous collective existed. In contrast, as this study has endeavored to show, "human rights" is an internally diverse and contested field, structured not only by top-down ideas and interventions but also by the manner in which different institutions function, the different forms of rights violation encountered in different times and places, and the innumerable struggles of individuals, organizations, peoples, and social movements, aimed at pushing back against injustices they encounter in their everyday lives. Recognizing the existent diversity among human rights visions is hence important, in order to be able to grasp contemporary dynamics of the field in their full complexity.

Greater attention to the diversity of approaches to human rights deployed across the regional contexts is also important in light of the lessons that may be drawn from the comparative successes, limitations, and possibilities inherent in each regional system. From a broad, heuristic perspective two approaches to human rights may be identified as having developed in the regional human rights context. On the one hand, there is the European approach, which has combined judicialization, an orientation toward the production of jurisprudence, a preference for individual cases and an individuated rights vision, and the articulation of more cautious judgments and remedies. On the other hand, a more systemic approach has evolved in the Inter-American and African systems, which have favored the combination of commissions and courts, an orientation toward serving as an advocacy partner for civil society in responding to the worst rights violations, a tendency to consider violations from a wide-angled perspective, and an assertive approach to judgment and remedies.

At the very least, awareness of these two alternative possibilities should help rights advocates consider more expansively the system design options available to them. Recognition of these differences should drive further reflection, however. In order to spell this out, it is necessary to step back and consider the successes and limitations of regional human rights work in broad perspective. In terms of successes, all three systems have grown over time, expanding their power and authority and entrenching themselves within their respective regions. Each has developed a substantial body of jurisprudential output – the European system above all – which has helped to give more extensive, detailed, concrete substance to general rights obligations in the regions and beyond. Each has tackled innumerable rights violations, and while numerous judgments in all three systems have not been complied with, many have been, resulting in progressive outcomes both for individual claimants and on a broader, structural level.

While all three regional rights systems have had successes, those successes have been limited. Most fundamentally, this is due to the fact that the systemic change toward which human rights work is oriented is by nature hard to achieve, as well as the fact that the power of supranational rights oversight mechanisms is significantly constrained. Even bearing such restrictions in mind, however, limitations of rights systems' own making may be observed as well. Most overarchingly, the historic tendency of many rights advocates to focus on the production of jurisprudence must be interrogated. This is not because the production of such jurisprudence is unimportant – quite the opposite, as developing clear standards against which conduct may be judged is a cornerstone of rights work more broadly. The reality, however, is that jurisprudential production represents a first, relatively easy to achieve step within the broader process of realizing rights-based reform. It is, moreover, an area in which the amount of work to be done will diminish with time – while standards may always be refined, and evolving concerns explored, it is a testament to the success of various human rights institutions in this area that extensive standards governing core civil, political, and due process rights, at the very least, may now be pointed to.

As such, it is important that in addition to jurisprudential production rights systems devote attention to the processes through which they seek to support efforts aimed at the reform of rights-violating systems. Most broadly, this requires pursuing a range of tasks over and above jurisprudential production – necessitating, in short, the less-judicialized sorts of approaches pursued by the Inter-American and African regional systems, in contrast to the European. More specifically, it means that rights institutions should recognize their place and role within the broader ecosystem of actors and organizations oriented toward reform. In short, rights institutions must recognize that meaningful systemic reform requires broad-based popular support, and that the optimal role for rights institutions in such a context is to support those efforts in the most effective manner possible. In the design of all their activities, therefore, regional rights institutions, like all other human rights bodies, should seek to maximize the extent to which they are responsive to and serve to magnify the efforts of social movements, civil society organizations, and rights advocates.

In addition, recognition of the existing diversity of human rights visions should lead both rights' supporters and critics to pause and reflect on the nature of rights claims made to date, and the potential for more expansive claims to be made in future. In this regard, three areas in which all three regional systems have failed to expand their visions of rights as broadly as might have been hoped may be highlighted.

First, the output of all three regional systems has been disappointing relative to social and economic rights. For many reasons, this is not surprising. In Europe, such rights were not included in the Convention.[1] Nonetheless, there is no shortage of manners in which the European Court might have interpreted Convention rights in a manner supportive of social and economic rights, and it has frequently been called upon to do so. In some instances, changes have been made: for instance, the European Court has developed its jurisprudence on the right to strike over time, though significant limitations remain.[2] In other contexts, as for instance relative to austerity policies, the Court has been less willing to venture outside its comfort zone.[3]

The Inter-American and African systems' disappointing records in regards to such rights are harder to explain, given that both systems have clearer mandates to address those issues, thanks to several provisions within the American Declaration of the Rights and Duties of Man and the African Charter. While both systems have issued important rulings on social and economic rights, the majority of such rulings have been linked to group-based rights claims; broader issues, pertaining to states' policies in relationship to healthcare, education, housing, welfare, taxation, environmental conditions, and other key socioeconomic rights issues have yet to be addressed with the degree of attention and detail they merit.[4] This

[1] Social and economic rights were included in another treaty, the European Social Charter. The European Committee of Social Rights that oversees that Charter has not had nearly the success of the European Court of Human Rights, however, not least because few states have allowed civil society organizations to access the Committee directly.

[2] See Karacay v. Turkey, App. No. 6615/03, Eur. Ct. H.R. (June 6, 2007); Enerji Yapi-Yol Sen v. Turkey, App. No. 68959/01, Eur. Ct. H.R. (April 21, 2009); Kaya and Seyhan v. Turkey, App. No. 30946/04, Eur. Ct. H.R. (September 15, 2009); Çerikçi v. Turkey, App. No. 33322/07, Eur. Ct. H.R. (October 13, 2010); R.M.T. v. UK, App. No. 31045/10, Eur. Ct. H.R. (April 8, 2014); John Hendy QC and Michael Ford QC, "RMT v United Kingdom: Sympathy Strikes and the European Court of Human Rights," Oxford Human Rights Hub (April 10, 2014); Laurens Lavrysen, "Strasbourg Court Fails to Adequately Protect Trade Union Freedom: Secondary Strike Action Only Considered to be an 'Accessory' Aspect of Article 11 (R.M.T. v. UK)," Strasbourg Observers Blog (May 12, 2014); Alan Bogg and K.D. Ewing, "The Implications of the RMT Case," 43 *Industrial Law Journal* (2014), 221–52.

[3] See Margot E. Salomon, "Of Austerity, Human Rights and International Institutions," 21 *European Law Journal* (2015), 521–45.

[4] Key cases relative to one or another of the above rights include Social and Economic Rights Action Center and Center for Economic and Social Rights v. Nigeria, Comm. No. 155/96, Af. Comm. H.P.R. (October 27, 2001); Purhoit and Moore v. The Gambia, Comm. No. 241/01, Af. Comm. H.P.R. (May 29, 2003); Yakye Axa Indigenous Community v. Paraguay,

has not been a fault of the systems alone, but also of regional human rights organizations, which too often have failed to prioritize social and economic rights claims. There are some signs attention to such issues may be increasing generally, and there have been some promising signs within the regional systems as well, including the Inter-American Court's 2017 decision in *Lagos del Campo v. Peru*,[5] in which the Court found that Article 26, the provision of the American Convention obliging states to progressively realize socioeconomic rights, is justiciable, opening the door to the development of the system's social and economic rights jurisprudence in the years to come.

Second, the regional human rights systems have struggled to adequately address cross-border rights violations. This has been most pronounced in the European system, linked to the limited visions of rights that developed thanks both to the system's emphasis on the superior rights protection enjoyed in Western Europe and its reluctance to tackle the widespread and systematic violations committed in the colonial context. The limitations of the European system's vision of rights have expressed themselves in recent years both through deeply questionable judgments regarding multiculturalism in general and Islam in particular,[6] and in the system's

App. No. 12.313, Int. Am. Ct. H.R., Merits, Reparations and Costs (June 17, 2005); Yean and Bosico v. Dominican Republic, App. No. 12.189, Int.-Am. Ct. H.R. (September 8, 2005); Centre on Housing Rights and Evictions (COHRE) v. Sudan, Comm. No. 296/2005, Af. Comm. H.P.R. (May 27, 2009); Xákmok Kásek Indigenous Community v. Paraguay, App. No. 12.420, Int.-Am. Ct. H.R., Merits, Reparations, and Costs (August 24, 2010); Mapuche Paynemil and Kaxipayiñ Communities, Case No. 12.010, Int.-Am. Comm. H.R. (February 5, 2013); Environment and Human Rights, Int.-Am. Ct. H.R., Advisory Opinion No. OC-23/17 (November 15, 2013); Poblete Vilches and Others v. Chile, App. No. 12.695, Int.-Am. Ct. H.R., Merits, Reparations and Costs (March 8, 2018); Cuscul Pivaral and Others v. Guatemala, App. No. 12.484, Int.-Am. Ct. H.R., Preliminary Objections, Merits, Reparations and Costs (August 23, 2018); Indigenous Community Members of the Lhaka Honhat (Our Land) Association v. Argentina, App. No. 12.094, Int.-Am. Ct. H.R., Merits, Reparations and Costs (February 6, 2020).

5 App. No. 12.795, Int.-Am. Ct. H.R., Preliminary Objections, Merits, Reparations and Costs (August 31, 2017). The Commission has also issued a number of important thematic reports addressing socioeconomic rights, including *Access to Justice as a Guarantee of Economic, Social, and Cultural Rights: A Review of the Standards Adopted by the Inter-American System of Human Rights* (2007) and *Guidelines for Preparation of Progress Indicators in the Area of Economic, Social, and Cultural Rights* (2008).

6 On the Court's reactionary jurisprudence in the area of multiculturalism in general, and on the question of headscarves in particular, see Christopher Belelieu, "The Headscarf as a Symbolic Enemy of the European Court of Human Rights' Democratic Jurisprudence: Viewing Islam through a European Legal Prism in Light of the Sahin Judgment," 12 *Columbia Journal of European Law* (2006), 573–623; Jill Marshall, "Conditions for

inability to adequately address Europe's "refugee crisis."[7] At least traditionally, moreover, the European system has been reluctant to recognize transnational responsibility, though the system has become more progressive on such issues over recent decades.[8] While the Inter-American and African systems do not share the sources of limitation inherent to the history of the European system in such regards, neither has yet explored issues of transnational responsibility as expansively as it might.[9]

Freedom – European Human Rights Law and the Islamic Headscarf Debate," 30 *Human Rights Quarterly* (2008), 631–54; Jilan Kamal, "Justified Interference with Religious Freedom: The European Court of Human Rights and the Need for Mediating Doctrine under Article 9(2)," 46 *Columbia Journal of Transnational Law* (2008), 667–708; Rachel Rebouche, "The Substance of Substantive Equality: Gender Equality and Turkey's Headscarf Debate," 24 *American University International Law Review* (2009), 711–38; Jennifer Heider, "Unveiling the Truth behind the French Burqa Ban: The Unwarranted Restriction of the Right to Freedom of Religion and the European Court of Human Rights," 22 *Indiana International and Comparative Law Review* (2012), 93–129; Sally Pei, "Unveiling Inequality: Burqa Bans and Nondiscrimination Jurisprudence at the European Court of Human Rights," 122 *Yale Law Journal* (2013), 1089–102; Eva Brems ed., *Diversity and European Human Rights* (Cambridge University Press, 2013).

[7] This is not to deny that the European human rights system has been a positive force on the issue, as in many instances the jurisprudence of the Court has helped to push for stronger standards for refugees and migrants' rights in Europe – on which issue see, e.g., Cathryn Costello, *The Human Rights of Migrants and Refugees in European Law* (Oxford University Press, 2015). The Council of Europe's Commissioner for Human Rights, too, has been a positive force; see, e.g., Nils Muižnieks, "Europe Can Do More to Protect Refugees," Open Democracy (September 2, 2015). Despite such positive influences, however, the Court's inability to adopt a more systemic viewpoint has significantly limited its ability to deal with the broader contours of the manner in which Europe has mistreated migrants and refugees, as well as the manner in which it has attempted to ensure that they cannot reach Europe in the first place – on which issue see, e.g., Isabel Mota Borges, "The EU-Turkey Agreement: Refugees, Rights and Public Policy," 18 *Rutgers Race and Law Review* (2017), 140–1.

[8] Relative to the latter development see Soering v. the United Kingdom (App. No. 14038/88, Eur. Ct. H.R. (July 7, 1989)); Loizidou v. Turkey (App. No. 15318/89, Eur. Ct. H.R., Judgment on Preliminary Objections (March 23, 1995)); Ilascu and others v. Moldova and Russia (App. No. 48787/99, Eur. Ct. H.R. (July 8, 2004)); Al-Skeini and others v. United Kingdom (App. No. 55721/07, Eur. Ct. H.R. (July 7, 2011)). For more on the European system's approach to such issues, see Miltner, "Revisiting Extraterritoriality." For more on the recognition of transnational and extraterritorial responsibility in human rights law generally, see Marko Milanovic, *Extraterritorial Application of Human Rights Treaties: Law, Principles and Policy* (Oxford University Press, 2011). For a collection of hopeful essays, outlining what a more progressive body of jurisprudence in this area might look like, see Mark Gibney and Wouter Vandenhole eds., *Litigating Transnational Human Rights Obligations: Alternative Judgments* (Routledge, 2014).

[9] The Inter-American system's jurisprudence on the rights of undocumented migrants represents one relative exception; see, e.g., Juridical Condition and Rights of Undocumented

Finally, more attention must be devoted to the intersection of the two issue areas – that is, to transnational violations of social and economic rights. In order for many of the most serious and systemic global rights violations to be addressed, it is crucial that human rights law find ways to more directly and effectively call out socioeconomic rights violating measures imposed by powerful states, including certain of the effects of international economic law and institutions, the transnational tax regime, and the massive and systemic harms caused by environmental degradation and climate change. There are reasons to be hopeful relative to human rights organizations' future ability to address such issues. While to date none of the regional human rights systems has been at the forefront of such efforts, the tools at those systems disposal – in particular the more flexible and inclusive ways of framing claims made possible by the systemic approach of the Inter-American and African systems – are crafted in such a manner as to enable such claims to be brought. Whether such claims will in fact be advanced and will prevail, of course, will depend both on the will and vision of human rights advocates, and on the broader political contexts in which the regional systems operate.

Migrants, Int.-Am. Ct. H.R., Advisory Opinion No. OC-18/03 (September 17, 2003); Undocumented Workers v. United States of America, Case No. 12.834, Int.-Am. Comm. H.R. (November 30, 2016).

# INDEX

For EU product safety concerns, contact us at Calle de José Abascal, 56–1°, 28003 Madrid, Spain or eugpsr@cambridge.org.

www.ingramcontent.com/pod-product-compliance
Lightning Source LLC
LaVergne TN
LVHW011812200926
848484LV00005B/1155